CW00796156

A PORTRAIT OF

Lincoln's Inn

A PORTRAIT OF

Lincoln's Inn

EDITED BY

Angela Holdsworth

EDITORIAL COMMITTEE

Andrew Collender, Mark Ockelton, Guy Holborn

THIRD MILLENNIUM PUBLISHING, LONDON III

A Portrait of Lincoln's Inn

Copyright © The Honourable Society of Lincoln's Inn and
Third Millennium Publishing Limited

First published in 2007 by
Third Millennium Publishing Limited,
a subsidiary of Third Millennium Information Limited

2–5 Benjamin Street
London
United Kingdom
EC1M 5QL
www.tmiltd.com

ISBN: 978 1 903942 54 3

British Library Cataloguing in Publication Data

A CIP catalogue record for this book is available
from the British Library.

All rights reserved

No part of this publication may be reproduced or
transmitted in any form or by any means, electronic
or mechanical, including photocopying, recording
or any information storage or retrieval system,
without permission in writing from the publisher

Designed by Matthew Wilson and Susan Pugsley
Production by Bonnie Murray

Reprographics by Asia Graphic Printing Ltd
Printed in China by 1010 Printing International

Contents

Foreword

FROM HIS ROYAL HIGHNESS THE DUKE OF KENT, KG

When I was kindly invited as Royal Bencher to write a few words encouraging advance support for this excellent project in the brochure at the end of 2005, the book had yet to be written, designed and produced. Now here it is. The Inn and the publishers cannot be accused of misrepresentation in any guise. Those who made the project possible by subscribing in advance will not be disappointed. Those who buy it now can see for themselves the care, imagination and thought that have gone into it.

The professionalism of the Editor and the creative and technical skills of the publishers have made possible a venture that the Inn would not have been able to tackle on its own. But the book remains very much an Inn project – nearly all the forty or so contributors are members of the Inn. Their enthusiasm and affection for the Inn, as well as their knowledge and expertise, are abundantly clear on every page.

Members of the Inn who read the book will doubtless share that enthusiasm and affection. However, an audience, it is hoped, will also be found beyond members of the Inn and the legal fraternity. Lincoln's Inn is after all one of the most unspoilt corners of central London, and as is shown in many of the chapters its history has impinged on many aspects of national life – political, literary as well as in art and architecture. A good deal of original research has gone into making the book a serious contribution to the history of the Inns of Court and the legal profession. There is of course much to entertain too, and the illustrations – some very striking, many unusual – have, I think, done more than justice to the Inn and to the variety of the contributors' essays.

Whether you are a student just about to be called – especially if you are returning to practise overseas – or a longstanding member who wishes to appreciate your connection with the Inn, or indeed a visitor or just a reader with a friendly interest in this fascinating corner of legal London, I am sure you will find something worthwhile to detain you in this admirably produced book.

March 2007

Philip Hardwick's design for the Great Hall built 1843–5.

Contributors

David Ainger (called 1961) practises at the Chancery Bar and is Chairman of the Library Committee.

His Excellency Judge Bola Ajibola KBE (called 1962) is a former Attorney General and Minister of Justice of Nigeria, and Judge of the International Court of Justice and an Honorary Bencher.

Roy Amlot QC (called 1963) is the Treasurer for 2007.

Elizabeth Appleby QC (called Gray's Inn 1965, ad eundem Lincoln's Inn 1975) is Master of the Library and of the Walks for 2007.

The Rt Hon Dame Mary Arden DBE (called Gray's Inn 1971, ad eundem Lincoln's Inn 1973) is a Lady Justice of Appeal.

Cherie Booth QC (called 1976) practises in employment, public and human rights law.

The Hon Sir Nicolas Bratza (called 1969) is a High Court Judge and has been the United Kingdom judge on the European Court of Human Rights since 1998.

Peter Castle (called 1971) practises at the Chancery Bar.

Edna Chayen (called 1954) lives in Israel where she is a published poet.

His Honour Judge Collender QC (called 1969) is a Circuit Judge.

His Honour Roger Cooke (called 1962) practised at the Chancery Bar and was a Circuit Judge from 1989 to 2005.

Sir George Engle KCB, QC (called 1953) was First Parliamentary Counsel 1981–6.

Desmond Fernando, President's Counsel, (called 1958) is an Honorary Bencher and was President of the International Bar Association.

Robert Fookes (called 1975) practises at the Planning Bar.

Hazel, Lady Fox CMG, QC (called 1950) is an academic and practitioner in international and comparative law.

Theresa Gibbs was born in 1920 in 24 Old Buildings, where her father, John Cudworth Whitebrook, lived and practised until 1960.

Sir Peter Graham KCB, QC (called Gray's Inn 1958, ad eundum Lincoln's Inn 1982) was First Parliamentary Counsel 1991–4.

The Hon Mr Justice Handley (called to the English Bar by Lincoln's Inn 1986) is a Judge of Appeal of the Supreme Court of New South Wales and an Honorary Bencher.

David Harris (called 1973) practises at the Revenue Bar.

Paul Heim CMG (called 1955) is former Registrar of the European Court of Justice.

Tessa Hetherington (called 2004) practises in public and employment law.

Colonel David Hills MBE is the Under Treasurer.

Guy Holborn is the Librarian.

Angela Holdsworth is the producer of many television history programmes and is the author of *Out of the Doll's House*, a history of women in the twentieth century.

The Hon Randy J. Holland is a Justice of the Supreme Court of Delaware and an Honorary Bencher.

Cenydd Howells (called 1964) is a Recorder and practises at the Chancery Bar.

Danish Iftikhar (called 2005) practises in Rawalpindi.

Nicholas Le Poidevin (called 1975) practises at the Chancery Bar.

Lesley Lewis (née Lawrence, called 1956) worked from 1940 to 1944 as Managing Clerk at her family's firm of solicitors, Lawrence Graham of 6 New Square.

Edite Ligere (called 2000) practises in public and employment law.

The Hon Mrs Justice Sujata V. Manohar (called 1958) is a former Judge of the Supreme Court of India and an Honorary Bencher.

Professor Alan H. Nelson is editor of the forthcoming volume on the Inns of Court in the *Records of Early English Drama* series.

The Rt Hon Sir Martin Nourse (called 1956) is a former Lord Justice of Appeal.

Mark Ockelton (called 1977) is Deputy President of the Asylum and Immigration Tribunal.

Peter Post was Clerk to Lord Denning from 1975 to 1982.

Collin Sequerah (called 1985) practises in Kuala Lumpur.

Thomas Sharpe QC (called 1976) practises in EU and competition law.

Nicholas Shaw is the Organist.

Sukhwant Singh (called 1981) practises in Perth, Western Australia.

The Rt Hon Sir Christopher Slade (called Inner Temple 1951, ad eundem Lincoln's Inn 1954) is a former Lord Justice of Appeal.

The Hon Mr Justice Stock (called 1968) is a Justice of Appeal in Hong Kong and an Honorary Bencher.

The Rt Hon Lord Walker of Gestingthorpe (called 1960) is a Lord of Appeal in Ordinary.

Richard Wallington (called 1972) practises at the Chancery Bar.

Sir Michael Wright (called 1957) is a former High Court Judge and was Treasurer in 2003.

Huijian Zhu (called 2005) is a former pupil at Essex Court and Fountain Court Chambers.

Editor's Note

The title of this book has been carefully chosen. It is not a comprehensive history but rather an anthology of articles and memories creating a portrait of the Inn past and present. Each chapter looks at a different aspect of the Inn – its history, its buildings, its people – and can be read on its own or as part of the whole. Most contributions have a historical perspective, so a strict chronology is impossible. In a very loose structure, profiles of the Inn's great figures are interspersed chronologically through the book and the more recent history is (mostly) covered in the later chapters.

The authors, whether writing from chambers in Old Square, Kuala Lumpur or Western Australia, are all closely affiliated to the Inn. They range from some of the Inn's most distinguished members to recent graduates. This is entirely their book. I have merely been the facilitator, aided and abetted at all times by the Editorial Committee – Andrew Collender, Mark Ockelton and Guy Holborn. Without their advice and enthusiasm this book would never have been produced. Their suggestions in the early days determined its content and shape and their continuing collaboration has ensured its distinctive Lincoln's Inn character. In particular, Guy Holborn's prodigious knowledge of the Inn's history, traditions and treasures has enhanced the text and appearance of every chapter in the book. I am grateful to them all for their time and their support.

I am indebted to David Hills and Eve Bedell at the Inn for their patience and help in dealing with my endless enquiries and to Chris Fagg and his team at Third Millennium Publishing. Bonnie Murray has ably co-ordinated the production and Matt Wilson, assisted by Susan Pugsley, has designed a beautiful book.

I hope the following pages will add to the reader's knowledge of the Inn's impressive history and that its splendid traditions are suitably celebrated.

Angela Holdsworth

A Community of Lawyers:
Six Centuries of an Honourable Society

ROBERT WALKER

Lincoln's Inn is a society of lawyers which has for more than six centuries occupied the same site in central London. It is bordered by Holborn and Gray's Inn to the north, by Chancery Lane to the east, by the Royal Courts of Justice, the Strand and the Temple to the south, and by Lincoln's Inn Fields to the west. Over the centuries the site has got bigger, and the buildings have changed a good deal, but there has been an essential continuity.

At the time of the Inn's origins, probably in the late thirteenth or early fourteenth century, the area was still quite undeveloped: even a sixteenth-century map shows Lincoln's Inn and Gray's Inn largely surrounded by fields, with cows grazing in the area that now includes Red Lion Square and Southampton Row. In their earliest days, the Inns of Court would have been described as lying between the City of London and the Palace of Westminster. The city skyline was dominated by the cathedral we call Old St Paul's, which replaced two earlier churches that had been destroyed by fire, one a century before the Norman Conquest, the other in 1086. The body of London's patron saint, Erkenwald (a seventh-century monk who became Bishop of London), survived both these early fires, and his shrine was a place of pilgrimage until the sixteenth century. In those days, long before the title of King's or Queen's Counsel came into existence, serjeants at law (members of 'the order of the coif') were the most senior members of the profession, and on their appointment, they used to walk in procession to St Paul's to venerate St Erkenwald's shrine.

Fires great and small feature prominently in the history of London, and Lincoln's Inn has had some narrow escapes. The Great Fire of 1666 destroyed the Old Bailey, Newgate, and Billingsgate on the second day of the conflagration, but it stopped at the top of Fetter Lane on the third day. After the fire, a team of judges was appointed to adjudicate on the multitude of disputes that resulted from it and they included two famous Lincoln's Inn men: Sir Matthew Hale, who features often in these pages, and Sir Richard Raynsford, who succeeded Hale as Chief Justice in 1676. (Raynsford gave the Inn one of its treasures, the Raynsford Cup,

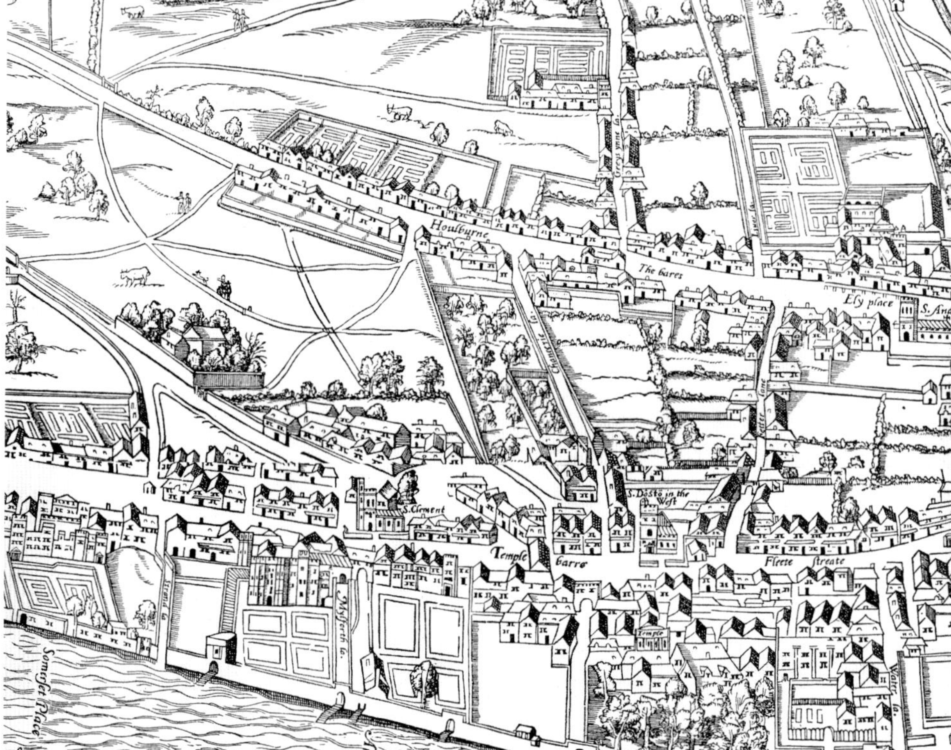

Holborn area c1561, from the 'Agas' map of London.

Charter granting the original site of the Inn to the Bishops of Chichester, 1228.

inscribed *hoc pignus amoris*, 'this [is a] pledge of love'; it is much prized since most of the Inn's earlier silver was sold during the Civil War.) During the Gordon Riots in 1780, William Pitt, then about to be called by Lincoln's Inn, wrote in a letter that the Inn 'was surrounded with flames on all sides'. There were fires in New Square (then Serle Court) in 1752, 1782, and 1849. Lincoln's Inn suffered bomb damage during both world wars but escaped relatively lightly compared with the other Inns.

The origins of Lincoln's Inn are obscure, and the cause of controversy among legal historians, but we can at least ask: Why 'Lincoln's'? Why 'Inn'? The second question is easier than the first. In the Middle Ages, the word 'inn' (like 'hôtel' in French) was used not only to describe a commercial hostelry but for the town house ('hôtel particulier') of a peer, bishop, or other magnate. An inn might consist of a group of buildings and would often include an imposing hall, large enough to house the owner, his family, his guests and his retinue. At some time during the thirteenth or fourteenth century, law students began to lodge at various inns situated between the City and Westminster, and some of these inns evolved into centres of legal education. It was a gradual process: unlike many Oxford and Cambridge colleges, Lincoln's Inn had no conscious foundation and no dated charter.

The origin of 'Lincoln's' is more debatable. The traditional answer is that the Inn is named after Henry de Lacy, third Earl of Lincoln, who died in 1311. But there are other candidates, including Thomas de Lincoln, a fourteenth-century serjeant.

The Inn's Arms

Azure semy of Millrinds and on a Canton Or a Lion rampant Purpure is the official blazon or description of the Inn's coat of arms in the Norman French used by heralds; others may refer to a blue background, scattered with gold millrinds and, on a gold rectangle in the top left corner, a purple lion standing ready to fight. Millrinds are schematic representations of the wrought-iron components fitted to millstones to give them purchase on the shafts of a mill. They appeared, as a 'cant' or pun on his name, in the arms of Richard Kingsmill, the leader of the group of benchers who in 1580 obtained the freehold of the land on which the Inn stands, and were evidently adopted by the Inn as a compliment to him. The purple lion on its gold background was previously used as the arms of the Inn, and may be seen on the Gatehouse in Chancery Lane. The lion was intended for the arms of Henry de Lacy, Earl of Lincoln, but old sources suggest that this device was only a part of his arms. In 1633, a challenge to the Inn's title to the land by a Stuart Bishop of Chichester was decided in favour of the Inn by Charles I sitting in person; the title to the arms was confirmed by certificate in 1969. No crest, supporters, or motto are recorded.

Mark Ockelton

A 1574 entry from the Black Books.

Whether or not it is the oldest of the Inns of Court, Lincoln's Inn has the earliest comprehensive records, its Black Books. These provide an unbroken chronicle starting in 1422. They show that in 1422 the society already had a settled social and educational routine and they enable us to trace the Inn's activities – educational, social and regulatory – over nearly six centuries. We learn from the Black Books that what we now call the Old Hall was built between 1489 and 1492 and that the Inn's arms were first carved over the Gatehouse in 1518.

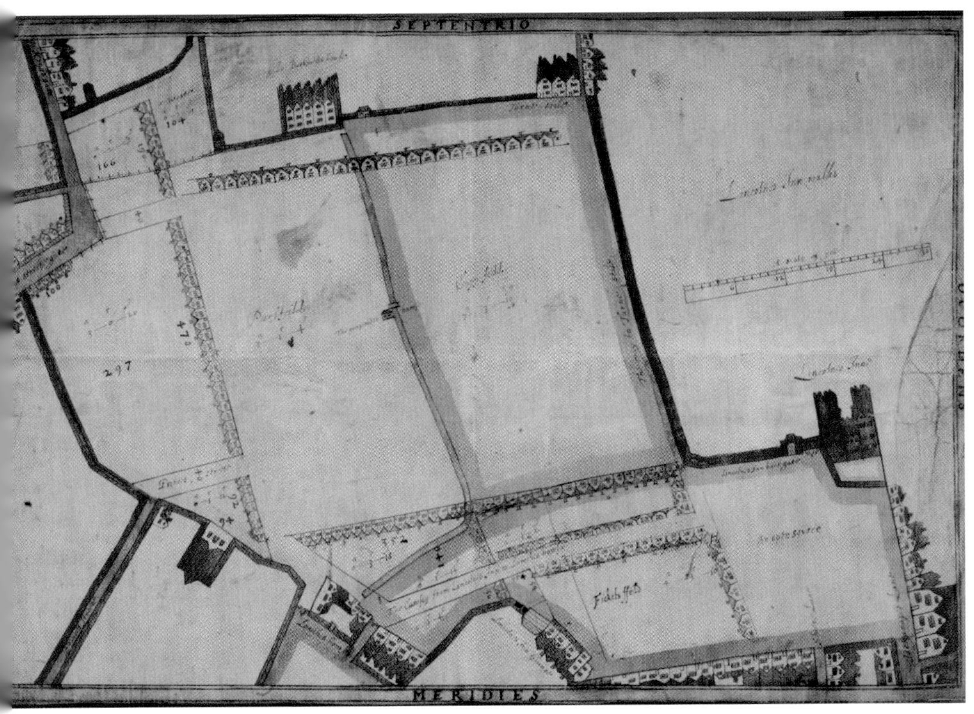

Plan attached to the agreement whereby the Inn acquired the eastern half of Lincoln's Inn Fields in 1657 to ensure control over development.

A wartime Treasurer, Sir Gerald Hurst, wrote of the Black Books in his *Short History of Lincoln's Inn* (1946), 'No narrative history could illustrate as forcibly the fundamental conservatism of human nature, especially among lawyers. The Masters of the Bench at various stages have altered their religion, shifted their allegiance, reversed their politics; but the Black Books record no cataclysm. The life of the Society flows on, serene and unruffled.'

There is some irony here, conscious or unconscious. The Inn has certainly come through some very troubled times, and at some of the most troubled times – much of the sixteenth and seventeenth centuries, and the period of the French Revolution and the Napoleonic Wars – Lincoln's Inn men have been very close to the heart of public life. (It is always men until the twentieth century: there is no hint of a Pope Joan or a Chevalier d'Eon at the English Bar.) During the Tudor and Stuart periods, times of bitter religious conflict heightened by fear of foreign invasion, and of civil unrest followed by civil war, there were undoubtedly many turncoats among those running the Inn's affairs; but there were others who stood out courageously for their beliefs, and others again who managed to survive violent regime change without obviously compromising their principles.

We shall in later chapters meet several of the Inn's most celebrated figures from this period, which, despite its unceasing conflict and violence, was in many ways the Inn's golden age. Passing mention of a few of them will show that if the Black Books appear to record a serene and unruffled life, they do not tell the whole story. One of the Inn's very greatest men, Sir Thomas More, succeeded Cardinal Wolsey as Henry VIII's Lord Chancellor. More was universally admired for his learning, integrity and humanity, but he was dismissed from office in 1533 and beheaded for high treason two years later for refusing to take the Oath of Supremacy. (In 1998, Sir Francis Jacobs, former UK Advocate General in Luxembourg, gave a memorable lecture in the Inn on More's trial, demonstrating its deficiencies in terms of Article 6 of the European Convention on Human Rights.) More is the only member of the Inn to have been canonized by the Roman Catholic Church, although another member, Cardinal Newman, has entered the *cursus*.

In 1634 William Prynne, a member of the Inn and a fierce opponent of royal absolutism, was ordered by the Star Chamber to have his ears cut off by the hangman, for a supposed insult to Queen Henrietta Maria. Three years later, by another order of the Star Chamber, he was branded on both cheeks as a seditious libeller. Prynne was also expelled from the Inn, where he had long been unpopular because of his fierce puritanical objections to revels, but he was reinstated when the tide turned against Charles I and he went on to prosecute Archbishop Laud in 1644 and serve as Treasurer of the Inn in 1657. Though he protested that he was 'no changeling, turncoat or apostate', he seems to have supported the Restoration and won the trust of Charles II. So did Sir Matthew Hale, who had defended Laud but accepted a judgeship under Cromwell, and was then successively Chief Baron of the Exchequer and Chief Justice of the King's Bench under Charles II. Prynne and Hale were more fortunate at the Restoration than the five members of the Inn who had sat as judges at the trial of Charles I – expulsion from the Inn was the least of the penalties they had to suffer.

Between More and Hale, chronologically, comes the Inn's greatest poet, John Donne, who was born early in the reign of Elizabeth I and died early in the reign of Charles I. As we shall see in a later chapter, his complex and contradictory character remains an enigma, despite the copious evidence of his poetry and prose. In terms of unfathomability he is in a class of his own.

By the fifteenth century, and throughout the Tudor and Stuart periods, the Inns of Court were regarded as the third university of England, where many noble families chose to send their sons for further education, even though they did not intend to live by the practice of the law. At that time Oxford and Cambridge taught only civil law (that is, Roman law) and canon law, and common law was regarded as a better training for future justices of the peace. So Bar students (then called inner barristers) included many of the *jeunesse dorée* of England. Many of them felt disdain for their less aristocratic colleagues who actually wanted to earn their living as barristers.

The mixed and mettlesome character of the students repeatedly produced disciplinary problems. By 1588 the benchers issued orders prohibiting the wearing of hats in Hall or in Chapel, and requiring the wearing of a gown in or outside the Inn. Later, playing cards or dice in hall was prohibited.

Legal education lay at the heart of the Inn's activities from its earliest days until the Civil War, and the content and form of the education were already well settled in Tudor times. As described in a later chapter, this education was practical, time-consuming, hands-on, and in-house. The whole membership of the Inn saw education as their professional duty, and for hundreds of years, including periods when printed books were unknown or a rarity, the system worked. The great constitutional historian F.W. Maitland commented:

> *Now it would, so I think, be difficult to conceive any scheme better suited to harden and toughen a traditional body of law than that which, while books were still uncommon, compelled every lawyer to take part in legal education, and every distinguished lawyer to read public lectures.*

This system of practical instruction was severely disrupted by the Civil War in the middle of the seventeenth century, and it did not really recover for at least two hundred (some would say three hundred) years. In the twenty-first century the participation of the Inns and the circuits in the vocational training of barristers – before call, during pupillage, and for the purposes of continuing professional development – with busy practitioners somehow finding the time to undertake this unpaid work, is a welcome sign that something of the old system is being recreated.

Legal scholars seem to be agreed that the same system of education in the common law was followed, with only minor variations, in all the Inns of Court. This is puzzling if you assume that Lincoln's Inn was from its earliest days

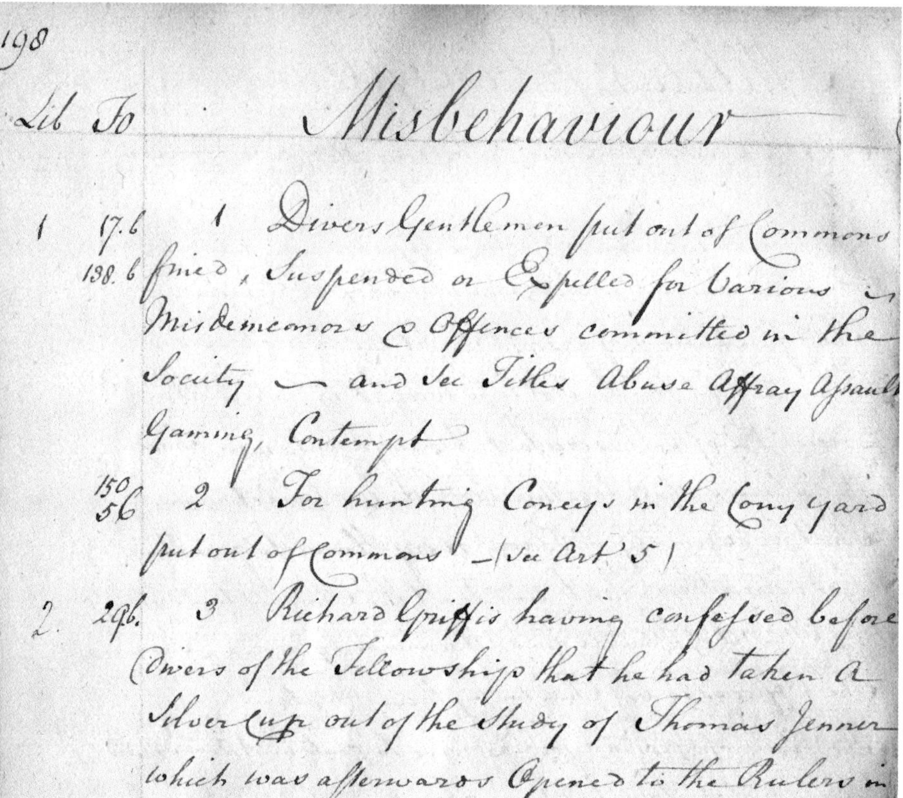

198

Lib Fo — Misbehaviour

1 17.6 1 Divers Gentlemen put out of Commons
138.6 fined, Suspended or Expelled for Various
Misdemeanors & Offences committed in the
Society — and See Titles Abuse Affray Assault
Gaming, Contempt

150/56 2 For hunting Coneys in the Cony yard
put out of Commons — (See Art 5)

2. 296. 3 Richard Griffis having confessed before
Divers of the Fellowship that he had taken a
Silver Cup out of the Study of Thomas Jenner
which was afterwards Opened to the Rulers in

John Coxe's Digest of Council Orders 1769 provides a catalogue from the sixteenth century onwards of offences committed by members, such as stealing wood from the kitchen, 'night-walking', and having women in chambers.

New Square 1741 (John Maurer).

associated with the Court of Chancery, and with equity and trusts. But equity and the law of trusts were still at an early stage of development when the educational system collapsed at the time of the Civil War. Lord Nottingham (Heneage Finch), the so-called father of equity, was Lord Chancellor from 1675 to 1682. It was only from 1733 that the Old Hall (as we now call it) was regularly used by the Lord Chancellor for sittings during the vacation, and this must have encouraged Chancery practitioners to concentrate themselves in Lincoln's Inn. It was well into the nineteenth century before the Chancellorship became almost a monopoly of Lincoln's Inn, and that near-monopoly did not continue in the twentieth century.

During the middle part of the eighteenth century the Inn's two most heroic figures were Hardwicke (born Philip Yorke) and Mansfield (a Scot, born William Murray). Hardwicke was Lord Chancellor from 1737 until 1756, having been Treasurer of the Middle Temple in 1721 (aged 30) and Treasurer of Lincoln's Inn in 1725 (this sort of plurality was later stopped). He was one of the great Chancellors who moulded and refined the doctrines of equity. Mansfield was Chief Justice of the King's Bench from 1756 until 1788. He was a man of wide learning and the loss of his library and papers (burned during the Gordon Riots) was a great blow to legal scholarship. He strove to bring equity and the common law closer together, and with his decision in *Moses v Macferlan* (1760) he could claim to be the founding father of the now fashionable subject of restitution. He even won praise from Jeremy Bentham, a Lincoln's Inn man who was not slow to castigate the errors and follies of the law.

We shall come back to Hardwicke and Mansfield. They were heroic figures at a time when Lincoln's Inn, in common with the other Inns of Court, had more or less abandoned what had for centuries been seen as its primary function: legal education. The sorry tale can be read in full in the reports of a Select Committee on Legal Education (1846) and the subsequent Royal Commission (1855). But the point is illustrated succinctly by a curious little volume, *The Student's Guide through Lincoln's Inn* (2nd edn, 1805) written by the Inn's Steward, Thomas Lane. It combines cloying obsequiousness to the benchers with a lively appreciation of all the charges, fines, and emoluments which were going to come the Steward's way from the students. But it deals with the actual content of legal education in one single uninformative sentence:

The Court of Chancery in the Old Hall 1808, Lord Eldon sitting (Pugin and Rowlandson).

Above: Opening of the Great Hall 1845: the Bar stands as Queen Victoria and the Prince Consort lead a procession of benchers.

'The student will be informed by the proper officer in the hall (who takes down the names for that purpose) of the method of doing exercises.'

The emphasis on charges and fines is a reminder that they were then a very important part of the Inn's total income. Even in the middle of the nineteenth century about half the Inn's annual income (then about £10,000) came from barristers' and students' dues of one sort or another, collected by an immensely convoluted and bureaucratic system. The other half came from rents. Today, by contrast, the great bulk of the Inn's income is rental income from the letting of barristers' chambers, solicitors' offices, residential flats, and a few commercial properties. The rent roll is large but the Inn spends huge sums on maintaining and, so far as Listed Building Regulations permit, modernizing its buildings. Other significant sources of income are parking charges, the letting of the Great Hall and the Old Hall for outside functions, and fees for filming. Students' dues produce a relatively trivial amount, and all the Inn's educational activities are either free or heavily subsidized.

Despite the collapse of legal education, the end of the eighteenth century was a great period in the Inn's history. Its outstanding figures included Erskine, possibly the very greatest of the Inn's advocates, and Eldon, who was not a Lincoln's Inn man but presided over the Court of Chancery in the Old Hall for twenty-five years and must be the most likely suspect for the Lord Chancellor described in the first chapter of *Bleak House*, which although published in 1851 seems to look back to an earlier period.

Eldon, born John Scott, is famous as a most learned, meticulous and deliberate judge. He himself admitted that he had 'somewhat of the cunctative' in his character, and he now appears as almost as a caricature of the old-fashioned Chancery lawyer. But he must, as a young man, have had some special spark in him. He was already a fellow of University College Oxford when, at the age of 21, he eloped and got married in Scotland. He was called in 1776, and in his first year he earned half a guinea, which he gave to his wife. He had agreed that he should keep his first eleven months' fees, and give her those of the twelfth month – the half-guinea was the only money he earned in the year. But in 1780, on a one-guinea brief to consent on an appeal heard by Lord Thurlow, he argued a fundamental point on the equitable doctrine of conversion, carried the day against eminent opponents, and found his reputation made.

By way of contrast, Lord Erskine, who served as Chancellor during the one-year gap between Eldon's long terms of office, was a Lincoln's Inn man but had nothing to do with Chancery work until he was appointed Lord Chancellor in 1806. His fame rests on his consummate skill as an advocate in what would now be called high-profile human rights cases. We shall come back to Erskine in a later chapter. In his day, law and politics were closely entwined. Lord Ellenborough (another Lincoln's Inn man who, as John Law, had defended Warren Hastings) sat in the Cabinet in 1806, in the Ministry of All the Talents, while also holding office as Chief Justice of the King's Bench.

In the east window of Lincoln's Inn Chapel are displayed the coats of arms of Treasurers from 1680 (the

Left: Lord Eldon 1751–1838.

office of Treasurer was ancient, but emerged as head of the Inn only at the beginning of the eighteenth century). From the stained glass you can see that at the turn of the eighteenth century there was a remarkable run of Treasurers: Pitt the Younger (1794), Erskine (1795), and Addington (1797). Pitt was Prime Minister from 1783 (aged 24) to 1801 and from 1804 to 1806, and Addington was Prime Minister during the intervening years: no doubt the responsibilities of the office of Treasurer were less onerous in those days.

The opening years of Queen Victoria's reign coincided with the rise of the Chartist movement, which aimed at political equality far beyond the modest progress achieved by the Reform Act of 1832. Chartism found expression in massive public demonstrations that caused great public alarm. Riots in some manufacturing towns were violently repressed. The culmination was the deployment of considerable forces to meet the civil unrest that was expected in London on 10 April 1848, when the Third Chartist Petition was to be presented to Parliament. Two of the biggest marches started in Russell Square and John Street and headed south, and Lincoln's Inn became a centre for the recruitment, marshalling, and refreshment of large numbers of special constables. But the Inn had many young men who strongly sympathized with the Chartists, while deploring the violence of some of their leaders and supporters; they included Charles Kingsley and Thomas Hughes who, under the influence of F.D. Maurice, Chaplain to the Inn, were committed to what came to be known as Christian Socialism.

Right: Roundell Palmer, First Earl of Selborne 1812–95, one of the great reforming Lord Chancellors of the Victorian era (G.F. Watts 1891).

The Victorian age was a period of long-overdue law reform, and the Court of Chancery had the most crying need for reform. Change came slowly, first with the appointment of Vice-Chancellors to take some of the Chancellor's work, and then in 1851 with the creation of the Court of Appeal in Chancery. The Council of Legal Education was established at about the same time, but Lord Selborne's ambitious plans for a Law University came to nothing, partly because of unified opposition from the Inns of Court, which saw it as a threat to their very existence. Selborne (Roundell Palmer, Lord Chancellor 1872–4 and 1880–5) identified three causes: 'jealousy on the part of the University of London ... the inert and suspicious conservatism of the Inns of Court, and a strong prejudice against bringing together under one system of education future Barristers and future Solicitors'. Selborne was, however, successful in his even more ambitious plans for the concurrent administration of law and equity, which resulted in the Supreme Court of Judicature Acts of 1873 and 1875.

The movement for this fundamental change in the civil justice system coincided with pressure for the building of new law courts on a unified site. The issues interacted and were the cause of much controversy. Soon after the middle of the nineteenth century the Old Hall had been divided into two to accommodate the Lord Chancellor and the Court of Appeal in Chancery (it was by then the Old Hall as the Great Hall, originally called the New Hall, had been built; it was opened by the Queen in 1845). There were also adjacent court buildings, long since demolished, for the three Vice-Chancellors, one where the War Memorial now stands, and the other, accommodating two Vice-Chancellors, immediately south of the Chapel. In this way the Inn housed five Chancery courts, and in 1859 the Inn offered to spend £100,000 on a new court building for all three Vice-Chancellors. But in the same year a Royal Commission recommended bringing all the common law and equity courts together on a single site. The original proposal, supported by the Inn, was for building between Carey Street and the Strand. Others were in favour of an alternative site on the Embankment. The original proposal carried the day and the Royal Courts of Justice were opened by Queen Victoria in 1882. As is well known, Selborne made a long speech in which he referred to the judges being 'deeply sensible of their own many shortcomings'; the original draft had said, 'Conscious as Your Majesty's Judges are of their own infirmities', but at a rehearsal Lord Justice Bowen had suggested that it should be 'of one another's infirmities'.

The changes in the civil justice system had a depressing effect on the Inn's prosperity at the end of the nineteenth century. The courts had not moved far, and the Inn was still the most convenient home for the Chancery Bar. But while the Common Law Bar prospered, and even began to venture into the newly formed Chancery Division, many young members of the Chancery Bar found that other law reforms, especially in the field of conveyancing, had taken away much of their bread-and-butter work. The membership of Lincoln's Inn remained static while the other Inns grew in numbers. The Inn's share of Bar students fell from 42 per cent in 1860 to 13 per cent in 1889.

Another important change in the membership took place around this time. Originally the benchers did not include the judges or the serjeants (broadly but not precisely equivalent to modern silks). On appointment as a serjeant, a barrister left his Inn and joined one of the two Serjeants' Inns, which merged in 1730 and disappeared completely in 1877. The common law judges were, until 1875, appointed only from among the serjeants, even if, as with William Murray, later Lord Mansfield, it meant formally admitting a barrister to the order of the coif immediately before his appointment as a judge. In 1877, the common law judges returned to their original Inns just after the new unified system of civil justice came into operation. Lincoln's Inn was less affected by this change than the other Inns because judges in the Court of Chancery were not chosen from among the serjeants.

Since then, all the Inn's members of the senior judiciary have been benchers and many have served as Treasurer, although the office is now much more demanding than it was. Real stamina is needed to fulfil the duties of Treasurer while sitting full-time in the Court of Appeal or conducting a busy silk's practice. A silk who is appointed as a High Court judge will almost always be a bencher, but just occasionally there has to be a rapid election. The numbers of the judiciary increase steadily, but so do the numbers of benchers: twenty-two in 1805; fifty-one in 1843; eighty-two in 1914; eighty in 1948 (including, as Sir Gerald Hurst's book records, eleven honorary benchers, but that was a low point in the fortunes of the Chancery Bar); today, there are over 300, including sixty honorary benchers. The Inn's policy is that the benchers should always include a sizeable majority of practising barristers, with a proper balance between silks and juniors.

In theory, the affairs of the Inn are governed by Council, a general meeting of all the benchers. Council meetings are normally held once a month in term time. But in practice most of the work is done by a series of committees, of which the most important are the

The Inn's last serjeant, Sir Richard Amphlett, being inducted in the Common Pleas in 1874.

The south end of the Great Hall from the Vice-Chancellor's Court (L.J. Wood).

Charles Barry's design for new law courts in Lincoln's Inn Fields c1841, the first of many abortive plans to build new courts on a unified site.

Treasurer's Committee (a sort of inner cabinet), the Finance Committee, and the Buildings Committee; and by the Inn's staff directed by the Under Treasurer, whose old-fashioned title disguises his crucial position as the Inn's Chief Executive Officer.

Selborne was probably the greatest of a line of reforming Lord Chancellors from the Inn in the Victorian age; among the others were Lords Brougham (Lord Chancellor 1830–4), Lyndhurst (John Singleton Copley, Lord Chancellor for three spells between 1827 and 1846), St Leonards (Edward Sugden, Lord Chancellor 1852), Cranworth (Robert Rolfe, Lord Chancellor 1852–8 and 1865–6), and Cairns (Lord Chancellor 1868 and 1874–82).

The will and eight codicils of Lord St Leonards made an interesting contribution to the law. After his death no one could find them, but his devoted daughter, Charlotte Sugden, was able from memory to give a detailed and credible account of their contents. This was the first time that a lost will had ever been proved on the strength of oral evidence alone, without any secondary evidence of a documentary nature. The remarkable circumstances were summarized by the President of the Probate Division in the leading case of *Sugden v St Leonards* (1876):

> *But Miss Sugden's position is exceptional ... she was the daily companion for many years of one of the greatest lawyers that ever lived; who was devoted to his profession; who to the latest years of his life delighted in carrying on his studies in that profession, and who took a pleasure in making plain to non-professional and otherwise uninstructed minds subjects of a somewhat complicated character in which he himself took an interest. Miss Sugden was his assistant and amanuensis in the preparation of the later editions of his works, and she appears to have been always with him upon the many occasions on which he dealt with his testamentary papers and dispositions.*

Reading between the lines, you feel Miss Sugden must have been as saintly a character as Dorothea Casaubon in *Middlemarch*.

The Inn produced many other great figures in the nineteenth century: space permits mention of just two more, Lord Kingsdown (born Thomas Pemberton) and Sir George Jessel. Pemberton was called in 1816 and quickly obtained a lucrative practice at the Chancery Bar. He seems to have been an archetype of the best sort of Chancery silk, having

> *a lucid simplicity and subdued strength, which seemed, without an effort, to assume the most appropriate forms of argument and language. Usually more succinct than the advocates of his own day, and infinitely less prolix than the advocates of our time, Pemberton marshalled the facts of his case, with an unerring perspicuity and then led the mind of the judge, by a natural train of thought, to the legal principles which ought to govern his decision.*

His career followed a strange course. By chance he was briefed on behalf of a distant relative, Sir Robert Leigh, and won the case in 1831. His client (who had an income of £14,000 a year) was so pleased that he changed his will to give his kinsman a life interest. On Sir Robert's death in 1842, Pemberton changed his name to Pemberton Leigh, retired from the Bar, and became a country gentleman and amateur scientist. But he was made a member of the Privy Council, and, while complaining that he would rather be at home on his estates, he made a huge contribution to the judicial work of the Privy Council, becoming an expert on all the topics which then came on appeal to the Judicial Committee of the Privy Council, among them ecclesiastical law, admiralty law, private international law as affecting marriages, imperial constitutional law and Indian land tenure.

Jessel was the first Master of the Rolls (1873–83) to preside over the newly established Court of Appeal. This marked the culmination of the ascendancy of the office of Master of the Rolls: originally a clerk, but an increasingly powerful clerk, in Chancery; later the Lord Chancellor's deputy; now the second most important judicial post in the English justice system. Moreover, it was no coincidence that the change took place at the time of Jessel's appointment: the Lord Chancellor could not find a Court of Appeal strong enough to hear appeals from Jessel.

Jessel had been called in 1847. He quickly gained a large Chancery practice, with a special expertise in bankruptcy law. Holdsworth describes him as 'a profound equity lawyer with the mind of an acute juryman, who by reason of that unique combination of qualities was able to apply to the rules of equity the touchstone of common sense.' At the Bar and on the bench he was known for his kindness to new practitioners and his abrasiveness to leaders of the Bar: 'His friendly zeal in helping young and nervous practitioners over the stiles of legal difficulties was only equalled by the fiery enthusiasm with which he thrust back the Attorney and Solicitor General and people of that sort.' He could also be caustic about cited authority with which he did not agree. As a judge he never reserved judgment; his saying was, 'I may be wrong, but I never have any doubts.'

By the 1870s the Black Books begin to show the admission to the Inn of students from India, which then extended to the whole subcontinent, and other parts of what was then the British Empire. The overseas students started as a trickle, and in the twentieth century became a strong stream which seems to have reached its high water mark in the 1960s. But overseas students still play an important part of the Inn's life and culture, as we shall see in a later chapter.

The history of the Inn during the twentieth century may still be too close for balanced judgment. During the first half of the century the Inn, like the legal profession generally, was slow to react to the enormous social and economic changes brought about by two world wars, women's emancipation, the welfare state, the end of empire, and the death of deference. During the second half of the century the Inn became rather more aware of the changing world outside, and rather better at adapting to it. Lawyers may remain prominent in public life, but are less likely to combine public office with their profession – it is now barely possible to practise at the Bar and be a member of the House of Commons. The Inn's two most recent Prime Ministers have shown little interest in the law, and not much respect for it. Practice at the bar has become much more demanding. Barristers are more professionally competent. Chambers are larger and better managed. They are also (on the whole) friendlier and more informal, and decisions on pupillages and tenancies are (on the whole) taken responsibly and fairly.

After a grim period in the 1950s, when the judges of the Chancery Division were so personally unpleasant as to

Sir George Jessel 1824–83, the first Master of the Rolls to preside over the Court of Appeal.

The Inn's oldest buidings at the heart of twenty-first century London.

drive most of the work away, the Chancery Bar has flourished and its work has greatly diversified. Since the 1960s, Chancery judges have, with rare exceptions, been quiet, courteous, and expert. Robert Stevens has compared them to the subalterns in the trenches during World War I who vowed that if they survived they would never behave as badly as the staff officers above them.

How has the Inn managed to survive through six centuries? The grandiloquent answer would be that each generation of lawyers has faithfully passed on to the next the lamps of justice, learning, integrity, and good fellowship. A humbler and truer answer would be that the Inn has (often only at the eleventh hour) shown itself capable of adapting to changing circumstances. Economic realism would say that the reason why Lincoln's Inn and the other Inns of Court survived, while the Inns of Chancery disappeared, is that the Inns of Court had a monopoly of admitting barristers to the practice of their profession. This right was finally established by the judges over 400 years ago. Solicitors' rights of audience in higher courts have so far made little impact on the Bar. But today monopolies are rightly subject to close scrutiny, and it is up to the Inns to be prepared to explain themselves to the new Bar Standards Board and to the general public.

Explain, not justify. The Inns have once again recognized their responsibilities in the practical training of young barristers, and they discharge their responsibilities with skill and enthusiasm. Dozens of busy practitioners somehow find the time to teach advocacy to the young, for no pecuniary reward and often at personal inconvenience. The scale and importance of this voluntary effort is not generally known, but it deserves to be.

So what of the future? It is inappropriate to indulge in self-congratulation or triumphalism. There are, as usual, some dark clouds in the sky: statutory regulation of the legal profession, the continuing dilemma of deferral of call, and restructuring of legal aid. Nevertheless there are reasons for optimism. The Inn is a much friendlier place than it was fifty, or even twenty-five years ago. Members and students and their partners and children are welcomed – really welcomed – to the Chapel, to summer parties, to Christmas parties, and at all sorts of social gatherings. The standard of young practitioners at the Chancery Bar, and the Bar generally, is far higher than it was fifty, or even twenty-five years ago. It would be gratifying to put this down to the strenuous efforts which all the Inns have made to promote advocacy training; but probably the real reason is market forces: ninety per cent increased competition, and ten per cent improved training is a more likely explanation. Nevertheless the Inn's future is as a regenerated place of legal education. The commitment to legal education must be paramount. Without that the fine wines and urbane talk, the old silver and the soft candlelight, delightful as they are, would become a quaint irrelevance. That must not happen.

The annual family picnic.

Great Figures

The Inn's copy of the famous painting by Hans Holbein of 1527 in the Frick Collection, New York. The Inn's miniature (to the right), on the other hand, is not a copy but an original sixteenth-century work, though now thought to be after Holbein rather than by him, one reason being that the collar of SS is the wrong way round, an error that Holbein himself is unlikely to have made.

SIR THOMAS MORE 1478–1535

Thomas More was born in London, the son of Sir John More, a barrister who later became a justice of the King's Bench Court. His education began at the city's best school of the time, St Anthony's, and in the household of John Morton, Archbishop of Canterbury, who was prompted to say of him, 'This child here, whosoever shall live to see it, will prove a marvellous man.'

At Oxford he developed his command of Latin and was drilled in logic before, at his father's command, taking up the study of law at an Inn of Chancery, New Inn. He was admitted to Lincoln's Inn in 1496, being called to the Bar about five years later (the exact date is not recorded).

Described by his friend Erasmus as *'omnium horarum homo'*, rendered later as 'a man for all seasons', and by G.K. Chesterton as 'the greatest historical character in English History', he was in turn a successful barrister, a statesman, Lord Chancellor of England, and, from 1935, a saint. But he was also a scholar, the humanist author of amongst other great works, *Utopia*, a wit, and a man of cultivated tastes who delighted in music and painting. In 1535 Henry VIII had this luminary beheaded as a traitor.

More was a man of the Renaissance. The 'old learning' of the Middle Ages decreed that established Church authority controlled the religious houses, the universities and the learned professions. The 'new learning' sought to re-vitalize theology with human reason and through the study, in the original languages, of the culture and scholarship of ancient Greece and Rome. The decade after More left Oxford was for him a period of intense intellectual, spiritual, and cultural ferment. His curiosity and capacity for work caused him to study the Bible, the Church Fathers, and the classics as well as to write widely. Before he finally bowed to his father's wish that he follow in his footsteps he tested his vocation for the priesthood, residing for four years with the Carthusians, subjecting himself to their discipline and learning a lifelong habit of mortification of the flesh.

Despite his attraction to the monastic way, he pursued the new learning and humanism under the influence of his Oxford friends and Erasmus, and decided to serve God and his fellows in a lay rather than religious capacity. Early in his career he wrote of his desire for temperance, patience, humility and hope; desires he often repeated during his career and echoed in a prayer he penned in his final hours.

More's legal career advanced steadily, and with the accession of Henry VIII in 1509 he began to play a part in public affairs. His handling of a notorious shipping case brought him to the attention of the royal court after which he received many commissions to represent England's interest abroad.

It was at this time that More wrote *Utopia*, a many-layered work that satirizes European society for its short-sighted love of gain, its lack of true Christian piety and charity, and its unreasonableness. Among the topics discussed by More in *Utopia* were penology, state-controlled education, religious pluralism, divorce, euthanasia, and women's rights.

More was admitted to the King's Council in 1518 and was with the King when he met François I at the Field of the Cloth of Gold and, shortly afterwards, the Emperor Charles V. In 1521 he was knighted and made Under Treasurer of the Exchequer; in 1523 he was elected Speaker of the House of Commons, and in 1525 he became Chancellor of the Duchy of Lancaster. During these years he was almost constantly in attendance upon the King.

Erasmus provides a pen portrait of More at this time. Calling him England's only genius and a man born and framed for friendship, he describes him thus:

> *He is not tall without being noticeably short. His complexion tends to be warm rather than pale with eyes rather greyish-blue, with a kind of fleck in them, the sort that usually indicates a gifted intelligence. His expression shows the sort of man he is, always friendly and cheerful, with something of the air of one who smiles easily, and disposed to be merry rather than serious or solemn, but without a hint of the fool or the buffoon.*

His household was known for its piety and erudition. Unusually for those times, More provided education equally for his daughters as for his son, writing to his children's tutor, 'women and men are equally suited for those studies by which reason is cultivated and becomes fruitful like a ploughed land on which the seed of good lessons has been sown.'

In 1521 Henry had written an anti-Lutheran tract that earned him the papal title of *Fidei Defensor*. By 1525 the war on heresy had begun in earnest. For More, heresy was corruption of the soul and he campaigned actively against it. Indeed, it is hard to defend More from the charge that on his orders men were tortured for heresy.

In 1529 More followed Wolsey to become Lord Chancellor of England. He streamlined outdated practices in the common law system and opened up access to the equity courts. He had particular expertise in common law, and demonstrated in his judicial role a fearless integrity based on his conviction that judges should act according to their judicial consciences.

But even as More took up his highest office the storm clouds were gathering. Wolsey had been stripped of his office by Henry for his failure to obtain the king's long-desired divorce from Queen Catherine. In 1532, when More saw that Henry was determined on marriage with Anne Boleyn, he resigned the Great Seal on grounds of ill-health and sought the happiness of a retired life.

But his time for quiet study was to be short. More refused to attend Henry's marriage to Anne in 1533. From that moment he was a marked man. He was required to swear to the Act of Succession, which he refused to do because it entailed a repudiation of papal supremacy; his arrest swiftly followed. After more than a year of cruel imprisonment in the Tower, More was brought to trial in Westminster Hall, not for refusing to swear to the succession but for denying King Henry VIII's new title of Supreme Head of the Church of England under the 1534 Act of Supremacy.

The outcome of the trial was never in doubt. He was sentenced to a traitor's death, commuted to beheading. Within a week of the jury's verdict, he was executed. His death shocked the country; continental Europe was appalled at the news and the Emperor Charles V made formal protests.

'Ye must understand', More said to his judges at his trial,

> *that in things touching conscience, every true and good subject is more bound to have respect to his conscience and to his soul than to any other thing in all the world beside. I am not bounden to conform my conscience to the Council of one realm against the general Council of Christendom. I have all the Councils made these thousand years. The discharge of my conscience enforceth me to speak. It is not for this Supremacy so much that you seek my blood, as for that I would not condescend to the marriage.*

Conscience for More was not simply an individual matter. As Lord Chancellor he was charged with the application of traditional principles of conscience to law. At his trial he asserted the primacy of the laws of God and reason. The dilemma of what is due to the individual conscience and what is due to the state is eternal. Sir Thomas More stands for us as an exemplar of the claims of conscience against the laws of the state.

Andrew Collender

VTOPIAE INSVLAE FIGVRA

VTOPIENSIVM ALPHABETVM.

a b c d e f g h i k l m n o p q r s t v x y

Tetraſtichon vernacula Vtopienſium lingua.

Vtopos ha Boccas peu la chama polta chamaan Bargol he maglomi baccan foma gymno ſophaon Agrama gymnoſophon labarembacha bodamilomin Voluala barchin heman la lauoluola dramme pagloni.

Horum verſuum ad verbum hæc eſt ſententia.

Vtopus me dux ex non inſula fecit inſulam
Vna ego terrarum omnium abſq; philoſophia
Ciuitatem philoſophicam expreſſi mortalibus
Libēter impartio mea, nō grauatim accipio meliora.

The Library's copy of the exceptionally rare first edition of Utopia, *1516.*

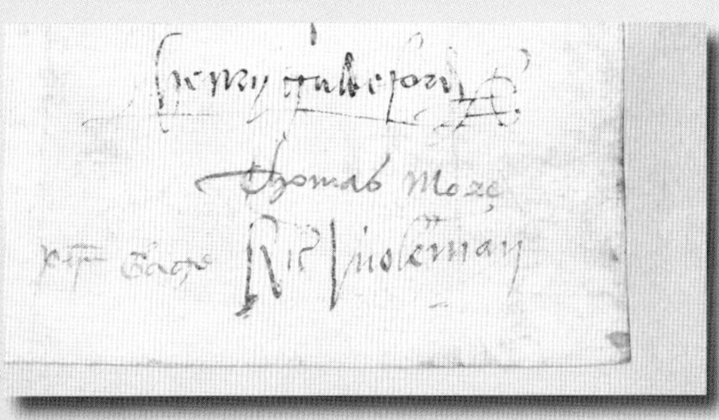

More's autograph on a 1527 document, now in the Library. Examples of More's signature, even in the Public Records, are uncommon. Had he not declined the office of Keeper of the Black Book, we would have more examples of his handwriting.

The Buildings:
Long History and Picturesque Variety

ROBERT FOOKES AND RICHARD WALLINGTON

The only surviving fabric of the medieval palace of the Bishops of Chichester.

The Inn has a picturesque variety of styles and periods of architecture, in a pleasantly haphazard juxtaposition. One reason for this is that twice a major rebuilding scheme was started but only partly carried out. Another factor is that the Inn did not lose any buildings in the two world wars.

The building history of the Inn before the twentieth century is a barometer of its prosperity. The booming sixteenth and nineteenth centuries were times of extensive building, while little was added to the fabric of the Inn in the leaner seventeenth and eighteenth centuries. The Inn was reasonably well-off in the twentieth century, perhaps very well off in the latter part, but for legal, cultural, and economic reasons it has done more rebuilding and refurbishment of old buildings than building new ones, and any new ones have been in unobtrusive locations.

From the left: 8 Old Square (c1875); the Chapel (1623 and, shown, 1882); Old Hall (1492 and 1928); 12 and 13 New Square (1535).

A feature of buildings of all periods is the presence of the initials of whoever was Treasurer when its construction or some major repair or reconstruction occurred, together with 'T' for Treasurer and the year. This practice goes back at least to the seventeenth century, and is similar to the practice of traditional owners of large landed estates putting their initials on new buildings. Dickens pokes mild fun at this practice in relation to Staple Inn in Chapter 11 of *Edwin Drood*.

BEGINNINGS

The medieval period is represented by Old Hall, and also in a sense by the whole of Gatehouse Court, the quadrangle of buildings with the Gatehouse to the east, Old Buildings to the south, Old Hall to the west, and the Chapel to the north. This is the original nucleus of the Inn. Like a piazza in an Italian town that preserves the shape of the Roman amphitheatre that preceded it, Gatehouse Court maintains the ground plan of the early medieval palace of the Bishop of Chichester, which was rented by the Society of Lincoln's Inn from some time before 1422. None of the fabric of the Bishop's palace survives apart from the remains of a pointed arch, with nailhead decoration, which was uncovered during nineteenth-century alterations and is now set in the external north wall of Old Hall.

In the Middle Ages there were many institutions where men lived in communities: monasteries, Oxford and Cambridge colleges, religious confraternities, craft guilds,

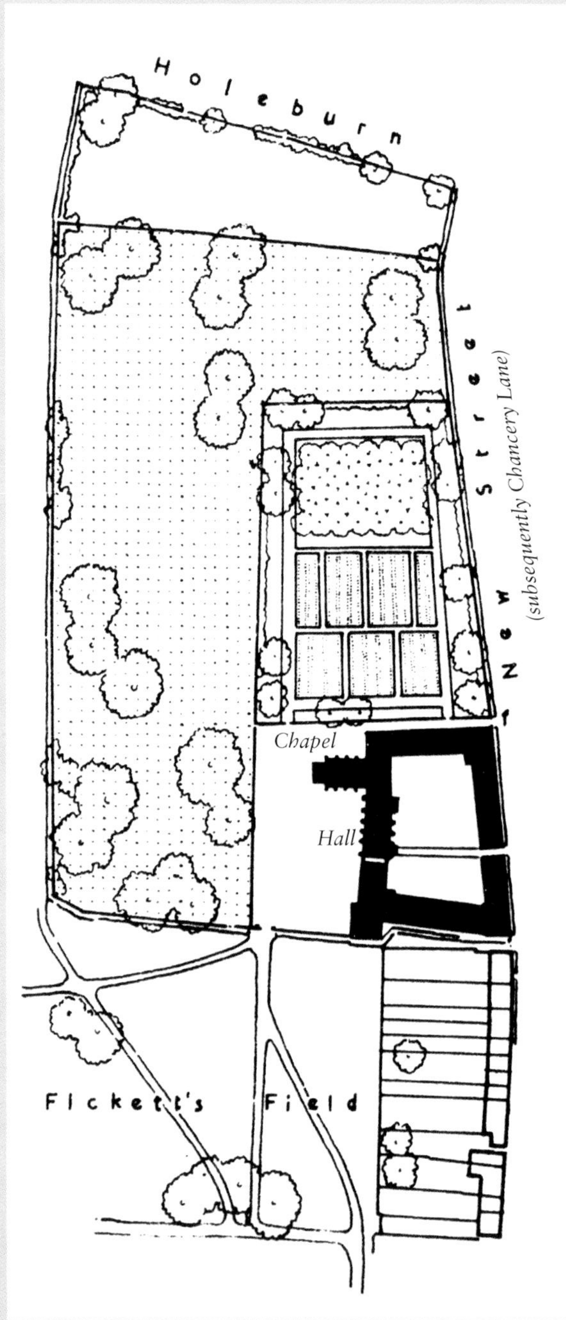

Above: Modern reconstruction of the ground plan of the Palace of the Bishop of Chichester, which the Society of Lincoln's Inn started to occupy before 1422.

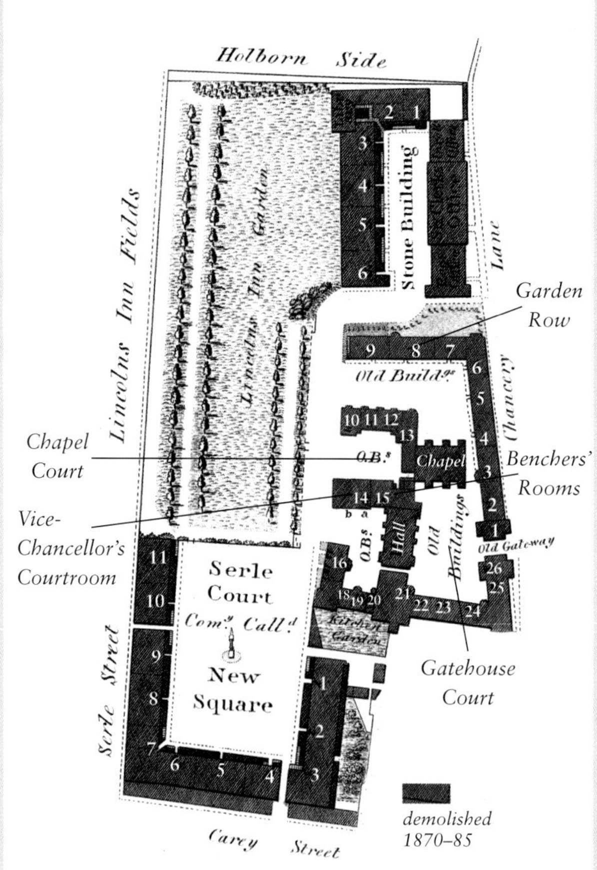

Left: Plan of Lincoln's Inn in 1823, before the Great Hall, Library and 7 Stone Buildings were built, and showing the buildings demolished 1870–85.

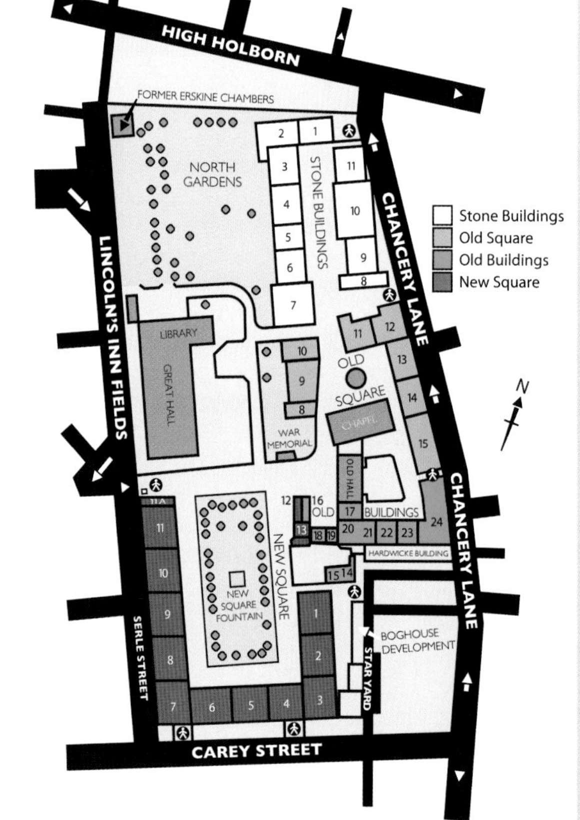

Left: Lincoln's Inn, 2007.

livery companies, Inns of Court. All had the same institutional and architectural geography: a chapel for communal worship, a hall for communal eating with associated kitchens, and rooms or 'lodgings' for individuals to live or work in arranged around staircases, the whole ensemble laid out around one or more quadrangles or courtyards. The palaces of great lords were similarly arranged, the lodgings being for their many counsellors, servants, and retainers. Thus the Society of Lincoln's Inn was able to make use of a bishop's palace, and the Societies of the Inner and Middle Temple could use former buildings of the Knights Templar.

Old Hall roof structure (1492).

Old Hall

In a period of prosperity between the late fifteenth and early seventeenth centuries the Society of Lincoln's Inn replaced all the buildings of the Bishop's palace in stages, built additional chambers to the north and west, and in 1580 acquired the freehold of the Inn. Old Hall (1489–92), replacing an earlier hall, is the earliest surviving building of this campaign of renewal, and the earliest surviving secular building in the Inns of Court, although rebuilt completely, but faithfully to the original design, in 1924–8. It is a standard mid to late fifteenth-century hall design. Old Hall's main glory is the timber roof structure, rediscovered in the 1920s after being hidden for 200 years. The main defining elements are the arch braces, collar beams, and wind braces. As built, Old Hall was shorter than it is now, lacking the bay windows at the southern end. It was extended, and the southern bay windows added, in 1582. The interesting Jacobean screen against the south wall is from 1624, while the miniaturized gothic vaulting in the passage behind the screen is from 1819, when the screen was probably moved back against the south wall (having it seems previously been located further to the north, with a gallery over). The kitchens were in what is now 17 Old Buildings, but these were demolished when the Great Hall was built in the 1840s. In about 1720 a plaster ceiling was inserted in Old Hall, which hid the medieval roof timbers, and in the late eighteenth century the exterior was covered in cement rendering like that on the Chapel (see illustration page 47).

THE SIXTEENTH CENTURY

The Gatehouse and south side of Gatehouse Court (now 20–24 Old Buildings) were rebuilt in the sixteenth century and then again in 1966–9, approximately preserving their original sixteenth century external appearance. Modern bricks were used and the effect is rather dull, but a contrast is provided to the nineteenth-century neo-Tudor of 15 Old Square. The Gatehouse still has its sixteenth-century door.

Surviving from the sixteenth century, though much altered, is the group between Old Hall and New Square: 12 and 13 New Square and Nos 16, 18, 19, and 20 Old Buildings. These date from about 1535, with new windows inserted in the eighteenth century. Viewed from the north they present a delightful appearance, with a skyline chaotic with chimney stacks and octagonal staircase towers, and with much surviving warm red brickwork of the period.

The Gatehouse (1518) viewed from Chancery Lane, from a print of 1800.

Several other ranges were constructed in the sixteenth century to the north and west of Gatehouse Court but were demolished in the nineteenth century to make way for new building (see the plan of the Inn for 1823).

THE SEVENTEENTH CENTURY

The Chapel

The Chapel dates from 1619–23 and is the subject of a separate chapter. It is remarkable for its undercroft, which was a graveyard for members of the Inn (confined to benchers from 1791), and as a fine example of early seventeenth-century gothic architecture.

New Square

The seventeenth century, especially the years of the Civil War, was hard for the Inn, and there was no new building by the Inn between 1623 and 1774. New Square, built around 1690, is not an exception as it was a private venture, mostly on land outside the Inn but over which Lincoln's Inn acquired a degree of control, and to which the Inn lent its name, or 'brand' as it would now be called. The square's history is of legal as well as architectural interest, since it has 'flying freeholds' with the mutual obligations of repair etc regulated by a private Act of Parliament.

In the late seventeenth century there was a house-building boom in the area between the City of London and Westminster, and pieces of open land became ripe for development. One of these was an area known as Fickett's Field or Little Lincoln's Inn Fields immediately to the south of the Inn's gardens. Henry Serle, a barrister but not a bencher of Lincoln's Inn, agreed in 1679 to purchase most of the rights to this land with a view to developing it. However, appropriately for something intended for lawyers, the venture began with complicated litigation, which delayed construction for about ten years. Serle had to fight on two fronts: against the benchers of the Inn over his development plan and against his former partner over the ownership of the land. The dispute with the Inn was resolved by an agreement of 11 July 1682 between Serle and the benchers, the latter headed by the memorably named Sir Harbottle Grimston. This determined how New Square was eventually developed. It defined the dimensions and location of the buildings to be constructed by Serle and the locations of gateways and walls, and provided that the land in the middle should remain forever open and unbuilt upon. The entrances to the chambers were to be from inside the Square, and the effect of the various provisions was to treat the new buildings as if they were part of the Inn, even though only 11 New Square (as it became) was on the Inn's land. Although the buildings on Serle's land were to be his to dispose of, he agreed that they were to consist exclusively of chambers for members of Lincoln's Inn or serjeants at law who had formerly been members, and that the occupants were to be subject to the regulations of the Inn. The buildings were to be known as Serle Court. It was in other words a superior private finance initiative under which the number of chambers available for members of the Inn was much increased at no cost to the Inn.

Etching of 1760 showing, from the left: part of Old Buildings and 12 and 13 New Square (1535), the former pillar in New Square (1696), and No. 1 and part of 2 New Square (c1693).

New Square (c1693) looking south in the early eighteenth century (Sutton Nicholls).

New Square looking south in 2007, with an extra storey, shallower pitched roofs, and gardens but no pillar in the centre.

Looking north-eastwards from New Square in about 1874. From the left: 9 Old Square (c1874) before 8 Old Square was constructed; the one-storey courtroom (1819), now demolished; 12 and 13 New Square (1535) with the now demolished shops to the south.

Serle's other, longer, fight over his ownership of the land was with Nicholas Barbon, a buccaneering businessman and an extremely colourful character. Barbon was the son of Praisegod Barbon, a prominent puritan during the Civil War who gave his name to the Barebones Parliament, one of Oliver Cromwell's unsuccessful governmental experiments. Nicholas Barbon rebelled against parental puritanism, lived extravagantly, and tried to make a fortune from property development, particularly in and around the Inns of Court. The litigation ended only in 1689, with a victory for Serle, but when he died in 1690 Barbon reappeared in charge of the building works, apparently as agent for the administrators of Serle's estate. Serle seems to have finished about half the development by the time of his death and Barbon completed the rest by late 1692 or early 1693.

What Serle started and Barbon finished was 1–11 New Square. We have already seen that 12 and 13 New Square are sixteenth-century buildings with later windows inserted, and numbered as part of New Square. New Square has had various misadventures since 1692, including major fires at Nos 2, 3, 4, 10, and 11. No. 10 was rebuilt in the nineteenth century, as was No. 11 in the twentieth century after war damage. The original appearance of the buildings is best seen in Nos 6–9. Even these were altered in the eighteenth century, when the original casement windows were replaced by sash windows, the original wooden cornice was removed, and an extra storey was added. No. 2 is different from the rest having segment-headed windows, the window frames set back from the wall surface, and vertical bands of red brick, which suggest that the front wall was rebuilt around 1730 in a more contemporary style. Other points of interest are the boundary stones displayed on the walls of Nos 1 and 11, and the artisan baroque decoration of the archway through to Carey Street in the south-east corner.

In 1722 the surviving partner of the partnership of goldsmiths, which then owned Serle Court, became insolvent. The property of the partnership was sold off freehold and piecemeal, often to the existing tenants. The result was the patchwork of ownership with many 'flying freeholds' that continues today, although the Inn has gradually acquired parts of New Square and now owns more than seventy per cent of the buildings. The Inn regulated maintenance and contributed to it from an early stage, in reliance on the 1682 agreement, until it promoted a private Act of Parliament, the Lincoln's Inn Act 1860, which has since governed the mutual obligations of proprietors. The combination of fragmentation of ownership and the 1682 agreement have preserved New Square from redevelopment, and it is probably the most complete late seventeenth-century London square to survive. It has little in common with the medieval courtyard layout of Gatehouse Court, something implicitly acknowledged by the name changing from Serle *Court* to New *Square*.

Left: A New Square basement area.

Right: The archway leading out of New Square to Carey Street (c1693) bearing the initials of Nathaniel Clarke KC, Treasurer in 1818 when the Inn purchased the shop premises.

T
CTS
1848
T
N . G . C.
1818.
T
N . G .
1818.
WILDY & SONS LTD
LAW BOOKSELLERS
VALUERS & EXPORTERS
LIBRARIES PURCHASED
Established 1830

THE EIGHTEENTH CENTURY

Stone Buildings

Stone Buildings are a noble fragment of a grander scheme for replacing and extending the Inn's buildings. The extension was built, but the rebuilding stage was never reached. The project began with Council in 1766 and 1768 ordering surveys of the existing buildings of the Inn with a view to rebuilding, and in 1769 deciding to sell Thavies Inn for £4,100 and use the money for improving Lincoln's Inn. The confusing events of the next few years are typical of an institution run by a committee. In April 1771 Council ordered that Robert Adam, James Paine, Matthew Brettingham, and Robert Taylor be asked to draw plans for rebuilding the old part of Lincoln's Inn. In December 1771 Council ordered that only Taylor be invited to submit plans, but in June 1772, on hearing that the other three still intended preparing plans, ordered the Steward to ensure they were all four delivered by the first day of the next Michaelmas term.

Adam, Paine, and Brettingham drew up plans in 1772, but Taylor still got the job. Four years later Paine was paid £200 and Brettingham £80 for their plans. Some of the drawings they supplied, long thought lost, were found in a clear-out of some of the Inn's cellars in 1988. The Inn paid nothing to Adam and he kept his drawings, which are now in the collection of Sir John Soane's Museum. The surviving drawings indicate that the brief was to replace everything except the Chapel and 1–11 New Square, to build out northwards into the gardens but leave the western part of the gardens as they were, and to include accommodation for the Six Clerks of the Court of Chancery.

Robert Taylor (1714–88), like Paine, belonged to an earlier and more Palladian generation of architects than Adam, but was open to new ideas. Taylor had inherited his father's bankrupt stonemason's business, and built up his own practice first as a sculptor and then as an architect. He was hard-working and a good businessman. By the 1770s he had a substantial architectural practice, his main clients being City of London merchants and the Bank of

Robert Adam's design for the Inn (1772): upper, the west front from the gardens; lower, the east front from Chancery Lane.

England. He was later knighted on becoming Sheriff of London. He named his only son Michael Angelo after another sculptor turned architect. Michael Angelo Taylor, after being admitted to Inner Temple in 1769, was admitted to Lincoln's Inn in October 1770, and called to the Bar by Lincoln's Inn in November 1774. A student's choice of an Inn of Court was often his father's, and it looks as though Robert Taylor was aware that rebuilding plans were in the offing and that it would do no harm for the Taylor family to be seen around the Inn.

Taylor's design, approved by a resolution of Council on 6 August 1774, was more interesting than Brettingham's, but more affordable than Paine's or Adam's. Clad in Portland stone, it was still going to be expensive. At the same Council meeting, the Inn's bricklayer was ordered to start constructing on the North Garden what are now 3–6 Stone Buildings in accordance with Taylor's plans. Taylor's plans show a new hall for the Inn on the site where 7 Stone Buildings now stands, and it is the central feature of the design. The plan then has a symmetrical repeat of what are now 1–6 Stone Buildings extending southwards from the new hall and turning east towards Chancery Lane south of the Chapel. The sixteenth-century buildings would have been demolished, including Old Hall.

At the same time the Inn was negotiating with the Accountant General and Registers, and the Six Clerks of the Court of Chancery to sell them the land in the North Garden along Chancery Lane for new court offices. The court offices were also designed by Taylor, and built under direct contract with the Court. These are now 8–11 Stone Buildings, which the Inn purchased in 1881 when the court officials were either abolished or transferred to the new Royal Courts of Justice. The buildings are a simplified version of Taylor's design for the Inn, with no giant columns, and clad in yellow brick rather than Portland stone in the case of Nos 8, 9, and 11.

The buildings opposite consisted entirely of new chambers for members of the Inn. To help finance the construction work the lessees were sold long leases for a premium and a ground rent. Down to this time all the chambers in the Inn were leased in this way, and it was only subsequently that the Inn started letting premises at rack rents. Nos 3–6 Stone Buildings were completed by late 1778, but it took until June 1780 for the initial leases to be granted, including a lease of the attic of 4 Stone Buildings to William Pitt for a premium of £161.3s.10¾d. The sale of these leases brought in a total of £13,000. Other sources of finance for Stone Buildings were the sale of Thavies Inn (£4,100) and the sale of the land for Court offices for a total of £11,089. The total of all these is £28,089, which was perhaps all spent on Nos 3–6, for in 1778 they were ordered to be insured for £28,000. However, the Inn still had to find other money to finance Nos 1 and 2.

Construction of the north range, now 1 and 2 Stone Buildings, took until 1785. The plan had originally been for the north range to extend to Chancery Lane, but it was not practicable to buy the small piece of land at the north-east corner of the garden. Accordingly the magnificent east facade of No. 1 is hidden behind a shop, and the building has a staircase immediately behind this façade, causing the windows in the facade to be false. Taylor designed the interior of the Inn's new library at 2 Stone Buildings and the books were moved there in 1787 from the old library, which had been in a now-demolished building that projected westwards from the area between

James Paine's design for the Inn (1772), west front.

The west front of Stone Buildings (1774–85) in 1800 (S. Ireland), the unfinished southern end hidden by a tree, also showing the west end of Garden Row (demolished 1870s) with the sundial now on 4 Stone Buildings attached to it.

Old Hall and the Chapel. The remainder of Nos 1 and 2 was again leased as chambers.

The next stage would have been the hall, but the Inn had probably used up most of its available resources at this stage. Then came the French Revolution in 1789, followed by the Napoleonic Wars, and it was not until the 1830s that the Inn started to think about doing any more building.

Stone Buildings was eventually finished off at the south end by the building of No. 7 to the designs of Hardwick (see below) between 1843 and 1845. On the garden front he copied the west facade of the north end, at last providing symmetry. The treatment most appropriate to the south and east facades of No. 7 will not have been as obvious. Hardwick chose to carry on the giant order as pilasters on the south wall, and to repeat on the east face Taylor's giant order of attached columns but without a pediment above. The result is that the east facade of No. 7 gives some idea of what Taylor's hall would have looked like from the outside, although it would have extended two more bays to the south and would have had larger windows at the first-floor level.

In the design of Stone Buildings the medieval courtyard has been left behind, even more than with New Square. Viewed from between the two ranges of Stone Buildings it is a London street, but viewed from the garden it is somewhere between a Palladian country house and a government building such as Somerset House.

The west front of Stone Buildings in 2007.

HARDWICKE
12 NEW SQUARE
OLD SQUARE

THE NINETEENTH CENTURY

The Great Hall Complex

By the 1830s Old Hall had become too small for its purpose despite various extensions. Similarly, the Library in 2 Stone Buildings was running out of room to expand. In 1839 the Inn considered a scheme by the architect John White to enlarge and extend the Old Hall to provide additional dining accommodation, a council room, and a new Library. A second opinion was requested.

The Inn turned to Philip Hardwick. He was by then the vice-president of the Institute of British Architects and had just shown his liking for the 'masculinity of Doric' in creating the Euston propylaeum (the 'arch' controversially demolished in 1962). His father, Thomas, had been a well-known architect and his elder brother John was a barrister member of the Inn. In a period of rapidly changing architectural fashions he was exceptionally versatile and able to design competently in English Baroque (Goldsmiths Hall) as well as neo-Grecian at Euston, the neo-Palladian of 7 Stone Buildings, and the neo-Tudor of the Great Hall. Hardwick's comment on White's plan was that the 'accommodation is inadequate for the business of the Society' and that 'if economy be the principal object I am not aware that a more economical plan could be produced'. He was asked to produce plans of his own. Meanwhile he started work at the Inn, and designed and supervised the construction of 7 Stone Buildings (see above). He also repaired and improved the Chapel.

In 1842 Hardwick gave his opinion on the way forward for the Hall and Library. He produced, in contrast to his mainly classically-inspired work elsewhere, a Tudor Gothic proposal that has been described as the first conspicuous metropolitan building 'in which the piquant possibilities of articulated Gothic composition were made strikingly evident'.

Hardwick reported to the Inn that:

> *The proposed building being thus entirely detached, it is unnecessary to adapt its style of architecture to any already in the Inn, but as the building is for a purpose to which the collegiate style of architecture is most appropriate, Mr Hardwick selected that for the design he has now the honour to submit, and of the period towards the end of the sixteenth century before the admixture of Italian architecture.*

The Great Hall, Council Room, and Library (1845) viewed from the south-east, before the extension eastwards of the Library (L.J. Wood).

He was probably influenced by the presence of the existing fifteenth- and sixteenth-century buildings in the Inn, and possibly also by the recent construction of neo-Tudor benchers' rooms in the Middle Temple and the late-Tudor splendours of Middle Temple Hall. There was already a Tudor revival style in architecture, mainly to be seen in country houses, and in some town and suburban houses.

Hardwick's plans were approved and went on to win a Gold Medal at the Paris Exposition of 1855 before returning to the Library. Work began on 1 February 1843 with the foundation stone being laid on 20 April. The initials PH and the year 1843 are picked out in burnt-ended 'blue' bricks on the south end of the Hall. Thereupon Hardwick senior was taken ill, as was his son Philip Charles Hardwick, who had been assisting him. Much of the work fell to another assistant, J.L. Pearson, subsequently an eminent church architect.

During construction, the extensive 'architect's instructions' resulted in many changes from the detailed working drawings. For example, the entrance to the Council Chamber and Library changed so frequently that

Right: The Great Hall lantern.

Below: The Great Hall roof structure.

Opening of the Great Hall 1845.

the engravings for the official opening of the complex depict the intention rather than what was built. The terraces were a late addition and a useful repository for material left over from the works. The roof to the Hall, which was originally described as formed wholly from oak, was found, during restoration by Donald Insall and Associates in 1986, to be a composite structure suspended from iron rods ingeniously threaded through it. It is, nevertheless, a fine confection resembling the roof of the Great Hall at Westminster, from which the unusual combination of arch braces and hammer beams is plainly derived. The decorative detail in the Hall timberwork is almost certainly derived from the hall of Hampton Court, which is early Tudor rather than late. New techniques were employed in other places as well as the Hall roof. The lower parts of the building use 'jack-arch' vaulting with the vaults springing from iron beams rather than from masonry walls or columns; also there are concrete footings and cement or plaster for skirtings and door surrounds.

Much of the internal decorative detail, particularly the stonework, is generic late gothic rather than specifically Tudor. The most original and imaginative element is the octagonal vestibule and clerestory between the two benchers' rooms, which both creates interesting space and lighting inside and livens up the skyline between the Hall and Library roofs when viewed from outside.

Roofscape of the Great Hall and Library (1845 and 1872).

The complex is mainly built of red brick on a stone plinth; the external stonework of the plinth and the decorations are of Ancaster stone whilst the internal masonry is from Caen. The internal finish has been praised for the admirable design and execution of every bolt, hinge, latch, escutcheon, and door-head spandrel, each of which was said to be different and to have the right feeling.

The original estimate was for £50,000, of which £45,000 was to be borrowed. The minutes of a Council meeting of May 1852 have a summary of the costs of the

new works in the 1840s: £83,367 for the Hall and Library including fittings but not furniture, and £17,163 for 7 Stone Buildings.

The Great Hall was opened with much ceremony by Queen Victoria on 30 October 1845. No major changes have been made to the appearance of the Hall and Library complex since it was built, apart from the Library extension. The Great Hall, the Library and the benchers' rooms are thus exceptionally well preserved Victorian interiors.

The Library Extension

Within twenty or so years the Library as designed by Hardwick was found to be too small. Sir George Gilbert Scott, the architect of the Midland Hotel fronting St Pancras Station, was commissioned to extend it. He produced a virtually seamless three-bay eastward extension mimicking precisely Hardwick's existing building (he was 'assisted' by E.B. Denison, later Lord Grimthorpe, of whom more follows). It was built in 1871–2. The building has armorial chimney stacks, one covered in the millrind motif from the Inn's arms, and the other by the lion.

Old Square and Old Buildings Area

Until the early 1870s the layout around the Chapel and Old Hall differed from that of today (see the plan of the Inn in 1823). The buildings were known collectively as Old Buildings and had been little altered since 1623. In the period 1870 to 1890 the rebuilding of this part of the Inn, which had been contemplated on and off for the previous hundred years, was started, and more than half carried out. One cause for the delay in rebuilding was the Inn's campaign to have the Chancery Courts permanently housed in its precincts. It became apparent by 1865 that this was not going to happen, and in that year Sir George Gilbert Scott was instructed to consider redeveloping the Inn with more chambers. He proposed chambers at the north end of the Garden. This scheme, after six years of redesign and deliberation, was rejected by Council in 1871 for no stated reason.

In 1872 Sir George Gilbert Scott was asked to produce designs for what are now 8–10 Old Square. The initial specification was referred to Mr E.B. Denison. As is apparent from comparing the plan of the Inn in 1823 with the plan of it as it is now, this block replaced the former Chapel Court (former 10–15 Old Buildings) and the western end of the former Garden Row, but it was aligned with Stone Buildings and was partly on land not previously built upon. This block seems to have been completed by 1874 or 1875. The replacement for the remainder of Garden Row (now 11 and 12 Old Square) was, however, scaled down, with simpler window tracery, and with the proposed towers and gateway linking it to Nos 8–10 removed from the design. Nos 11 and 12 Old Square were erected 1876–9.

These buildings were constructed to a high specification and remain some of the least altered buildings in the Inn. They are in Tudor revival style to

Lord Grimthorpe's unrealised design for the Gatehouse.

Nos 2–4 Old Buildings (J.R. Emslie) before demolition to make way for 13–15 Old Square.

Lord Grimthorpe in 1889.

match the Great Hall complex. Sir George Gilbert Scott's son John Oldrid Scott supervised construction after his father died in 1878.

John Oldrid Scott then proposed a redevelopment of Chancery Lane Row (formerly 2–6 Old Buildings) down to the Gatehouse. This was carried out in two stages: first the current No. 13 between 1879 and 1884 to his design, then the current Nos 14 and 15 between 1885 and 1887 to a self-build design by the Inn. The self-build was undertaken by Kaberry, the Inn's Clerk of the Works, under the direction of Lord Grimthorpe.

Lord Grimthorpe was the E.B. Denison, later Sir Edmund Beckett, to whom the original designs for this area had been referred in 1872. He was Treasurer in 1876. He specialized in railway private bills and became leader of the Parliamentary Bar in 1860. He was an ecclesiastical controversialist, an amateur but widely practised architect, and a practical horologist. The clock on the Great Hall dates from 1884 and has a Beckett–Denison double three-legged gravity escapement. As an architect he concentrated on ecclesiastical projects, decreeing precisely what works were necessary, and often funding

No. 13 Old Buildings, demolished c1875, with the Chapel entrance arch of 1737.

these himself. The restoration of the Chapel in 1882, when he was acting Dean of Chapel in place of Sir George Jessel, who was Jewish, is reported to have been poorly received – yet the Inn may well have benefited from his involvement elsewhere by acquiring medieval oak for the Chapel, possibly from St Albans. As a quid pro quo Grimthorpe employed his own builder, William Longmire of St Albans, to extend the Chapel in 1881–3. That is how the arch forming the entrance to the Chapel, installed in 1737, came to be in the garden of Longmire's old house in St Albans – somewhat to the mystification of the current owner until recent researches explained the connection.

Controversy centred upon Grimthorpe's determination, in driving the building scheme on, not to stop to the north of the Gatehouse but to sweep away both the Gatehouse and the buildings to the south of it. These would have included 21–26 Old Buildings. Saving the Gatehouse became a rallying call to early building conservationists in 1886–90, and the biographer of Grimthorpe records that 'his contemplated demolition of Sir Thomas Lovell's gatehouse in Chancery Lane was happily frustrated'.

Grimthorpe described himself as 'the only architect with whom I have never quarrelled', and is famous for his remark in connection with 14 and 15 Old Square that 'You do pay me (and you should add our Clerk of the Works) the compliment that I have built more substantial and convenient chambers than Architects did while we employed them.' He has received a consistently bad press, culminating with the Inn's declining the offer of his portrait in 1917.

Perhaps now is the time for a reappraisal of 8–15 Old Square and for a comparison with the much-renovated shells of the Gatehouse and 21–24 Old Buildings. The buildings have worn well, were original in design and appearance and represent an important statement of the optimism of the period. They compare favourably with the neighbouring retained facades of older buildings.

A further legacy of the incompleteness of the Old Square/Old Buildings rebuilding scheme is the confusing combination of two different numbering schemes going in opposite directions. Nos 1–7 are missing from the Old Square sequence and Nos 2–15 from the Old Buildings sequence. The new buildings were given numbers in a completely new sequence in a clockwise direction, on the assumption that the sequence would continue past the Gatehouse, and replace what are now No. 1 (on the north side of the Gatehouse) and 16–24 Old Buildings (west to east) with 1–7 Old Square (east to west).

The arch in St Albans, still bearing the initials of Marmaduke Alington, Treasurer 1737.

Left: War Memorial (1921) with 8 Old Square (c1875) in the background.

Right: Old Hall reconstruction nearing completion c1928, with the south bay (1582) and screen (1624).

THE TWENTIETH CENTURY

The Inn sustained damage in both world wars, as described in a later chapter, but was extremely fortunate to have suffered relatively little permanent damage to its fabric.

The War Memorial was erected and unveiled in 1921 on the site of the former Vice-Chancellor's Court. The siting was only resolved upon after much consideration. It was designed by the Inn's Architect Mr (later Sir) John Simpson, extended in 1949–50, and substantially restored in 2006.

Old Hall refurbishment

Sir John Simpson was asked to consider the dilapidated state of the under-used Old Hall in 1924. He wrote, in the vein of one builder reviewing a previous builder's job:

> *Who was responsible for those criminal doings of the XVIII century? Official records are discreetly silent as to his name; but we may guess it to have been James Wyatt who, 'restoring'* more suo *in 1790–6, removed the timber roof from the Chapel and, there too, substituted a plaster ceiling. On this work he is known to have employed one Bernasconi, doubtless an expert at the dreadful business of string and stucco ... He was, at any rate, but an accessory of Wyatt, whose handiwork at certain cathedrals has left such a reputation as even his misdeeds at Lincoln's Inn cannot smirch.*

Simpson, at the same time as he was designing Wembley Stadium, set about his own restoration methodically and with a painstaking attention to preservation wherever possible. The work was carried out by in-house masons. In the rebuilding of Old Hall the rendering was discarded, the bricks were re-used, most of the exterior stonework was replaced, and the eighteenth-century ceiling was destroyed to reveal the timber roof structure, which was repaired and re-erected. The panelling was designed by Simpson and was based on fragments found when the Hall was taken apart. The result is a charming interior, dripping with nostalgia for the Middle Ages, without the original inconveniences of being heated by a fire in the centre of the Hall or the floor being covered with straw.

The1960s

In the 1960s the Inn started developing once more. Rebuilding of 21–26 Old Buildings retained the impression of the original exteriors but only Nos 22–23 reflected the original internal features. The scheme involved a new building on the site of the old Chancery Lane post office. This was variously called Mansfield Court, then Hale Court, and finally Hardwicke Building.

The new building is clad in Portland or similar artificial stone, to a modern but restrained design which blends well with Old Buildings. As built it has residential accommodation with mansard windows on the fifth floor under a Westmorland slate and copper roof.

The 1970s

The 1970s were marked by a proposal for a radical assault on the North Garden. In this period the increasing numbers practising at the Bar meant that there was a shortage of space for barristers' chambers within the Inns of Court, and it was thought by many that the solution was to build more accommodation within the Inns.

In 1972 Lincoln's Inn applied for planning permission to develop the North Garden for office space. The proposal was for two buildings at right angles running all the way along the northern edge of the gardens and down the Walks on the western side. The buildings, designed by Sir Hugh Casson, were to be four storeys high over a basement car park and the intention was to free up space within existing buildings within the Inn by decanting solicitors into 73,600 square feet of new, purpose-built office space. The *Architect's Journal* was unconvinced: '...the impression is still of a long horizontal slab. The garden elevations are questionable – that of the north building is intended to be unpretentious but did it have to be so undistinguished?'

Unsurprisingly, the objectors at the public inquiry in January 1974 were led by the very solicitors it was proposed to decant. The evidence for the proposal included the dire warning that if permission was refused, the Inn would have to consider accommodating barristers in vessels on the Thames. The Inspector and the Secretary of State were unimpressed.

Nothing daunted, a more modest scheme was taken to Inquiry in 1983 and permission was granted. Unfortunately, the Minister had taken so long in producing his decision that the adjoining joint developer had proceeded alone. Consequently, a less ambitious application was made in 1986. This building, a further Casson & Conder design, was permitted, built and originally occupied by Erskine Chambers. In external appearance it takes its inspiration from the nearby Sir John Soane's Museum, simplifying further an already stripped-down classical style.

Next came the Boghouse redevelopment, the new building hidden between the back of 1 and 2 New Square and the wall flanking Star Yard.

THE TWENTY-FIRST CENTURY

The New Square Fountain

In 1999 it was decided to replace the existing ornamental pond in the centre of New Square. The central feature of New Square has changed several times. On completion of Serle Court and its open courtyard, Cavendish Weedon was permitted in 1696 to erect a central pillar and clock only. In fact, this had a fountain at its base and an engraving suggests that it had jets spraying into a basin at its pedestal. In Kip's engraving of 1720 the jets can be seen but not a pool. In 1823 Charles Lamb recorded that 'Four little winged marble boys used to play their virgin fancies, spouting out ever fresh streams from their innocent-wanton lips ... They are gone and the spring choked up.' The original dial clock had been replaced by a sundial, the basin had become stagnant, and in 1817 the pillar was taken down to pedestal level and replaced by a gas light. All were removed in 1845, when the lawns were laid and a central hexagonal reservoir was created, which was intended to have a fountain.

The fountain in New Square (2002).

Finally, over 150 years later, a fountain, designed by the celebrated sculptor William Pye, was commissioned for the Queen's Golden Jubilee in 2002. The laminar jets aptly form a water crown. As might be expected, Lincoln's Inn is included in the Royal Academy's architectural tour of London, but it is the Queen's Jubilee Fountain that is responsible.

The Kitchens

Changing times in the guise of health and safety finally caught up with Hardwick's kitchens in 2004. A major refurbishment of the Great Hall complex at basement, first and second-floor levels was undertaken in two phases. Very few noticeable alterations were made to the Hall itself or to the Library. Virtually nothing below them was left unchanged. The opportunity was taken by the architects, Acanthus Clews, to put in a new mezzanine floor in the top half of the kitchens, to create the new Members' Common Room.

The top of the Great Hall kitchen fireplace (1845), now in the Members' Common Room.

The kitchen fireplace in its original state.

The Library's eastern staircase turret (1872).

The Future

The planning laws and the fact that most of Lincoln's Inn is listed make it very unlikely that any major new buildings will be constructed in the Inn in the foreseeable future. The only practicable method for the Inn to increase the accommodation it owns is to purchase freeholds in New Square and property outside the Inn. The Inn recently bought 33 Chancery Lane, and refurbished it to provide seminar and meeting rooms and a set of barristers' chambers. There will continue to be alterations and refurbishments to maintain and improve the Inn for the needs and functions of the future.

It is to be hoped that the Inn's buildings will continue for many years to provide a tranquil working environment and communal meeting place for lawyers and law students, a subject of study for architectural historians, a ready-made set for film and TV costume dramas, and a visible witness to the historic roots and continuity of England's legal system and constitution.

The Chancery Connection

ROGER COOKE

'Chancery', a word which really means 'Chancellorship' and so 'to do with the Chancellor', comes into the history of Lincoln's Inn in several ways. The Inn's eastern boundary is Chancery Lane. Like many thoroughfares it started life as 'New Street'. From the fourteenth century it began to be known as 'Chancellor's Lane', since it was the street where the Lord Chancellor, then essentially the minister for administration, kept many of his offices. The main repository of the Chancery records (in the form of long rolls of parchment) was on the site of a religious house which included a chapel. This office, and later court, thus became known as the Rolls Chapel, or simply 'the Rolls', presided over by the Master of the Rolls, the Chancellor's principal deputy. Opposite, where the Law Society now stands, was the house of the Six Clerks, officers of the Court of Chancery. In time the name evolved to the present Chancery Lane.

Then there were the Inns of Chancery. Lincoln's Inn was not an Inn of Chancery. This title belongs to our small neighbours which long ago prepared students for entry to the four great Inns of Court. Two such Inns were linked to Lincoln's Inn and are described at the end of this chapter, but Lincoln's Inn is the Inn particularly associated with both the old Court of Chancery and the Chancery Bar.

THE COURT OF CHANCERY

The Court of Chancery was the Court of the Lord Chancellor and also later of his deputies. It administered a system of law, known as 'equity', operating alongside the common law and on occasions superior to it. The way equity developed is, of course, familiar to lawyers, but readers not steeped in the law may not know the history. In the medieval world the superior courts of common law were rigid and formulaic, both in the rights they recognized and the remedies they were prepared to give. In particular, they were unable to deliver justice in the new forms of property arrangement becoming common in the fourteenth and fifteenth centuries. The medieval king, looked upon as the fountain of justice, was frequently petitioned by litigants unable to obtain relief in the common law courts. As time went on, and such petitions grew in number and complexity, the King referred them to the Chancellor. Medieval Chancellors were clergy, and so the idea of making orders which 'bound the conscience' of the defendant, central to the development of equity, came naturally to them.

The Old Hall.

The Court of Chancery in the Old Hall c1840 (T.H. Shepherd).

Left: Lord Ellesmere (Sir Thomas Egerton 1541–1617) who as Lord Chancellor 1603–17 famously battled with Sir Edward Coke over the respective jurisdictions of Chancery and the common law courts.

By the end of the Middle Ages Chancellors had begun to devise remedies unknown in common law, such as making orders (known as injunctions), restraining unlawful conduct, and recognizing new rights, most famously and importantly through what became the trust. The old informal arrangement for hearing petitions to the king became a regular court with its own judges and, in time, a vast amount of judicial business. It continued in existence until all the old superior courts were abolished by the Judicature Act of 1873 which created the modern High Court and fused common law and equity. The High Court was devised to sit in divisions, which loosely followed the jurisdictional arrangements of the old courts, and the modern Chancery Division of the High Court is the successor of the Court of Chancery.

Sittings in and around Lincoln's Inn

From their medieval beginnings until the opening of the Royal Courts of Justice in 1882, the superior courts sat in, or around, Westminster Hall. The Court of Chancery did so during the short legal terms (much shorter than today). However, by the mid-sixteenth century the Master of the Rolls was also exercising judicial functions as a 'vice-chancellor'. Although it was not until the nineteenth century that the Master of the Rolls sat concurrently with the Lord Chancellor as a separate court, much Chancery business was from early times conducted just across the street from Lincoln's Inn, at the Rolls Chapel, where King's College Library now occupies the former Public Record Office building. The Lord Chancellor himself continued to sit during vacations, presumably at Westminster, until in 1737 the more convenient solution of regularly sitting in the Old Hall of Lincoln's Inn was established.

It appears that in 1717 Sir Joseph Jekyll, Master of the Rolls, was invited by the benchers to sit in the Old Hall for the seven years it took to rebuild the Rolls House. This presumably was remembered, and in 1733 Lord Chancellor Talbot came to sit in the Old Hall on an

LAW INTELLIGENCE.

COURT OF CHANCERY, Nov. 6.

This being the first day of Term, the Judges and King's Counsel were with the Lord Chancellor in Lincoln's Inn Hall until near one o'clock, when his Lordship took his seat, and partially heard one motion. At half-past two the Court rose, it being necessary to have the hall prepared for the students of law to dine.

To-morrow at ten was positively fixed for the Portsmouth cause.

1822

CURIOUS ADVERTISEMENT.

(FROM a PAPER *in the* WEST *of* ENGLAND.)

WANTED in an ATTORNEY's office, a young man as a Clerk. He must write a good hand and expeditiously, and understand the practice of the Courts of Chancery, King's Bench, Common Pleas, and Exchequer. If he is conversant in Conveyancing, so much the better.—Before, between, and after office-hours, he must milk a cow, look after two horses, clean his master's shoes, shave him, and dress his hair. He must wear a livery on Sundays, and attend his master and mistress to the parish church.—Wages ten guineas a year: but if he can draw bills, answers, exceptions, interrogatories, demurrers, and other pleadings in the Court of Chancery, another guinea will not be considered as an object. Apply by letter (post paid) to Mr. &c.

1791

Above: The Old Hall to the right with the (first) Vice-Chancellor's Court just protruding to the left. The Court and the arcade were built in 1817. Drawn by the American landscape painter Gilbert Munger in 1879.

Far right: Old Hall c1874.

occasional basis. The Black Books record that benchers were content that he should 'use the same so long as his Lordship shall so please', promising also to make alterations if there 'be anything wanting to make it more commodious and convenient.' Three years later the next Lord Chancellor, the famous Lord Hardwicke, came to sit here more regularly. The buttery (between the Hall and the Chapel) was fixed up as the judge's withdrawing room. In 1770 the Hall was ordered to be 'new floored' and elevated in the area where the Lord Chancellor sat. In 1794 the Black Books recorded that hours of 'exercise' within the Hall had to be varied when the Lord Chancellor sat there. The 'exercise' referred to gentlemen members of the Armed Association of Lincoln's Inn learning the use of arms following declaration of war with France the previous year.

The use of the Old Hall for sittings in vacation might suggest that it was rarely used. But throughout this period law terms were extremely short, barely twenty per cent of the calendar year, so vacation sittings represented periods of considerable length and importance. It might be thought that the practicalities of using the Hall as a court rested on the fact that during the vacations the Inn did not require the Hall, but eighteenth-century timetables of court business show that the Lord Chancellor also sat in the Hall during term time on Wednesday and Friday afternoons. Furthermore, for a period from 1820 to 1826 the Court sat in the Hall throughout the term while new courts at Westminster were being built, without, it would seem, unduly disrupting the everyday life of the Inn.

By 1778, the Court had established an even more permanent presence within the Inn. There were long and complex negotiations for building the offices of the court officials within the Inn, most notably those of the famous Six Clerks. A deal was eventually struck in 1775. However, negotiating with government departments was no quicker in the eighteenth century than it can be now. In 1786 there was trouble over payment for the Six

The Old Hall, Council Chamber, Library, and (half-height to the left) the Vice-Chancellor's Court. From a drawing of 1880, shortly before the Court and adjacent buildings were demolished (Alan Stewart).

Clerks' office site and the money was not received until 11 May 1787, though the buildings (which now form 8–11 Stone Buildings) had been completed nine years earlier. Large and impressive, the Six Clerks' office, now the headquarters of the Inns of Court & City Yeomanry, formed the middle of the range. Interestingly, contemporary maps show all the public entrances to the Chancery offices in Stone Buildings on Chancery Lane, possibly at the insistence of the Inn to preserve amenity and keep out the general public.

The 'temporary' courts erected for the additional Vice-Chancellors in 1841, still standing in 1880 (Alan Stewart).

In the nineteenth century the Court of Chancery grew with the appointment of three Vice-Chancellors as additional first instance judges and two Lords Justices to hear Chancery appeals. Space was found for all of them within the Inn. The accommodation in temporary-looking structures or partitioned areas of the Hall seems not to have been of the best. One observer compared the exteriors to dockside sheds and the interiors to 'the appearance of a third-rate Dissenting Chapel in a fourth-rate provincial town'.

By 1860 Lincoln's Inn had really become the regular seat of the Court. The Royal Commission charged with bringing all the courts together on one site reported:

> *practically the Courts of Equity have ceased to sit at Westminster and now sit in convenient neighbourhood to each other in Lincoln's Inn ... Their offices and chambers, fourteen in number, are scattered about in Chancery Lane, Quality Court, The Rolls Yard, Lincoln's Inn and Staple Inn ....*

Temporary building in New Square for exhibiting the competing designs for the new law courts 1867.

Above left: Sir Edward Fry 1827–1918 (Roger Fry).

Above: Sir Robert Megarry 1910–2006, Vice-Chancellor 1976–85, the title having been revived after a gap of eighty-five years in 1970.

The building of new but inadequate courts next to Westminster Hall had not solved the accommodation problem and there was a strong movement which gained impetus as the century progressed to find a new site for all the courts. There were long disputes between many interested parties about the appropriate site. Eventually the choice fell on the Carey Street site where the Royal Courts of Justice now stand

After the opening of the Royal Courts of Justice in 1882 the new Chancery Division moved there. Before the final move, there was one last new connection with Lincoln's Inn. The reforms of the courts preceded by nearly a decade the completion of the new building. In the meantime an extra Chancery judge had been appointed and, therefore, extra space was needed for another court. So from 1877 to 1882 the new judge, Mr Justice Fry, sat in a courtroom constructed in the basement of the east end of Lincoln's Inn Library apparently intended as a lecture room. This was not wholly successful. Complaint was made of it being 'unwholesomely close' and that witnesses were kept standing in the rain. After many years as a book stack, this court room has been resurrected. Now known as the Old Court Room, it is one of the Inn's reception and committee rooms, containing a fine portrait of Mr Justice Fry, a member of the Bristol Quaker family, painted by his son Roger, a well known painter of the time and a member of the Bloomsbury Group. Mr Justice Fry went on to be one of the great figures of the Chancery bench and later of the Court of Appeal, playing a leading part in the adaptation of Chancery law and practice to the new conditions.

There has been occasional judicial use of the Old Hall in later years. Most recently on 30 July 1973, the Old Hall was briefly revived as a court when Mr Justice Megarry sat there as a judge of the Chancery Division to hear proceedings involving a large number of bond holders. More people were expected than any of the courts in the RCJ could hold. In the event few attended.

Relinquish all I hold most dear,
Full Sixty Thousand Pounds a Year,

PAUL PRY'S peep into CHAN
An overwhelming Suit.

HOW THE MONEY GOES, OR FOR WHAT POOR SUITORS ARE ROBBED.

Salaries of the Officers of the Courts of Chancery.

Lord Chancellor (including his salary as Speaker of the House of Lords ....
Master of the Rolls (Lord Langdale)................ 14,000 0 0
Vice-Chancellor of England (Sir L. Shadwell) 7,000 0 0
Two Vice-Chancellors (Sir J. L. K. Bruce & Sir J. Wigram) 6,000 0 0
£5,000 each ....
Accountant General, Chancery (W. Russell) 10,000 0 0
Nine Masters in Chancery (J. E. Dowesdell, W. Wingfield, 3,814 0 0
J. W. Farrar, Sir Giffin Wilson, W. Brougham, N. W. Senior, Sir W. Horne, Sir George Rose, R. Richards, and two vacant in December last), five £3,225 each, four £2,500 each 26,125 0 0
Ten Registrars of Chancery (J. Collier £2,900; R. O. Walker, £2,150; F. N. Davis, £1,900; H. E. Bicknell, F. R. Bowdwell. H. Hussey, and H. Wood, £1,850 each: E. D. Colville, £3,100; E. D. Colville, junr. £1,350; C. Munro, £1,350.) ....
Secretary to the Lord Chancellor (H. J. Perry) 18,150 0 0
Master of the Rolls (Right Hon. J. B. Smith)........... 2,060 6 0
Masters in Chancery, W. Curry, £2,769; T. Gould, £2,769; 3,964 0 0
W. Henn, (including pension) £3,309; J. Townsend, £2,769........................
Door Keeper, (see Extract from Punch)* 11,616 0 0

PENSIONS.
Late Lord Chancellor, (Lord Brougham) 3,218 0 0
Retired Master, Francis Cross 5,000 0 0
Late Lord Chancellor, Lord Lyndhurst.................. 1,500 0 0
5,000 0 0

£117,447 6 0

By the Six Clerks' Compensation Act, passed in 1843, for the purpose of abolishing a nuisance in the shape of a lot of waiting clerks in the court of Chancery, who did no duty whatever, but simply exacting Fees of the suitors there. In the usual style of aristocratic legislation "compensation" was granted to these legalized Turpins. New offices were at the same time created under the act, and of course a new set of highly paid officers appointed. The salaries of the new officers amount to 37,700*l*. per annum; and the "compensation" to the discharged clerks to 44,793*l*., making a total of no less than 76,000*l*. per annum. There are now four of the clerks who divide among them, as compensation, not less than 30,000*l*. yearly! Mr. Watson, M.P., brought this subject before Parliament in May, 1846, in moving for a select committee of inquiry. The Ministry, however, strenuously opposed him, and his motion was lost by a considerable majority. Where an abuse is to be preserved, the Aristocratic House of Commons is not generally found wanting.

On the occasion referred to, Mr. Watson stated that "there were no less than from 300 to 400 persons who were employed to collect fees in the Courts of Equity; that between 300,000*l*. and 400,000*l*. was paid in Salaries to the Officers of the Court of Chancery alone, part of which was a tax on the suitors and the rest on the country at large. There was one individual in the Court of Chancery who held a sinccure office of 7,700*l*. a year, another one of 5,496*l*. a year, and there were numerous

Above: 'Legalised Turpins'.

Left: This print of June 1826 was published shortly after the first Chancery Commission reported. Chaired by Lord Eldon, the Commission was singularly obtuse as to the need for reform.

THE REPUTATION OF THE OLD COURT OF CHANCERY

In the first chapter of *Bleak House*, Dickens paints a dismal picture of the Court of Chancery sitting in the Old Hall. But the reason for this picture and indeed for the book is the serious malaise into which the old Court fell. A great deal of the work of the Court in its later years involved the administering of the estates of deceased persons, some of which were very large. The rule was that if any question or difficulty arose, the Court had to take over the entire administration of the estate. This was inevitably a lengthy business – and an expensive one. Indeed cases might start which never finished and it was not unknown for estates to be wholly eaten up by costs, as portrayed in the great case of *Jarndyce v Jarndyce* in *Bleak House*. With this came a proliferation of expensive paper, ridiculed by Dickens as 'mountains of costly nonsense', much of which was quite probably never read. Contemporary statistics suggest that in this period the number of cases handled by the Court actually fell, though the amount of interim applications

The Institute

Freemasons Tavern

Monday 13 March 1815

At a Meeting for the purpose of Establishing a Conveyancers Club.

Present

P.B. Brodie Esq. in the Chair

John Hodgson Esq.

Geo Morley Esq.

John Tyrrell Esq.

R.H. Coote Esq.

J. Tomkyns Esq.

It was Resolved.

One can hardly talk of Lincoln's Inn and the Chancery Bar without mentioning the Institute. 'Institute of what?' people often ask. The informative, but not strictly correct, answer is 'Institute of Conveyancers'. In fact when the Institute was founded in 1815, really as a conveyancers' dining club, it was resolved that 'the Club be called the Institute unless a better name be proposed at the next meeting'. No such proposal was made and the Institute remains as originally named. A number of changes were made to the qualifications for membership as practice changed in the nineteenth century and although the requirement to practise as a conveyancer has long gone, along with the conveyancers themselves, it remains necessary in order to be elected to be a junior barrister practising at the Chancery Bar. Note, juniors only. It often takes some while between being proposed for membership and there being a vacancy. If the candidate takes silk in the meantime, he or she is struck off the candidates' list.The core membership is forty juniors, which number has been fixed since 1870, hence the soubriquet 'the forty thieves'.

The Institute nowadays holds its meetings three times a year, mostly in Lincoln's Inn. Occasionally it ventures outside. Twice it has been down the river to dine at Greenwich and it once dined whilst cruising on the Thames, ending up at a firework display commemorating the centenary of Tower Bridge. The writer's first meeting was at one of the Greenwich outings in 1983. It was an unusual sight on a fine summer's evening to see thirty or forty middle-aged and elderly men, some in bowler hats (by then already a little passé) walking in file through the streets of Greenwich. A casually dressed young man leaning on a doorway turned to his girlfriend and said, 'What's this, a bleeding undertakers' convention?'

The Institute has always been a respectable organization. So far only one member has been tried for murder and he was acquitted. In 1821 J.H. Christie successfully fought a duel. He had chivalrously fired his first shot in the air and had only responded with a second in self defence. His friend, Sir Walter Scott, insisted he was the innocent party in the quarrel. Christie lived to become one of the first Conveyancing Counsel to the Court and had a string of distinguished pupils, including Wolstenholme, who with Sir Benjamin Cherry, the draftsman of much of the 1925 property legislation, wrote one of the conveyancers' 'bibles'.

Although the gatherings are always referred to as 'meetings', they are really dinners, and the business that is transacted is usually of a light-hearted kind. Notably, newly elected members are expected to 'entertain the company' and the spring meeting, which traditionally features a guest speaker, has seen a law lord reciting high-quality doggerel of his own invention and a judicial married couple singing an adaptation of a Beatles' song. But the Institute has a serious side. It represents a formidable concentration of learned and highly technical expertise in specialist areas of the law which on a number of occasions over the years has proved highly influential in the reform of the law.

Roger Cooke

That the Club be called "The Institute." unless a better name be proposed at the next meeting.

John Hodgson Pres.

within each case had risen substantially and kept the lawyers in active business.

In one of the greatest of all Chancery cases, *Thellusson v Woodford* (a likely model for *Jarndyce*), the Court made 950 orders, received 780 reports, and heard more than 100 counsel. In fact, almost every member of the Chancery Bar had appeared in the case at some point in his career. The case involved an eccentric will which directed the income of the estate to be accumulated for so long that most of the beneficiaries would never see it, whilst the eventual inheritors would be unimaginably rich. The case was first heard in 1798. The Court's initial decision that the accumulation was valid provoked the Accumulations Act 1800, the basis of the modern law. That did not, however, prevent the case dragging on until 1863, when the final order was made.

The court had an extraordinary myriad of officials to whom fees were payable. An order on fees of 1743 shows over sixty separate officers or offices. They ranged from the Six Clerks to the 'Porter at the Rolls', who apparently received two shillings 'upon every cause heard by consent at the Rolls, wherein a decree is made'. All of this attracted strong public criticisms and the attention of the Victorian law reformers, leading later to sweeping reforms. Their success may well be measured by the ensuing serious recession in Chancery work.

Bleak House: *the old man of the name of Tulkinghorn (1901 edn).*

THE CHANCERY BAR

There is a long and strongly believed tradition that the Chancery Bar practises in Lincoln's Inn and that most of its members are members of the Inn. Like many such traditions there is a lot of truth in it but it is not wholly accurate. It is not known with any certainty whether the link goes back before the arrival of the Lord Chancellor in the Old Hall in 1737 or is earlier, possibly connected with the proximity of the Rolls Court, which may have led to the Lord Chancellor being invited into the Inn in the first place. However, the existing evidence does not give much support to the latter theory.

The proximity of the Court of Chancery in the Old Hall and of the Rolls Court for such a substantial part of the year after 1737 must have made it attractive for regular practitioners in the Court of Chancery to practise from chambers in the Inn. Certainly the Court of Chancery attracted a specialist Bar, many of whom practised almost exclusively in that Court. Then, as later, they combined court practice with complex drafting of documents affecting trusts and property; many of the junior counsel at the Chancery Bar being referred to as 'equity draftsmen'.

They came to be linked with another specialist element of the Bar: conveyancers. These were barristers who specialized in complicated questions relating to the title to land. They were basically technical advisers and draftsmen and rarely went into court. Some conveyancers, although members of an Inn of Court (often Lincoln's Inn) were not called to the Bar but were known as certificated conveyancers. In the eighteenth century such 'practice under the bar' was the only option available to Roman Catholics, as before 1791 call to the Bar entailed taking the Oath of Supremacy. Others who were called to the Bar were often referred to as conveyancing counsel, but probably likewise seldom went into court.

The 1792 *Law List* is the earliest to identify conveyancers and equity draftsmen as a separate class of barrister. It shows about forty practising from Lincoln's Inn addresses and fifteen from addresses nearby, as

Inns of Chancery

The origins of the Inns of Chancery are even more obscure than those of the Inns of Court themselves. It is not even known why they should have been referred to as Inns 'of Chancery' – they had no connection with the Court of Chancery. Nor it is clear how they came to be subsumed under the control of the Inns of Court, and to act as preparatory schools for them. Of the nine Inns of Chancery identifiable by 1500, two became associated as satellites of Lincoln's Inn, a relationship later cemented by its acquisition of their sites as landlord. It is possibly to the chagrin of those currently in charge of the finances of Lincoln's Inn that those sites were disposed of long ago: they would be extremely valuable assets today. The site of Thavies Inn is now occupied by the neat neo-Georgian office block at the north-west corner of Fetter Lane (known as Thavies Inn House), in the shadow of Sainsbury's. Waterhouse's Gothic extravagance on the other side of Holborn, formerly occupied by the Prudential Assurance Company, was the location of Furnival's Inn.

The name of the first comes from John Thavie (or Davy), a previous owner of the premises who is commemorated in St Andrew's Holborn. Lincoln's Inn bought the premises from Gregory Nicholas for £75 in 1551. They were described as being near the Earl of Lincoln's house in Shoe Lane. Furnival's Inn is mentioned by John Stow (in his *Survey of London,* 1598), as formerly belonging to Sir William Furnivall and his wife, Thomasin, in the reign of Richard II. It was bought by Lincoln's Inn from Francis, Earl of Shrewsbury, Lord Talbot and Furnival for £120 in December 1547. Thavies Inn was sold in 1769 for £4,100 to Thomas Middleton, a member of Lincoln's Inn. Since the proceeds helped to finance the erection of Stone Buildings, it was not an entirely misjudged liquidation of assets. Furnival's Inn came to an end as a Society in 1817, when its membership had shrunk to a mere six ancients and sixteen juniors, and it could not afford to renew its lease on our unsentimental terms. A developer, Henry Peto, rebuilt the site on a building lease. The freehold was retained until 1888, when it was sold to the Prudential for £150,000.

The relationship between Lincoln's Inn and its Inns of Chancery is not entirely clear. The former had the right to appoint the Principal (the equivalent of the Treasurer) though this was usually done by election among the members of the inferior Inns, and the Reader, who, it seems, was always a member of Lincoln's Inn. Sir Thomas More was among those appointed to the latter office in Furnival's Inn. Moots were held in Furnival's Inn every Monday, Tuesday and Thursday, and in Thavies' Inn every Tuesday, Thursday and Saturday. Members of Thavies and Furnival's Inn might proceed to membership of Lincoln's Inn itself, often on favourable financial terms, but this was not always the case. Nor was membership of Lincoln's Inn restricted to those who had served their 'apprenticeship' in Thavies or Furnival's Inn. More himself, for example, had been a student of New Inn, which was attached to the Middle Temple.

The benchers of Lincoln's Inn frequently struggled to maintain order and standards in the inferior societies, with decreasing success as the years went by and their character changed. The original role of the Inns of Chancery was already in severe decline by 1600. Instead they became inhabited by attorneys and solicitors who, by social exclusion and ultimately by formal regulation, became unwelcome at the Inns of Court. Unlike the Inns of Court, underpinned by having the exclusive right of call to the Bar, the Inns of Chancery, with no such equivalent,

Left: Furnival's Inn 1754 (Sutton Nicholls).

Above: Furnival's Inn just before the demolition and rebuilding by Peto in 1818 (Robert Wilkinson, Londina Illustrata*).*

Thavies Inn from the Holborn end. From Hogarth's 1751 engraving Second Stage of Cruelty, *the carriage collapsing under the weight of barristers.*

stagnated. In fact, not counting the early demise of Strand Inn in 1549, Thavies Inn and Furnival's Inn led the sad but inevitable march to extinction, being the first two of the remaining eight to go; the last, Clifford's Inn belonging to Inner Temple, limped into the twentieth century, being dissolved in 1903.

Members of Thavies Inn include Nicholas Skeres, who, with Matthew Roydon, a minor poet and resident of Thavies Inn, and Thomas Edwards, was concerned in the murder of Christopher Marlowe. Edwards later shared chambers in Lincoln's Inn with Christopher Brooke, a friend of John Donne. Thomas Fidell, of Furnival's Inn, one of the attorneys of the Court of Common Pleas, was author of a book entitled *A Perfect Guide for a Studious Young Lawyer, being Presidents for Conveyances*, published in 1654. Charles Dickens wrote *Pickwick Papers* while living in Furnival's Inn, and places there John Westlock in *Martin Chuzzlewit*.

By 1804, Thavies Inn had been burned down 'some few years since', but it is not known whether this was during the ownership of Lincoln's Inn. In the same year, Furnival's Inn is described as follows: 'The street front is an uncommonly fine specimen of brick-work, being adorned with pilasters, mouldings, and various other ornaments, and extends a considerable length. It contains a range of very good chambers, and beneath a handsome arched gateway leading to the interior parts of the inn. It appears to have been erected about the time of Charles II.' Unfortunately, the chronicler found the place dirty and neglected and states that it was shortly to be demolished.

David Harris

against twenty-five elsewhere. By 1851 the Chancery Bar had expanded massively to about 620 in all, with a very large proportion within or near the Inn – only about 170 of those had addresses elsewhere.

So although by no means the whole Chancery Bar practised in the Inn, a very large proportion did. A piece of contemporary evidence suggests that, as one might expect, there were positive advantages in Chancery men practising within the Inn. Sir Samuel Romilly, a member of the Chancery Bar and of Gray's Inn, says in a letter of 1791 that he has just moved from Gray's Inn to New Square, Lincoln's Inn as 'much the better as a situation for business' though lacking the view of the gardens that he had enjoyed in Gray's.

By the middle of the twentieth century, the domination of the Inn by the Chancery Bar was almost complete. The 1967 *Law List* shows the whole of the London Chancery Bar, about thirty-two sets of chambers, as being in Lincoln's Inn, the only exceptions being three sets of tax chambers and three sets of intellectual property chambers, both then rather separate specialisms. Conversely, there was only one non-Chancery set within the Inn. A few years earlier the only London Chancery chambers not in the Inn were in New Court Carey Street. Most of the members of two distinguished Chancery sets there nevertheless gave 'new [sic.] Court Lincoln's Inn' as their address from about 1929 until New Court was demolished in 1964 and the chambers moved into the Inn.

Once they find chambers here many Chancery barristers originally called by one of the other Inns choose to join Lincoln's Inn as their second Inn – or *'ad eundem'* in the Latin phrase still used (some simply for practical reasons connected with their chambers being in the Inn, such as car park, library, lunch, and, in the past, use of the Inn's lavatories). As is apparent just from the details of some of the contributors to this volume, a substantial number of those have become benchers, and some have held office as Treasurer. This has contributed to the belief that none but Chancery practitioners belong to Lincoln's Inn. The Inn has, however, always contained a strong common law membership, including in recent times such distinguished figures as Lord Hailsham, Lord Denning (despite his development of equity, not originally a Chancery practitioner), and Lord Widgery. And some of the great figures of the Chancery Bar and bench remained with their 'mother' Inn, notably in Middle Temple, among them Lord Lindley and also in more recent times Lord Wilberforce, Lord Cross, Lord Templeman, and Lord Nicholls.

For a long time the Chancery Bar retained a distinct character of its own. Much of the work called for a high degree of precision and scholarship and a great deal of it was done on paper rather than in court. For many years there were to be found the legendary figures of 'rising equity juniors', men in late middle age or older, with a vast knowledge of property and trust law who drafted complex settlements and only went into court in cases that involved issues of law and construction. The folklore of the bar held that none of them would have known what a witness was, much less how to deal with him. There is a legend that when, after the Judicature Act, all judges became judges of the High Court and liable to go on circuit to try crime, the Chancery judges sent out were so horrified at seeing real criminals that in each case they asked what was the maximum sentence and gave it.

The view held by many outsiders about Chancery practice was encapsulated well in a verse to be found in *The Conveyancer's Guide* by John Crisp (1832), which Sir Robert Megarry used to quote to students. In the eighteenth or early nineteenth century a mature conveyancer, a bachelor in his fifties, in whose veins there flowed not blood but the best quality Indian ink, was struck by what used to be called the 'tender passion'. He sought, as was the custom, to address his beloved in verse. Having as the best tools to hand those of his trade, he addressed her thus ('fee' was a term for describing an estate in land):

Fee simple and conditional fee,
And all the fees in tail,
Are nothing when compar'd to thee,
Thou best of fees – female.

The modern Chancery Bar differs from its ancestors in many important ways. For one thing, recent mergers have seen the rise of fewer but much larger chambers at the Chancery Bar. Conveyancers and equity draftsman no longer exist as a distinct breed, though there remain some practitioners who have great expertise in matters such as land law and the modern law of trusts (almost always related to taxation problems). But in other fields the work has expanded, most notably in the directions of company law (including shareholders disputes and directors' breaches of duty), many forms of commercial and financial contract (including especially banking securities), and landlord and tenant work. There is an observable division between what is increasingly being called 'the Property Bar' and others. As the Chancellor of the High Court commented in the introduction to the latest Chancery Bar Directory, 'Nowadays almost any civil dispute not involving personal injuries, clinical negligence or ships may be resolved in the Chancery Division ....' Much of the old complex and specialized procedure which was peculiar to the Chancery Division has gone, in part following Lord Oliver's review in the early 1980s and also following the Woolf reforms. Nevertheless it is still an area of work where the procedure needs to be carefully moulded to suit the complex problems with which the court may have to deal. 'You have been at the Chancery Bar long enough', said Mr Justice Walton once to the writer of this piece 'to know that you mould the practice to suit the occasion.'

Paintings

Francis Hargrave
by Sir Joshua Reynolds (1723–92)

Francis Hargrave (1741–1821) entered Lincoln's Inn as a student in 1760, but was not called to the Bar until 1771. Within two years of call he made a name for himself in Somerset's Case, in which, on an application for habeas corpus, he successfully persuaded Lord Mansfield that the state of slavery 'is neither allowed nor approved by the law of England'. Soon after this he was made a King's Counsel, but his subsequent practice was largely confined to chambers, as a draftsman and writer of opinions – perhaps because his speeches in court, though painstakingly accurate, were 'prolix and tortuous'. His reputation rests on his extraordinary learning rather than his advocacy.

Hargrave became a bencher in 1802, and was Treasurer in 1813; but soon after suffered a mental breakdown. His wife petitioned Parliament to buy his legal manuscripts and printed books (many of them marginally annotated in his own hand), and his legal library was purchased for £8,000 and deposited in the British Museum. In 1843 a number of his manuscripts, mostly containing unpublished works by Sir Matthew Hale, were bought by the Inn from one of his sons.

His publications include eleven volumes of *State Trials* (1776) and a number of *Tracts relative to the Law and Constitution of England* (1791–2). These last combine edited texts, opinions, articles, case notes and lists of recent publications, thus anticipating the content of law journals of later times.

Hargrave died in 1821 and was buried in the Undercroft of Lincoln's Inn Chapel. This portrait, painted by Sir Joshua Reynolds in 1787, was bought by the Inn from Hargrave's son Francis in 1839.

George Engle

Paul before Felix
by William Hogarth (1697–1764)

In a trial scene from the Bible, Paul defends himself and the Christian religion. The Roman Procurator of Judaea, whose adulterous wife, Drusilla, sits on the bench beside him, is too much of a coward to make a prompt decision and so allows injustice to hold sway while he hopes to be bribed to allow the case to fail.

The commission was one of Hogarth's most profitable, but has not usually been regarded as a great work. The accomplished portrayer of eighteenth-century London in all its joy and squalor failed to rise to contemporary demands for monumental style in a historical scene. The converse, however, is that the artist never allows his public to forget that those in authority (whether in the past or the present) are first and foremost mere humans. The money for the commission was a bequest of £200 from Lord Wyndham, Lord Chancellor of Ireland, and it was probably Lord Mansfield who suggested the artist should be allowed to choose the subject. Hogarth's receipt dated 8 July 1748 and his detailed advice on framing and hanging survive. He clearly knew his picture of an unjust judge would hang over the senior Chancery judges of the day as they sat at dinner in term and in vacation above the Lord Chancellor presiding in his court in the Old Hall.

Mark Ockelton

Sixteen Prime Ministers

RICHARD WALLINGTON

The coats of arms of fifteen Prime Ministers are proudly displayed on the panelling in the Great Hall of Lincoln's Inn. The sixteenth would be Tony Blair's if he had a coat of arms. The Inn could even lay claim to a seventeenth: George Grenville, Prime Minister 1763–5, was a student at Lincoln's Inn but really belongs to the Inner Temple, where he was called to the Bar and became a bencher. The office of Prime Minister has been filled by persons with a Lincoln's Inn connection for 122 of the 285 years that have elapsed since 1721.

SIR ROBERT WALPOLE (1676–1745)

The story begins with Sir Robert Walpole (PM 1721–42), great both in girth and political genius, and known at court as 'le gros homme'. He is conventionally regarded as the first Prime Minister. There is no memorable historic measure attached to his name, except perhaps theatre censorship (Prime Ministers have had bad relations with the media from earliest times). His great achievement was to bring about a period of peace, and political and financial stability, after a period of domestic and international turmoil. He established a workable political system by using government patronage, together with alliances with Whig magnates who controlled groups of MPs, to maintain a working majority for the government in the House of Commons. Walpole was the first chief minister to sit in the Commons rather than the Lords.

Walpole became a student of Lincoln's Inn in 1697, but abandoned the law after the deaths of his elder brothers made him heir to the family estates. In 1726 he came to the Inn's Candlemas feast, and was elected a bencher five days later.

WILLIAM PITT THE YOUNGER (1759–1806)

There is a cluster of Lincoln's Inn politicians at the end of the eighteenth century and the beginning of the nineteenth, several of whom made it to Prime Minister, and most of whom are connected with William Pitt the Younger. The eighteenth-century political system was manned to a considerable extent by the younger sons of the aristocracy or landed gentry: owing to the practice of primogeniture, they needed an occupation. Apart from government office, the Bar was one of the few socially acceptable ways of earning a living for them, and it was also an occupation which it was possible to combine with politics when out of office. Pitt the Younger, like his father, was a younger son, as were Grenville (later Lord Grenville) and his father George Grenville, Spencer Perceval, and F.J. Robinson (later Lord Goderich). Melbourne, like Walpole, was a younger son who, on the death of an elder brother, became heir to the family estates.

William Pitt the Younger (PM 1783–1801 and 1804–6) is remarkable for having become Chancellor of the Exchequer at the age of 23 and Prime Minister at the age of 24. By the time of his death he had been Prime Minister for a total of eighteen and a half years, a tenure of office exceeded only by Sir Robert Walpole.

Pitt was called to the Bar by Lincoln's Inn in June 1780, when he had already agreed to lease chambers in the attic of the newly completed 4 Stone Buildings. He practised at the Bar on the Western Circuit in 1780. He entered Parliament in November 1780, and caused a sensation by the brilliance of his maiden speech on 26 February 1781. He returned to practice on the Western Circuit in the summer of 1781 during the Parliamentary recess.

The sundial repainted in 1794, so bearing Pitt's initials as Treasurer for that year, and moved to 4 Stone Buildings in about 1873. The inscription means: 'Ye do not know the hour he returns'.

W.P
1794
VIII
VII
VI
V
I
II
III
IIII
QUA REDIT NESCITIS HORAM

On enlarging this photograph we discovered the words 'Gallows Billy' which seem to have been added surreptitiously by the glass painter, G. Judge, when he painted these arms for the Treasurers' window in the Chapel in 1796. They must refer to Pitt's role in the various sedition-suppressing measures and treason trials of the mid-1790s.

On becoming Chancellor of the Exchequer in July 1782 Pitt abandoned practice at the Bar, but it meant that he was elected a bencher of Lincoln's Inn in November 1782. He served as Treasurer in 1794, and in the other offices of the Inn between 1789 and 1796, all while he was Prime Minister. In his year as Treasurer he did not attend a single Council meeting, but he did have the excuse of the war with revolutionary France, and the need to suppress subversion at home (many of those prosecuted for subversive activities were acquitted, defended by Pitt's fellow bencher Thomas Erskine). The sundial on 9 Garden Row was ordered to be repainted by Council in July 1794, and thus bears Pitt's initials as Treasurer. It is now on the west face of his old chambers, 4 Stone Buildings, to which it was moved in the nineteenth century when Garden Row was demolished.

In his personal life Pitt was a total contrast to Walpole: he was thin, socially diffident, celibate, and high-mindedly indifferent to the acquisition of wealth, while Walpole was fat, self-assured, lived with a mistress, and amassed a fortune from government office. On the other hand Pitt as politician and statesman is reminiscent of Walpole. Pitt was essentially an enthusiast for peace, stability, and prosperity, and not a natural war leader despite the country being at war for much of his time in office. Like Walpole, he had a particular genius for government finance, and the eventual victory over Napoleon owed much to his improvements to it. Also like Walpole he carried through no great measure or reform (despite various attempts), apart from the introduction of income tax (see below) and the union with Ireland. The latter, despite giving us our national flag and seeming a good idea at the time, did not endure in the long term, and two other Lincoln's Inn Prime Ministers, Gladstone and Asquith, devoted much of their political careers to trying to reverse it.

HENRY ADDINGTON (1757–1844)

Henry Addington (PM 1801–4) was put into bat as Prime Minister by Pitt when the latter resigned in 1801. He had been called to the Bar in 1784 after becoming an MP the previous year. He practised at the Bar for a few years before becoming Speaker of the House of Commons in 1789 at Pitt's request. He and Pitt had known each other from childhood as Addington was the son of the Pitt family's doctor. Addington was the first Prime Minister to come from the professional middle classes and was nicknamed 'the Doctor'. He was elected to the Lincoln's Inn bench in 1792, and served as Treasurer in 1797. While in office as Prime Minister he suffered the disadvantage of Pitt's and Pitt loyalists' critical remarks, the most famous being Canning's 'Pitt is to Addington, as London is to Paddington'.

Henry Addington, Prime Minister 1801-4 (artist unknown).

The most memorable achievement of Addington's premiership is income tax. Pitt had introduced the tax in 1798, but it had been repealed in 1802 when peace was made with the French. Addington re-introduced the tax in an improved form in 1803 when war broke out again. He was an inferior orator to Pitt, but he managed to devise a much more workable system of income tax, including the Schedule system of classifying kinds of income, and deduction at source. Addington's income tax was abolished at the end of the Napoleonic Wars. It was brought back by Peel in 1842, to finance reductions in customs and excise duties, and has remained ever since. Peel re-used Addington's legislation, and chunks of it remained embedded in the tax legislation until the current tax law rewrite project began to replace it. It is a sobering thought for all members of Lincoln's Inn, as they fill in their tax returns, that all three Prime Ministers responsible for income tax were members of the Inn. It does not stop there, because graduated income tax (now the forty per cent higher rate) was introduced by Asquith's government.

LORD GRENVILLE (1759–1834)

William Wyndham, 1st Baron Grenville (PM 1806–7), had been admitted a student of Lincoln's Inn in 1780, but became an MP in 1782 and then concentrated on politics. He was a first cousin of Pitt and the same age. He was an important member of Pitt's ministry between 1789 and 1801, but went into opposition after that apart from his year or so as Prime Minister at the head of a Whig administration. The historic achievement of his ministry was the outlawing of the slave trade.

SPENCER PERCEVAL (1762–1812)

Spencer Perceval (PM 1809–12) is memorable for being the only British Prime Minister to be assassinated. He has the interest from a Lincoln's Inn perspective that he had a long career at the Bar of twenty years or so, five of which were as Solicitor General and then Attorney General. Of the careers at the Bar of barrister Prime Ministers, his is the second longest (Asquith's being the longest), because he needed to earn a living and had twelve children to support. He was called to the Bar by Lincoln's Inn in 1786, was elected a bencher in 1796, the year he entered Parliament, and served as Treasurer in 1803. He is unique in that instead of the usual career progression of law officers to Chief Justice of a common law court and then Lord Chancellor, he went from being a law officer in 1801–6 to become Chancellor of the Exchequer in 1807, and then Prime Minister in 1809.

Spencer Perceval was a most effective Prime Minister in the Pitt mould, and noted for his integrity, fervent evangelical Anglicanism, and Christian charity. His religious convictions made him implacably opposed to Catholic emancipation and Napoleonic France. Under his premiership the tide began to turn decisively against Napoleon in the land war, and Perceval would probably have continued in office for many years had he not been shot dead in the lobby of the House of Commons on 11 May 1812. His assassin was John Bellingham, a Liverpool merchant who had been ruined by the war, and who despite a plea of insanity was convicted of murder and hanged on 18 May. As a mark of respect for Perceval's memory the benchers of Lincoln's Inn offered to admit two of his sons without fee, and put up the memorial tablet with a lengthy Latin inscription which can still be seen at the entrance to the Chapel.

The assassination of Spencer Perceval by John Bellingham in the lobby of the House of Commons 11 May 1812.

GEORGE CANNING (1770–1827) AND LORD GODERICH (1782–1859)

George Canning (PM 1827) had had a long and distinguished political career, starting as an enthusiastic young friend and supporter of Pitt, in whose administrations he held junior posts from 1796, and who had a sideline in writing satirical verses. He was Foreign Secretary in the Portland administration (1807–9), but was then out of office until 1816 after fighting a duel with Castlereagh. He had a particularly important tenure of office as Foreign Secretary 1822–7. He took office as Prime Minister on 10 April 1827, was elected a bencher of Lincoln's Inn on 14 May, but died on 8 August of the same year. He had been admitted as a student of Lincoln's Inn in 1787 but was never called to the Bar. He was succeeded as Prime Minister by F.J. Robinson, recently ennobled as Viscount Goderich (PM 1827–8), who resigned after about five months in office. He had been admitted as a student of Lincoln's Inn in 1802.

LORD MELBOURNE (1779–1848)

William Lamb, 2nd Viscount Melbourne (Whig/Liberal PM 1834, 1835–41) is remembered for the passion of his half-mad wife, Lady Caroline Lamb, for Lord Byron, pursued with much drama in public though it is uncertain with how much intimacy in private; more significant was the fact that he was Prime Minister when Queen Victoria came to the throne and became a mentor and father figure for her. He was called to the Bar by Lincoln's Inn in November 1804. He then had a brief, probably a one-brief, career at the Bar on the Northern Circuit before the death of his elder brother in January 1805 made him the heir to the Lamb estates and title. He then abandoned the Bar.

Melbourne was very much a leftover of the eighteenth-century aristocracy: indolent, ironic, cultured, and well read, contemptuous of religious enthusiasm and the middle classes, and he was generally thought to be the son of his mother's lover rather than of her husband. Like Pitt, Melbourne refused all honours, even the Garter. His administration carried on from that of Earl Grey, which had been responsible for the 1832 Reform Act. However, in the best eighteenth-century tradition, Melbourne believed in doing as little as possible, and the main legislative achievements of his premiership are the introduction of civil marriage, the registration of births, marriages and deaths, and the Wills Act 1837.

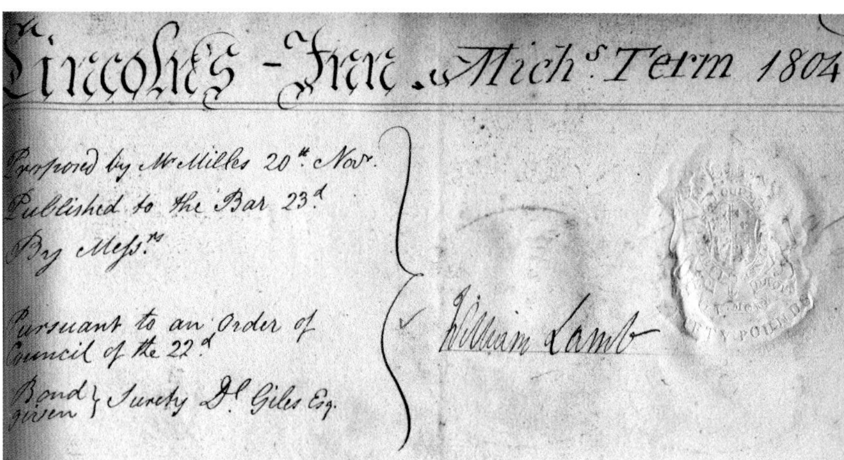

Lincoln's Inn . Mich.s Term 1804
Proposed by Mr Milles 20th Nov.
Published to the Bar 23d
By Messrs
Pursuant to an Order of Council of the 22d
Bond given } Surety Ds Giles Esq.
William Lamb

The signature of William Lamb (Lord Melbourne) in the Bar Book November 1804.

SIR ROBERT PEEL (1788–1850), BENJAMIN DISRAELI (1804–81), WILLIAM GLADSTONE (1809–98)

Sir Robert Peel (Tory/Conservative PM 1834–5, 1841–6), was a politician of the new age, from the factory-owning rather than the land-owning classes, industrious, high-minded, a moderate reformer and good at public finance, and, like Gladstone, a man who split his party over a matter of principle (Peel over repeal of the Corn Laws, Gladstone over Home Rule for Ireland). William Gladstone (Liberal PM 1868–74, 1880–85, 1886, 1892–4), the great Liberal leader, is arguably the most remarkable man ever to occupy the position of Prime Minister. He had enormous energy and grasp of detail, while also being a charismatic leader and formulator of policy. Benjamin Disraeli (Conservative PM 1868, 1874–80), his Tory opponent, was a complete contrast: opportunistic, with no interest in detail, but a political orator and tactician of genius. All three were admitted as students of the Inn, Peel in 1809, Disraeli in 1824, and Gladstone in 1833, but were never called to the Bar.

In later years Gladstone came to dinner in the Inn from time to time. Earlier, in 1853, Gladstone was grateful to the Inn for its support of his friend F.D. Maurice when the latter was dismissed from his chair at King's College London because he questioned whether the punishment of the wicked in the next world is eternal. The benchers of Lincoln's Inn, although probably in favour of the maximum punishment of the wicked, were more tolerant, and kept Maurice on in his post as the Inn's Chaplain.

In contrast to Pitt, Gladstone first became Prime Minister at the age of 58, and resigned as Prime Minister for the last time at the age of 84. His achievements, particularly in his first administration, were enormous,

Disraeli and Gladstone in Punch, *1857.*

and his administrations reformed just about everything, including the legal system, merging the superior courts into a single High Court by the Judicature Act 1873.

LORD SALISBURY (1830–1903)

Robert Cecil, 3rd Marquis of Salisbury (Conservative/Unionist PM 1885–6, 1886–92, and 1895–1902), like Peel, Gladstone and Disraeli, is a major political figure who never progressed in the law beyond being a student of Lincoln's Inn (admitted 1850). He is the last Prime Minister to have operated for any length of time from the House of Lords rather than the Commons, and is unusual in having been Foreign Secretary rather than First Lord of the Treasury. Although he was one of the last Prime Ministers to come from an old landed family, he did not conform to the stereotype of his class, as he was intellectual, high-minded, and religious, and had been a younger son living off meagre earnings as a journalist and annoying his father by marrying a social inferior (the daughter of a judge), before the death of an elder brother made him the heir to the family title and estates.

HERBERT HENRY ASQUITH (1852–1928)

Towards the end of the nineteenth century there was another cluster of politicians in Lincoln's Inn, mostly Liberal, but Asquith (Liberal PM 1908–16) was the only one to become Prime Minister. Asquith was yet another younger son, but his father died when he was eight leaving very little, and primogeniture was not an issue. Asquith probably had humbler origins than any of his predecessors as Prime Minister, and he represents the beginning of the opening up of high political office to persons who lack the advantages of inherited wealth or aristocratic connections.

Asquith chose the Bar as a career because it was a method of earning a living which could be combined with politics. He was called to the Bar by Lincoln's Inn in June 1876, and had a common law and commercial practice, taking silk in 1890. It was through Lincoln's Inn that he became a close friend of Richard Haldane, who persuaded him to stand for Parliament in 1886 and helped him to be adopted as Liberal candidate for East Fife. Asquith was Home Secretary in the Liberal government of 1892–5, and was unusual for a Home Secretary in being a success in that office, but on the fall of the government he returned to the Bar in 1895 and spent ten years doing profitable work such as Privy Council appeals and tax cases. He practised at the Bar until December 1905 (when he became Chancellor of the Exchequer), a total of twenty-six years, and never as a law officer.

H.H. Asquith in 1908.

History has been unkind to Asquith as Prime Minister, and what tends to be remembered is the nickname 'Old Squiffy' (like Pitt, he drank too much), and his emotional dependence on friendships with young women to whom he wrote copious letters. He is overshadowed by the more forceful personalities in his government, in particular Churchill and Lloyd George. He was a good committee chairman, a very effective Parliamentary speaker with a gift for encapsulating arguments with great conciseness and clarity, and a steady hand on the tiller in times of crisis. His ministry laid the foundations of the modern welfare state, and in the Parliament Act 1911 produced a solution to the problem of the House of Lords in a typical British compromise, which endured little altered until the introduction of life peers in 1958. By December 1916 Asquith's conduct as war leader was becoming increasingly unpopular and he was manoeuvred out of power after he had been Prime Minister for eight and a half years, the longest continuous period of office of a Prime Minister between 1827 and 1979.

Asquith had been elected a bencher of Lincoln's Inn in 1894 (in place of his former pupil-master, the recently deceased Lord Bowen), and served as Treasurer in 1920. He attended eight Council meetings as Treasurer, and at least one call night. In a letter to Mrs Harrison of 29 April 1920 he wrote: 'I went last night to Lincoln's Inn to receive in my capacity of Treasurer the new men being "called" to the Bar. I dined afterwards in Hall with my brother Benchers who are not a very lively lot – mostly judges and ex-judges and hoary KCs, whose conversation is as "shoppy" in its way as that of a table full of golfers or hunting men.' He unveiled the Inn's War Memorial on 16 March 1921, and a banquet was held in his honour by the Inn in 1925 to celebrate his elevation to the peerage as Earl of Oxford and Asquith by his fellow bencher, King George V.

NEVILLE CHAMBERLAIN (1869–1940)

Neville Chamberlain (National Government PM 1937–40) came from a political dynasty reminiscent of the Pitts or the Grenvilles, save that the Chamberlains were Nonconformist (Unitarian) manufacturers whose power base was the City of Birmingham rather than country estates. Neville Chamberlain (another younger son) was practical and pragmatic and showed great

The Prince of Wales (first row far left) and Neville Chamberlain (first row far right) dining in the Inn March 1925.

Lady Thatcher, Prime Minister 1979–90 (June Mendoza, 1990).

ability and dedication in matters of administrative and social reform. He had recurring bad luck, beginning with being sent by his father to grow sisal in a remote corner of the Bahamas for five years, losing a great deal of money, and continuing with his failure as organizer of national service in the First World War. He became head of a government of National Unity in 1937. His memorable words on 30 September 1938 describing the agreement he had reached in Munich with Hitler – 'This is the second time in our history that there has come back from Germany to Downing Street peace with honour. I believe it is peace for our time' – were soon contradicted by events. Like Pitt and Asquith, he found himself Prime Minister at the outbreak of a major European war which he would have preferred to avoid.

Neville Chamberlain was elected an honorary bencher of Lincoln's Inn in May 1937, when he was about to become Prime Minister.

MARGARET THATCHER (1925–) AND TONY BLAIR (1953–)

Margaret Thatcher (Conservative PM 1979–90) was called to the Bar by Lincoln's Inn in 1954 and practised at the Bar as a tax practitioner until elected as an MP in 1959. She was made an honorary bencher of Lincoln's Inn in 1975 after becoming Leader of the Opposition. Tony Blair (Labour PM 1997–) was called to the Bar by Lincoln's Inn in 1976, and practised at the Bar doing common law and employment work until becoming an MP in 1983. He was elected an honorary bencher of Lincoln's Inn in 1994 after becoming Leader of the Opposition.

It is too soon to assess the historical importance of Margaret Thatcher or Tony Blair as Prime Ministers, but there are some facts no amount of historical reassessment can alter. Margaret Thatcher was the first woman Prime Minister. Her government reversed the Keynesian economic policies which had been the orthodoxy since the Second World War. Tony Blair is the first leader of the Labour Party to win three general elections in succession. Both have had longer continuous terms of office as Prime Minister than Asquith.

Tony Blair on his Call Day July 1976.

Great Figures

SIR MATTHEW HALE 1609–1676

Matthew Hale, one of the greatest scholars of the English law and a model of judicial impartiality in a turbulent and partisan age, was born in 1609 in Alderley, Gloucestershire, the son of a retired barrister. Hale was orphaned at the age of five and educated under the direction of a Puritan vicar. In 1626 he entered Magdalen Hall, Oxford with a view to taking holy orders.

Attracted by a company of strolling players, Hale threw aside his studies in favour of fencing and gambling. He considered enlisting in the service of the Protestant cause in the Netherlands but an eminent lawyer, Serjeant Glanville, persuaded him to turn to the law.

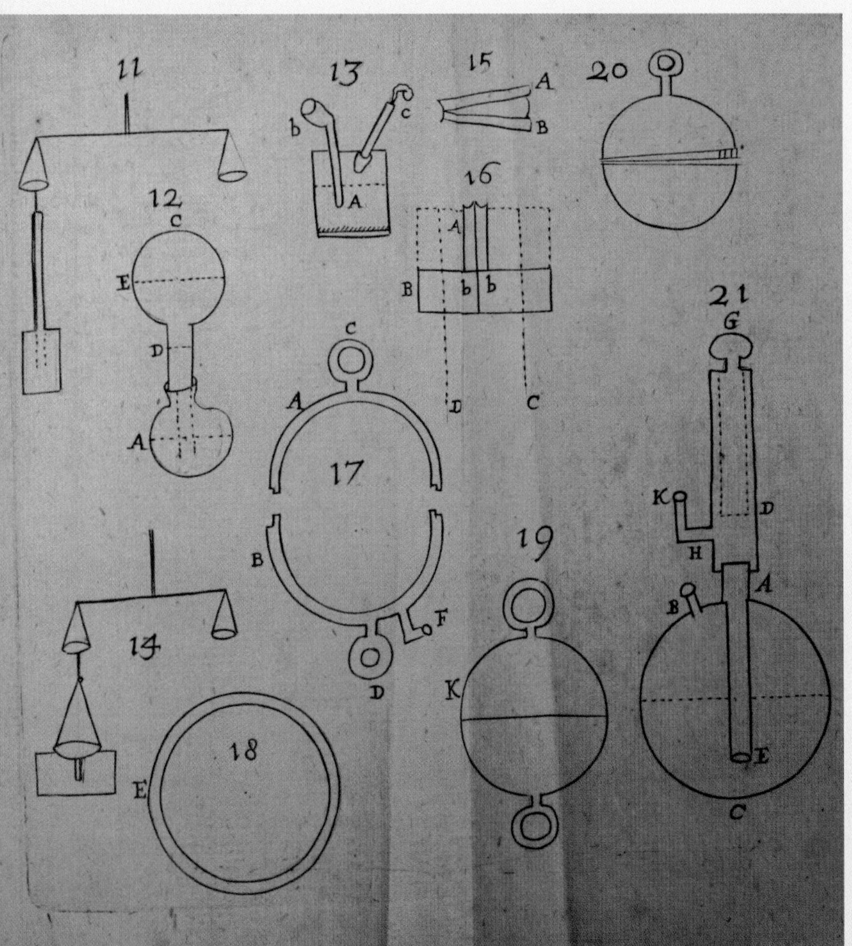

From Sir Matthew Hale's Difficiles nugae, or, Observations touching the Torricelliam experiment *(1675).*

Sir Matthew Hale by John Michael Wright 1671.

In 1629 he was admitted to the Inn, studying under John Selden, who greatly influenced him. Apart from law, Hale studied pure mathematics, physics, chemistry, anatomy, and architecture, working sixteen hours a day. He was called to the Bar in 1636, and within a few years he was at the head of his profession.

Hale entered public life at perhaps the most critical period of English history – the Civil War. Hale modelled himself on a writer and thinker from an earlier age of similar strife, Cicero's friend Pomponius Atticus. Atticus thought a man could best serve his country by avoiding partisanship. Hale avoided taking sides, and as a result was respected by both Royalists and Parliamentarians.

In 1654 he was appointed by Oliver Cromwell a judge of the Common Pleas, and at the Restoration in 1660 he was appointed Chief Baron of the Court of Exchequer. In 1671 he became Chief Justice of the King's Bench. In failing health he relinquished office in February 1676 and retired to Alderley, where he died on Christmas Day.

Hale's reputation rests upon his modesty and integrity as a man, his impartiality as a judge, and his erudition as a writer. He was a charitable man and took an interest in and wrote about social problems. He favoured cheap, drab clothing. Even as Lord Chief Justice his behaviour took lack of pretension to the verge of eccentricity. He disapproved of any sport involving killing animals for pleasure.

After the Restoration, he enjoyed virtually universal reverence, although some Royalists suspected him of pro-Puritan bias. Hale was certainly relaxed when national security was said to be threatened. In *Tonge's Case* in 1662 he was one of only two judges to refuse to convict a radical Puritan printer; in *Messenger's Case* in 1668, which arose from an apprentice riot seen to be anti-government, he was the only judge to oppose the decision to treat the rioters as traitors.

Hale took a restrictive view of the use of martial law and disliked the practice by which courts attempted to control jurors by fining them for returning verdicts considered perverse. Dryden records that King Charles believed that 'the King's servants were sure to be ruled against in any trial that was heard before Hale: not that he thought the judge was possibly to be bribed: but that his integrity might be too scrupulous'.

Hale was the driving force behind the Fire Court instituted in 1667 after the Great Fire of London to deal speedily with disputes arising from the destruction. So successful was the Court that the bulk of private re-building work was completed by 1670.

Even Hale was not entirely free of the prejudices of his age. In 1664 two elderly widows, Amy Duny and Rose Cullender, were charged before Hale with witchcraft. They were said to have bewitched seven children. It was alleged that some victims suffered fits in the course of which they vomited pins; others lost the faculties of hearing, sight, and speech. During the trial, three of the children suffered fits and were struck dumb. A mother of one of the children blamed her need to use crutches on the women. The jury found both women guilty. Before the women were sentenced, the children were restored to full health, and the mother abandoned her crutches, circumstances that might suggest to our modern minds hysteria rather than witchcraft. Nevertheless Hale sentenced the women and, still protesting their innocence, they were hanged. The trial presaged and gave an air of legitimacy to the accusations of witchcraft in Salem, Massachussetts in 1692.

But Hale is principally remembered not as a judge but as a jurist. He formed an extensive collection of manuscripts, the bulk of which were bequeathed by him to the Inn. The work by which Hale is best known is his *Historia placitorum coronae, The History of the Pleas of the Crown*, dealing with the law of crimes punishable by death – a long list in Hale's day. The book is a tour de force. Hale succeeded in reducing a mass of material to a coherent account of the criminal law. Published posthumously in 1736, it was the main authority on English criminal law for at least a century – the first edition of *Archbold on Pleading and Evidence in Criminal Cases*, published in 1822, still cited it extensively, and indeed from time to time it is referred to in the courts today.

The Great Fire of London: the City of London acknowledged the contribution of Hale and his fellow judges on the Fire Court by commissioning portraits of them, five of which hang in the Great Hall.

As a judge Hale demonstrated integrity, impartiality, intellect and diligence but there was more. Sollom Emlyn of Lincoln's Inn, the publisher of the first edition of the *Pleas of the Crown*, writes of him:

> *He was possessed in a high degree of that qualification so peculiarly necessary to a judge, I mean patience, (without which the most excellent talents may become insignificant), no considerations of his own convenience could prevail with him to hurry over a cause, for which reason he made it a rule, to be short and sparing at meals, that he might not either by a full stomach unfit himself for the due discharge of his office, or by a profuse waste of time be obliged to put off or precipitate the business that came before him. In every character of life he was a pattern well worthy of imitation: he was a public blessing to the age he lived in, and not to that only, but a bright and amiable example to succeeding generations.*

Andrew Collender

Poets, Playwrights, and Novelists

NO MAN IS AN ISLAND: JOHN DONNE, POET AND PREACHER

Robert Walker

John Donne (1572–1631) was a great poet and a great preacher. Some of his most passionate poetry was written when he was a student of Lincoln's Inn, and some of his most eloquent sermons were given when he was the Inn's Preacher.

This copy of a painting by an unknown artist hangs in the Chapel. The original was recently acquired by the National Portrait Gallery from the Marquis of Lothian.

Today many critics would place Donne among England's greatest poets. But his reputation has fluctuated remarkably; as John Hayward wrote, 'No English writer has provoked such passionate like and dislike.' Dr Samuel Johnson was particularly acerbic about him. Some of Donne's poetry, full of extravagant praise of women he had never set eyes on, was written to curry favour with the rich and powerful. Even the best of it often has tortured syntax and word order, and there are recurrent, almost obsessional themes, which resonate in his sermons also: the sun, angels, maps and globes, spheres, body parts, bodily dissolution, very large numbers, death, eternity.

Yet this strange man – at once scholarly and passionate, worldly and other-worldly – wrote poetry of startling imagination and power, especially in his *Songs and Sonnets* and his *Elegies*. *To His Mistris going to bed*, probably written soon after 1592 when he was admitted as a student of Lincoln's Inn, was regarded as so risqué that it was not published for some time: here are some well-known lines:

Licence my roaving hands, and let them go,
Before, behind, between, above, below.
Oh my America! My new-found-land,
My kingdome, safeliest when with one man
man'd,
My Myne of precious stones, my Emperie,
How blest am I in this discovering thee!

And here is the first verse of *Song*, probably written a few years later:

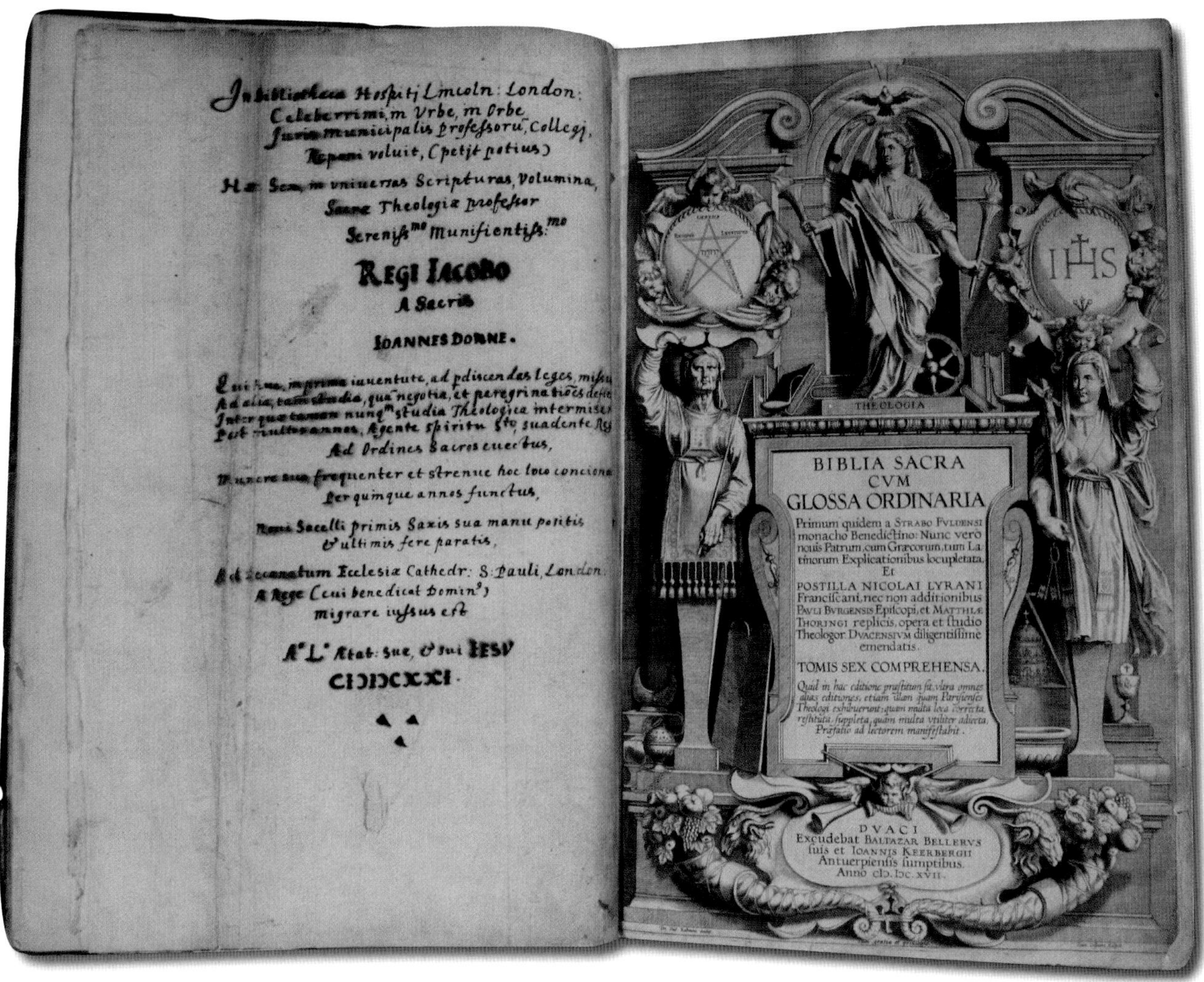

The bible inscribed and presented by John Donne to the Inn – 'the most celebrated college in the city, nay in the world, of the professors of common law' – when he left to become Dean of St Paul's in 1621.

Goe and catche a falling starre,
Get with child a mandrake roote,
Tell me, where all past yeares are,
Or who cleft the Divels foot,
Teach me to heare Mermaides singing,
Or to keep off envies stinging,
And finde,
What winde,
Serves to advance an honest minde.

Later Donne put his colourful youth behind him. During the last sixteen years of his life he was in holy orders. He preached in Lincoln's Inn, at St Paul's, and sometimes before the King at Whitehall. The language of his sermons is often as memorable as that of his poems. The most famous passage has a particular resonance for members of the Inn, as the Chapel bell is still tolled to mark the death of a bencher:

No man is an Iland, intire of it selfe; every man is a peece of the Continent, a part of the maine; if a Clod bee washed away by the Sea, Europe is the lesse, as well as if a Promontorie were, as well as if a Mannor of thy friends or of thine owne were; any man's death diminishes me, because I am involved in mankinde; and therefore never send to know for whom the bell tolls; It tolls for thee.

Although Donne had, in the years after the Guy Fawkes plot, written some anti-Catholic works (*Pseudo-Martyr* and *Ignatius his Conclave*), the writings of his maturity were often ecumenical in tone, 'I never fettered nor imprisoned the word Religion, not … immuring it in a Rome, or a Wittenberg or a Geneva; they are all virtual beams of one sun… They are not so contrary as the North and South Poles.'

What are we to make of this extraordinary man? Professor John Carey has written (in *John Donne, Mind and Art*), 'The first thing to remember about Donne is that he was a Catholic; the second, that he betrayed his Faith.' Donne was related through his mother to Sir Thomas More. Two of his uncles were Jesuits. One was hanged, drawn, and quartered for high treason. As a boy of 12 he was taken by his mother, together with another disguised Jesuit, William Weston, to visit his uncle in the Tower. He had a younger brother, Henry, who was also a student of the Inn. During the reign of Elizabeth I, Lincoln's Inn Fields were rumoured to be a haunt for priests, whose mere presence in England constituted the offence of high treason. In 1593 a suspected priest was found in Henry's room in or near the Inn. Both were arrested and Henry, faced with torture, betrayed the priest, who suffered the awful death reserved for high treason. Henry died of fever in Newgate. All these horrific events occurred by the time John Donne was 21. As Carey comments, 'Some readers may ask what all this has to do with Donne's poetry, but I imagine they will be few.'

Donne abandoned the Catholic religion and left Lincoln's Inn without being called to the Bar, although he continued to take an interest in both canon and civil law, as is apparent from his poetry and sermons. He spent some years abroad, including military service with the Earl of Essex. On his return to London in 1597 he obtained an appointment as secretary to the Lord Keeper, Sir Thomas Egerton. In 1601, under Egerton's patronage, he became Member of Parliament for Brackley. But at the end of that year he recklessly destroyed his prospects by a clandestine marriage to Lady Egerton's niece Ann, then barely 17. Donne lost his job and was for some time imprisoned in the Fleet. So again Donne exiled himself abroad, returning to London in 1607 to try to restore his social and public position. Meanwhile his unfortunate wife (who eventually bore him at least twelve children) was left in needy circumstances. During the next decade Donne worked hard, with considerable success to re-establish his position. His *Holy Sonnets*, and most of his prose works, other than sermons, date from this period.

He took holy orders in 1615 and became Preacher, then called reader in divinity, of the Inn in 1617, just after his wife's death. In 1619 he was a member of a diplomatic mission which James I sent to Heidelberg, where he preached before the Elector and Princess Elizabeth, for whose marriage he had written a poem seven years before. The mission was intended to promote James I's strategy of a liberal Protestant alliance, but it ended in the disaster of the Thirty Years War. Donne returned to the Inn in 1620. A year later he was made Dean of St Paul's. On Ascension Day 1623 he preached in Lincoln's Inn at the dedication of the new Chapel. He died in 1631, a few weeks after preaching an extraordinary sermon, *Death's Duell*, before King Charles I at Whitehall. It was widely regarded as his own funeral sermon. He spent the last weeks of his life preparing for death, even posing in his shroud for the monument which now stands in St Paul's.

The Library has two books owned by Ben Jonson, who in his youth helped his bricklayer stepfather with building works in the Inn. Jonson's motto tanquam explorator, *written in his own hand, is in the top right corner of Drayton's* Poly-Olbion *and a copy of Juvenal's* Satires *bears his signature.*

SHAKESPEARE'S DEBT

Paul Heim

The Library's copy of the second folio, 1632. *As You Like It* did not appear in print in any quarto edition during Shakespeare's lifetime, being first published in the first folio of 1623.

It is not to decry Shakespeare's world-bestriding genius to recall the debt he owes to a Lincoln's Inn man, Thomas Lodge.

Lodge entered Lincoln's Inn in 1578, fourteen years before John Donne, his parallel in many striking ways. Like Donne, he had some difficulty in finding his place in the legal world. The pleasures of London vied with the pleasures of the law. Like Donne, his circumstances, and the call of the times, led him to the profession of arms. The wars with Spain were continuing, the zest for exploration was in the air. The Inn had publicly pledged its loyalty to the Queen in a memorandum signed by ninety of its members. No mere words: at least three young members of the Inn, John Donne, Thomas Egerton, and Thomas Lodge, volunteered for service abroad. The first two joined the expedition led by the Earl of Essex and Sir Walter Raleigh to raid Cadiz. Thomas Lodge went on voyages to the Azores, and to Brazil.

While the ships were becalmed, Lodge took to writing sonnets, mainly in the classic Petrarchan mode, but also in his own longer model.

You sacred sea-nymphs pleasantly disporting,
Amidst this watery world wherein I sail...

This sets the more agreeable scene although later he describes his voyage, no doubt in heavier seas, as 'this travel desolate and hellish'. Essays and prose love plays also flowed from his pen, whetted by the torrid doldrums.

His greatest work, written at sea, was the prose tale, *Rosalynde, Euphues Golden Legacie*. In France, in the mystical, mythical Forest of Arden, Rosader, suffering at the hands of his unpleasant brother, but accompanied by his faithful servant Adam, has a number of adventures while he seeks and finds the entrancing Rosalynde.

This is no bread and butter miss. 'Of all her gifts, her wisdom pleases most' is the first description of her, but she may be 'most amiable, and yet unkinde: full of favour, and yet froward: coy without wit, disdainful without reason'.

Lodge found his original creation fascinating. So did his contemporary, Shakespeare, who lifted her as she was, witty and wise, versatile and constant, beautiful and contrary, to make her the captivating central figure of *As You Like It*.

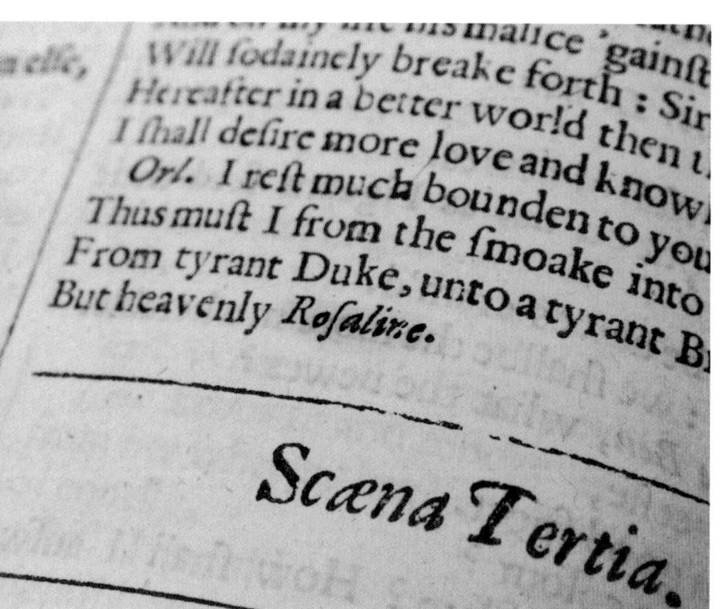
Will ſodainely breake forth : Sir
Hereafter in a better world then t
I ſhall deſire more love and know
Orl. I reſt much bounden to you
Thus muſt I from the ſmoake into
From tyrant Duke, unto a tyrant B
But heavenly Roſaline.

Scæna Tertia.

Shakespeare's Rosalind.

She is probably Shakespeare's own best monument. Harold Bloom, in his charmingly entitled book, *Shakespeare, the Inventor of the Human*, finds her to be 'the most admirable personage in the whole of Shakespeare', but even Shakespeare could not improve on Lodge's model. He kept her in the setting of the French Forest of Arden, no relation to sober Warwickshire, in spite of what commentators say, although he may have moved the dark, oppressive Ardennes somewhat to the South to ensure that his protagonists, while suffering from hunger, were not too cold to feel passion.

He also kept the main characters, although the transposition of Lodge's soulful and sensitive Rosader to Shakespeare's wooden Orlando is hardly an improvement. One could not take the well-meaning, abrupt, keep-fit enthusiast Orlando to be a Lincoln's Inn man. Rosader would have found a welcome in the Old Hall at any time.

Shakespeare was fascinated by Rosalynde. Her character traits are evident in so many heroines. Is she Kate? Is she Portia, beautiful, learned, faithful, and eloquent? She peeps out, unseen but irresistible, from the pages of *Romeo and Juliet*.

Lodge returned from his voyages a new man, with new horizons. The law held no more attractions. To the South of France he went, now to study medicine. After a visit to the Low Countries, he returned to London and established himself as a doctor, well-known and successful. He wrote a number of valuable medical treatises, but is remembered for Rosalynde, his golden legacie.

LITERARY ASSOCIATIONS IN THE VICTORIAN AGE

Robert Walker

Lincoln's Inn is rich in literary associations. Many famous authors have been members of the Inn, especially in the Victorian age. Some of them, such as Disraeli and Cardinal Newman, appear in the Inn's history only on their admission as students; they were never called and never practised. Others, notably, of course, John Donne, were more closely involved in the Inn's affairs; one, as we shall see, was appointed as a County Court Judge twenty-five years after publishing his most famous work.

If we are to pick a Lincoln's Inn literary first eleven, the first two places, chronologically and no doubt in stature, must go to Sir Thomas More as author of *Utopia* (published in Latin in 1516) and John Donne. Then we have nine Victorians, some famous only for their literary works, others more celebrated in other fields. They are (in chronological order of birth, not in order of literary stature) John Henry Newman, Benjamin Disraeli, Charles Reade, Charles Kingsley, Thomas Hughes, Wilkie Collins, Rider Haggard, John Galsworthy, and Sir Henry Newbolt. The last three spanned the Victorian and Edwardian ages, though Haggard did his best work as a young man, and Galsworthy published little until he was nearly 40. Newbolt's coming in at number eleven is appropriate for the author of *Vitae Lampada*:

There's a breathless hush in the Close tonight,
Ten to make and the match to win,
A bumping pitch, and a blinding light,
And an hour to play, and the last man in.

Thomas Hughes, author, also had a successful career at the Bar, practising from chambers in Old Square and becoming a County Court Judge in 1882.

We need not spend long here on Disraeli, who also features in the chapter on Prime Ministers. At the beginning and at the end of a tempestuous political career he found time to write some substantial novels which combined political ideas with vivid characterization, notably the early works *Coningsby*, *Sybil* (the origin of 'Two Nations' conservative thought), and *Tancred* and, towards the end of his life, *Lothair* (described by A.N. Wilson as a 'high camp fantasy', with its caricature of Cardinal Manning), and *Endymion*. His novels are not now widely read, and have missed the popularity which television has given to Trollope and Galsworthy.

The next six members of the team were broadly contemporaneous, producing most of their best work between about 1855, when Kingsley's *Westward Ho!* was published, and 1868, when Wilkie Collins's *The Moonstone* appeared. There were some friendships among them – notably between Kingsley and Hughes, both devotees of F.D. Maurice, one of the Inn's most famous Chaplains. But there were also some strong antagonisms – notably between Kingsley and Newman, leading to the publication in 1864 of the latter's *Apologia pro Vita Sua*.

The young Newman was not an altogether appealing character: self-absorbed, valetudinarian, too consumed by study of the Fathers of the Church to be aware of the social ills that surrounded him. That is perhaps reflected in his only substantial novel, *Loss and Gain* (1848), which many now find unreadable. His *Apologia* is a mixture of dated controversy and genuinely touching reminiscence:

> *Trinity had never been unkind to me. There used to be much snap-dragon growing on the walls opposite my freshman's rooms there, and I had for years taken it as the emblem of my own perpetual residence even unto death in my University. On the morning of the 23rd [February 1846] I left the Observatory. I have never seen Oxford since excepting its spires, as they are seen from the railway.*

But Newman could write beautiful verse (and gave us *Lead Kindly Light* and *The Dream of Gerontius*); he bore his disappointments with fortitude; and he did see Oxford again, because he was made Trinity's first honorary fellow in 1877, two years before he got his cardinal's hat.

Kingsley, his adversary, was also deeply religious but his faith was of a very different sort. He was for Christian manliness and Christian Socialism, and against Rome and clerical celibacy. In 1860 he was appointed to the chair of Modern History at Cambridge, though his historical scholarship was sometimes questionable. He is now best known for his didactic fantasy, *The Water-Babies* (1863).

Charles Kingsley's The Water-Babies: *the Professor and Ellie capture Tom (1916 edn illustrated by Jessie Wilcox Smith).*

Kingsley and Newman would therefore avoid each other in our notional dressing-room, and might well run each other out from time to time. Kingsley and Hughes, however, would be good friends on and off the field. Hughes was admitted in 1845 and though in the event called by Inner Temple he practised from chambers in Old Square for a number of years. He was a devout, conscientious, unselfish character. After he had written his famous book, *Tom Brown's Schooldays* (1857), a contemporary of his described him as 'on the whole very like Tom Brown, but not so intellectual'. The book made him a great deal of money, but in 1880 he generously

Thomas Hughes's Tom Brown's Schooldays*: 'The Night Fag' (1871 edn).*

invested (and lost) £7,000 in a plan to set up a Christian co-operative in Tennessee. Finding that he had to work again at the age of 60, in 1882 he obtained an appointment as a County Court Judge. It was said of him that 'his rough and ready justice became a byword for constant reversal on appeal'. But he was certainly a good team player.

Charles Reade was called in 1848 but never practised. He began as a dramatist but soon had great popular success with his novels, of which the best-known were *It's Never Too Late to Mend* (1856), *The Cloister and the Hearth* (1861), and *Hard Cash* (1863). They addressed important social issues, including the state of the medical profession in Victorian England, but Reade devised melodramatic plots and had a sensationalist style. He ran into trouble over accusations of plagiarism (he was said to have 'odd notions of *meum* and *tuum*'). On one occasion he obtained six cents damages in New York proceedings when he complained that he had been defamed as a plagiarist. He also quarrelled about plagiarism with Trollope, which was unfortunate as they were both members of the Garrick.

David Garrick 1717–79, actor and playwright, joined the Inn in 1737.

Mention of the Garrick Club sends us on a detour back to the eighteenth century, since David Garrick, the country's greatest actor, was also a member of the Inn. The plays which he wrote do not quite get him into the first eleven, but his talents as an actor-manager and society wit make him a distinguished twelfth man. He was born in Lichfield in 1717, a few years after Samuel Johnson, and he attended Johnson's short-lived school nearby. They came to London together in 1737 and Garrick joined the Inn in that year. But he was soon launched on a hugely successful theatrical career, much of it as actor-manager at Drury Lane, though he also spent some years in Dublin where he collaborated with Sheridan. He played all the great Shakespearean roles – Hamlet, Lear and Richard III each more than eighty times – in a natural and unaffected style which reflected his natural warmth and conviviality. Johnson had him in mind when he said to Boswell, 'Depend upon it, Sir, vivacity is much an art, and depends greatly on habit.' His friends included many leading figures of the time, including Edmund Burke, Joshua Reynolds and John Wilkes. In 1749 he married the beautiful Eva Maria Veigel, a Viennese dancer who was a protégée of Lady

Burlington. His *joie de vivre* lives on in the Garrick Club, founded in 1831, about fifty years after his death.

Wilkie Collins was called in 1852. He never practised but had a keen interest in the law, which appears in his work. He was a friend of Dickens, whose daughter, Kate, married his brother, and also of Reade. His best-known works are *The Woman in White* (1860) and *The Moonstone* (1868), intricately-plotted novels which are still read.

Henry Rider Haggard had already had a colourful career when he was called to the Bar in 1883. As a young man he had gone to South Africa as ADC to the Lieutenant Governor of Natal, and stayed on as an ostrich farmer. Before he left England he had fallen in love with a beautiful young heiress, but she could not wait for him to make a fortune in ostrich farming and married another. Haggard returned to England and entered practice at the Bar. He wrote *King Solomon's Mines* (1885) for a bet that he could not write a book as good as *Treasure Island*. The publisher offered him the choice of £100 or a ten per cent royalty, and he opted for the latter on the advice of a clerk (not his own barrister's clerk, but the publisher's clerk, while his principal was out of the room). This book, together with *She*, written in three weeks in 1887, made his fortune.

John Galsworthy's Loyalty: *De Levis accuses Dancy of being a thief (1930 edn illustrated by S. van Abba).*

John Galsworthy was the son of a prosperous solicitor who also had business interests. He was called in 1890 and took chambers in the Temple but was reluctant to practise at the Bar. As a young man he travelled abroad a good deal on family business; in 1893 he met Joseph Conrad on a ship bound for Cape Town, Galsworthy being a paying passenger and Conrad the first mate; they became friends for life. In 1905 he married Ada Pearson, formerly the wife of his first cousin, after a ten-year affair which he managed to conceal from his father during his lifetime: some of this turmoil may be reflected in the trials undergone by Young Jolyon and Irene, wife of Galsworthy's greatest character, Soames Forsyte. Galsworthy wrote three trilogies of novels, the first two very successful: *The Forsyte Saga* (the first book in the series, *The Man of Property*, was published in 1906), *A Modern Comedy*; and *End of the Chapter*.

The Forsyte Saga has twice been adapted as a television serial and was extremely successful; Galsworthy's depictions of the tensions between property and art, and between propriety and passion were as relevant in the 1960s as they were in Edwardian England. Galsworthy was liberal in his views and spoke out for causes he believed in (penal reform, votes for women and reform of the House of Lords) and against those he opposed (theatrical censorship and the Boer War). He was awarded the Nobel Prize for Literature in 1932, and was the Inn's only Nobel laureate until Nelson Mandela (an honorary bencher) won the Nobel Peace Prize.

As last man in we have Newbolt. He was called in 1887 and practised for twelve years. His poems were much admired at the time, but are now generally regarded as museum pieces of late-Victorian public-school patriotism and decency. It is therefore surprising to learn that his wife, Margaret, consented to their marriage in 1889 only if her cousin and close friend, Ella, could come and live with them. Their married life was in every sense a *ménage a trois*; Newbolt recorded in his diary which nights he had spent with each, which was hardly playing the game.

That the Inn produced so much literary talent in the Victorian age is no doubt a reflection of the numbers of gifted young men who were called to the Bar without intending to practise. It also no doubt reflects the voracious public appetite for reading novels in an age before cinema and television. It is quite surprising that so

Rider Haggard's King Solomon's Mines: *the party pretend to be gods to avoid execution (1912 edn illustrated by A.C. Michael).*

few of the Inn's Victorian novelists made the law, or lawyers, a central feature of any of their books. For that we have to go to two of the very greatest nineteenth century novelists, Charles Dickens and Anthony Trollope.

Dickens was not a lawyer but he knew a good deal about the law, the seamy side of life, and the horrors of being caught up in litigation. His idyllic childhood in Chatham and Rochester came to an abrupt end when his father, a government clerk, got into financial difficulties and Charles was taken away from school. His father's financial difficulties got worse, and in 1824, when Charles was 12, his father was committed to the Marshalsea Prison as a debtor and Charles was found a job sticking labels on blacking bottles for six shillings a week. His father's imprisonment lasted for three months, and Charles got a better job as a solicitor's clerk, but he never forgot these experiences. At the age of 16 he taught himself shorthand and became a freelance law reporter in Doctors' Commons.

To many well-read people the mere mention of Lincoln's Inn produces the free association of that wonderful but dreadful first chapter of *Bleak House*, which many regard as Dickens's finest work. Space permits only abbreviated quotation:

> *London. Michaelmas Term lately over and the Lord Chancellor sitting in Lincoln's Inn Hall ...*
> *Fog everywhere. Fog up the river, where it flows among green aits and meadows; fog down the river, where it rolls defiled among the tiers of shipping, and the waterside pollutions of a great (and dirty) city. Fog on the Essex marshes, fog on the Kentish heights. Fog creeping into the cabooses of collier-brigs; fog lying out on the yards, and hovering in the rigging of great ships; fog drooping on the gunwales of barges and small boats ...*
> *The raw afternoon is rawest, and the dense fog is densest, and the muddy streets are muddiest, near that leaden-headed old obstruction, appropriate ornament for the threshold of a leaden-headed old corporation: Temple Bar. And hard by Temple Bar, in Lincoln's Inn Hall, at the very heart of the fog, sits the Lord High Chancellor in his High Court of Chancery.*
>
> *Never can there come fog too thick, never can there come mud and mire too deep, to assort with the*

Oliver Twist: *'Evidence destroyed' (1838 edn illustrated by George Cruikshank).*

Pickwick Papers: *Serjeant Buzfuz 'a driving, chaffing, masculine Bar orator' (1880 edn).*

groping and floundering condition which this High Court of Chancery, most pestilent of hoary sinners, holds, this day, in the sight of heaven and earth.

This is the Court of Chancery; which has its decaying houses and its blighted lands in every shire; which has its worn-out lunatic in every madhouse, and its dead in every churchyard; which has its ruined suitor, with his slipshod heels and threadbare dress, borrowing and begging through the round of every man's acquaintance; which gives to monied might, the means abundantly of wearying out the right; which so exhausts finances, patience, courage, hope; so overthrows the brain and breaks the heart; that there is not an honourable man among its practitioners who would not give – who does not often give – the warning, 'Suffer any wrong that can be done to you, rather than come here!'

The Hall was of course what we now know as the Old Hall. The Great Hall had been built by the time *Bleak House* was published (first by instalments in 1851, then as a book in 1853), but the book looks back to an earlier period, perhaps 1827, the last year of Eldon's Chancellorship. It mentions passenger railways as just starting to be built, and Sir Leicester and Lady Dedlock visit the Hotel Bristol in Paris. Dickens's powerful scorn must have hastened the process of Chancery reform which was already getting under way in 1851.

The law appears in many other works of Dickens. In *A Tale of Two Cities* the hero, Sydney Carton, was an unsuccessful barrister, devilling for the successful but unattractive Mr Stryver; together they are the defence team in the treason trial near the beginning of the book, which recalls some real-life defences conducted by Erskine. *Oliver Twist* paints such a grim picture of criminal justice in the 1830s that the eminent critic Professor John Sutherland at first found it incredible, but his pieces, 'Why was Fagin hanged?' and 'Does Dickens lynch Fagin?' conclude that Dickens's picture was indeed accurate. *Pickwick Papers* contains the famous breach of promise action (Sir Gerald Hurst suggests that Mr Pickwick made a serious mistake in choosing Serjeant Snubbin, a 'lantern-faced, sallow-complexioned' Lincoln's Inn man, as his counsel for such a case), while *David Copperfield* depicts the workings of Doctors' Commons, where David is enrolled for the enormous fee of one thousand guineas, and the struggles of Thomas Traddles to make his way at the Bar without independent means. But it is in *Bleak House* that Dickens makes his fullest and most savagely entertaining assault on the law, and in particular on the bad old days of the Court of Chancery.

Bleak House is in every sense a big book, intricately constructed, with many sub-plots that grow into each other. There is a large cast of characters, some, such as Mrs Jellyby, Mrs Pardiggle, Mr Skimpole, and the Reverend Mr Chadband, introduced mainly for comic relief. The central plot concerns the endless, ruinously expensive action of *Jarndyce v Jarndyce* and the mystery surrounding a young woman, Esther Summerson. She becomes the companion of the Jarndyce wards in Chancery, and lives with them and their guardian, Mr John Jarndyce. By Chapter 3, the first of many chapters narrated by Esther, we learn that she is illegitimate, and knows nothing of either of her parents. Gradually various clues, such as family resemblances, an affidavit engrossed in a familiar hand, and a veiled lady who says she is a servant but gives a sovereign to Jo, the crossing-sweeper, link Esther to the grand Lady Dedlock. By the end of Chapter 29 the reader's suspicions are finally confirmed (though there are another 38 chapters to come) as Lady Dedlock cries, ' O my child, my child! Not dead in the first hours of her life, as my cruel sister told me ....'

The Dedlocks' country mansion is in Lincolnshire and Bleak House is near St Albans, but Lincoln's Inn is at the heart of the story. That is where the Lord Chancellor holds countless hearings, always adjourned, in *Jarndyce v Jarndyce*, and interviews the wards and their companion in his private room. It is where Miss Flite, a half-demented litigant in person, continues to hope for a judgment, and Mr

Gridley, 'the man from Shropshire', another litigant in person, tries (but always fails) to be heard. The solicitors Kenge and Carboy (whose clerk, Mr Guppy, first propositions Esther and then tries to blackmail Lady Dedlock) have their office near the Chapel, probably in Old Square. The much more sophisticated, and much more sinister, Mr Tulkinghorne, the solicitor to Sir Leicester and Lady Dedlock, has his office in Lincoln's Inn Fields.

And on the other side of the Inn, in the maze of sordid alleys east of Chancery Lane, are the humble workplaces and lodgings of others who play an important part in the story. Mr Snagsby, the law stationer, has premises at Cook's Court (possibly Took's Court?) in Cursitor Street. Across the alley is Mr Krook's marine store, or 'rag and bottle shop', where one room is let to Miss Flite and another to 'Nemo', an impoverished copier, whose handwriting on an affidavit is recognized by Lady Dedlock in Chapter 2, and who dies of opium poisoning in Chapter 11. Later we learn that he was a gallant officer and Esther's father. Lady Dedlock's letters to him, which Mr Guppy wishes to use against her, are believed to have been burned in the course of Krook's spontaneous combustion in Chapter 32.

The melodrama continues with more deaths, some unnatural, and some births and new beginnings. The case of *Jarndyce v Jarndyce* comes to an abrupt end in Chapter 65: 'Over for good! ... It seemed too good to be true. Alas, it was!' The case ends not because a final judgment has been delivered, but because the estate, in course of administration by the Court of Chancery, has been exhausted by costs. The true significance of the new will, found in Chapter 62, is never determined. In any event it could not have been proved in solemn form in the Court of Chancery, but would have had to go, as Dickens must have known, to Doctors' Commons and the Court of Arches.

Charles Dickens towards the end of his life.

Trollope shared with Dickens the experience of a miserable childhood. Unlike Dickens, he had strong Lincoln's Inn connections. His father was called to the bar by Middle Temple in 1804 and moved in 1806 to 23 Old Square, Lincoln's Inn, where Anthony was born. At the same time his father acquired an interest in the second and third floors of 8 New Square from which he practised – not very successfully, because he did not gladly suffer fools, a category in which he seems to have included most of his clients. By 1830 he had lost almost all his clients because of his uncontrollable bad temper, which was probably a symptom of mental illness, aggravated by dubious medication. Meanwhile Anthony was miserably unhappy at a succession of schools, Harrow, Winchester, and then Harrow again, as a poor day scholar whose father was known to be unable to pay his fees. Finally in 1834 his father fled to the Continent to escape his creditors and died there. Anthony was deeply scarred by these experiences, although they were not widely known until his autobiography was published posthumously in 1883.

Anthony married, obtained a responsible job in the Post Office, and began to write. *The Warden*, the first of the Barsetshire novels, was published in 1855 and has a strong legal interest. It shows the scrupulous Mr Harding, 'a good, almost saintly man who unwittingly finds himself in the position of receiving high pay for little work' as warden of an old folks' home, attending the chambers of Sir Abraham Haphazard in Lincoln's Inn in order to take his advice as to the law of charitable trusts. Similarly Lady Mason attends at Mr Furnival's chambers in the Inn in *Orley Farm* (1862). But of all Trollope's novels the one most centred on the law is *Doctor Thorne* (1858). It is a melodramatic tale of passion and disgrace, but it has a happy ending. As in *Bleak House*, its heroine is an attractive young woman of illegitimate birth, whose nearest relatives do not know of her existence. Her mother, Mary Scatcherd, has been persuaded to emigrate to America, and her mother's brother, who has been sent

Anthony Trollope's signature on the conveyance of his father's chambers at 8 New Square 1864.

to prison for manslaughter (a fatal blow in a fight with her seducer) is told that the child has died. So she is brought up by Dr Thorne, an unmarried but well-respected medical man, as his niece. The girl's real uncle makes good and, rather like Mr Rouncewell, the ironmaster in *Bleak House*, makes a fortune as an engineering contractor. He becomes Sir Roger Scatcherd, Baronet.

Dr Thorne, attending Sir Roger as his doctor, learns that he has made a will leaving everything to his son, Louis at 25, but if he dies without issue to Mary's eldest child; and Dr Thorne is to be the executor. Dr Thorne anxiously tries to persuade Sir Roger to be more particular, without explaining the reason for his anxiety. Later Sir Roger learns the truth. After his death it is discovered that he made a codicil saying that Dr Thorne, and only he, knows who is Mary's eldest child. It all ends happily in Chapter 46 after advice from all the top names in Lincoln's Inn – 'Sir Abraham Haphazard, and Sir Rickety Giggs, and old Never Say Die and Mr Snilam; they are all of the same opinion.' Mary Thorne gets the testator's fortune.

Trollope wrote the Barsetshire novels from 1855 to 1867, overlapping with his other great series, the Palliser novels, written from 1865 to 1880. He achieved this prodigious output by methodical habits: 250 words a page, forty pages a week. Most of his novels were published in instalments. It is said that one day at his club he heard two bishops discussing the latest Barsetshire instalment, and agreeing in their dislike of Mrs Proudie. Trollope introduced himself and promised to kill her off; and he promptly did so.

As Trollope noted, a lawyer's parlour-game is to find anachronisms and anomalies in how the law is treated in literature. *Doctor Thorne* is the subject of an interesting (but rather inconclusive) article by the great Australian judge, Sir Owen Dixon. There has been no discussion, so far as I know, of Squire Vavasour's will in Chapter 55 of the earliest Palliser novel, *Can You Forgive Her? (*1865). Alice Vavasour has broken off her engagement to Mr Gray, and become engaged to her cousin George, whose ambitions are larger than his means. He hopes to inherit the estate of his grandfather, who is dying. But when the will is read it contains a devise of the whole estate to George's eldest son – should George ever marry and have a son – as soon as he might reach the age of 25. George is very angry and insults the family solicitor, Mr Grogham. The lawyer is affronted and declares, 'It's as good a will as ever was made. If he can set that aside, I'll give up making wills altogether.' Mr Gogham was right in that the Squire had testamentary capacity and the will was properly witnessed. But the primary trust of the landed estate was for an unborn person contingently on attaining the age of twenty-five years, and section 163 of the Law of Property Act 1925 had no counterpart in earlier legislation. The devise was void for perpetuity.

This chapter has concentrated on writers of the Victorian age. The twentieth century seems to have produced a sparser crop. But we may note the prolific detective novels of Michael Gilbert, who was for thirty years a partner in a firm of solicitors within the Inn, and the sadly few books by Sarah Caudwell, Sarah Cockburn to some of us who were relatively young forty years ago. We may also notice in passing a Dickensian pastiche, Charles Palliser's *The Quincunx*, published in 1989. Its intricate plot hinges on the legal technicality that an incompletely barred entail produced a base fee (an absolute interest continuing until the failure of heirs of a single individual). The consequence, in the circumstances vividly described in the book, is that the hero, a young orphan, is in a position where one branch of an extended family wishes him dead, and another branch has an equally strong interest in his continued existence, though neither side wishes him well. Despite this erudite foundation the book displays considerable misunderstanding of the relationship between law and equity. But it is a good read for a really long journey.

Learning the Law

NICHOLAS LE POIDEVIN

Above: One of the early sixteenth-century playing cards (the earliest to be discovered in Britain) dating from the building of the Gatehouse where they were found.

Left: Last moments as a student – waiting in the Library before Call.

For as long as there has been a Lincoln's Inn, it has held students; but some have been more studious than others. A writer in Shakespeare's time advised law students not to study at night, because when the stomach was full the abundance of humours, unable to escape, lay 'like a lump of lead upon the brain'. They needed no telling. Then and earlier they played ball in the Old Hall and broke the windows; they indulged in absurd pranks; they gambled at cards – some have been found under the floorboards – and at dice; they committed casual violence, and they were found introducing women into chambers. The young Inns of Court gentleman, said a caricaturist, 'When he should bee mooting in the Hall, he is perhaps mounting in the Chamber …. He is roaring when hee should be reading, and feasting when hee should be fasting ….' Once patience was exhausted, the exasperated authorities might be driven to write to father about his son's misdemeanours. There is a long record of fines, remissions, suspensions and expulsions.

If they sound like university students, we should not be surprised: they were. The Inns of Court together comprised the Third University of England – third, that is, after Oxford and Cambridge – a phrase that goes back to the sixteenth century. But English law was not taught at Oxford or Cambridge; the only law on offer there was civil or Roman law and, until Henry VIII banned it, canon law. For many years young men had been coming to the Inns of Court, some to qualify themselves for practice, some to pick up enough law to hold their own in due course as landed gentlemen in a litigious society, some to polish themselves in the company of other young men of similar upbringing. Chief Justice Fortescue, a former governor of Lincoln's Inn, writing towards the end of his life in the 1470s, described the students as mostly the sons of gentlemen, on the ground that the common people could not afford the cost and merchants rarely wished to reduce their stock with the burden of it. Sir John saw the Inns in part as a form of finishing school, though judging from the Black Books the finish achieved was uneven. A century and more later, the function was much the same, the numbers greater. Nowhere but the Inns offered the glitter and variety of metropolitan life alongside the discipline of learning.

For those willing to take advantage of it, the legal instruction the Inns provided was anything but superficial. The student of the fifteenth or sixteenth century began not at one of the Inns of Court but at one of the ten or so Inns of Chancery, subsidiary legal colleges where the rudiments of the law were taught. Once in

Sir John Denham

Admitted to the Inn 1579, appointed judge in Ireland 1609:

> *He was generally temperate as to drinking; but one time when he was a student of Lincolne's-Inne, having been merry at the taverne with his camerades, late at night, a frolick came into his head, to gett a playsterer's brush and a pott of inke, and blott out all the signes between Temple-barre and Charing-crosse, which made a strange confusion the next day, and 'twas in Terme time.*

John Aubrey, Brief Lives *(ed. Anthony Powell, London 1949)* possession of the basics, the student passed on to an Inn of Court. There he was expected to play his part in a rigorous educational system which hinged on readings, or lectures, and moots.

Both are still with us. But the moot of yesteryear was not the brief exercise in appellate advocacy it has become. It was the prime method by which the detail of the law was driven into the heads of its future practitioners. Before the invention of printing, law books were few, expensive and hard to digest. Thomas Littleton, a serjeant and then a judge, wrote a classic introduction to land law for his son Richard; but like most classic introductions *Littelton's Tenures* was more admired by those who did not need it than those who did, and it inspired no emulators. To get a grip of legal principle you attended moots; you listened and in due course you argued yourself. You argued in so-called law-French: French, long the language of the Court, shrank to being the language of the courts, barbarously pronounced, and, when the courts dropped it, merely the language of moots. The moot-case, the problem to be argued, was intended to provide material to chew over for days, even weeks, on end. The Butler of Lincoln's Inn, today's Under Treasurer, seems to have kept an official or semi-official moot-book, containing a collection of moot-cases, and it was his job to assign one of them to those due to argue. The problems were devised to raise a string of knotty points, and the same ones were used for 200 years or more; one of the shorter, *Kyppocke's case* devised in the middle of the fourteenth century and still in use under Queen Elizabeth, is shown alongside. Modern students would blench at what their forbears were expected to master.

An early moot – *Kyppocke's case*

'A man has issue a son and a daughter by one marriage and a son by another; the elder son marries and purchases certain land to him and his wife and their heirs in fee; and then he aliens this same land to his sister in tail, with warranty; and afterwards the father, the elder son and his sister purchase certain land unto the father in fee, the son in tail and the sister for life; the father and son die; the sister holds over, against whom the son's wife brings *cui in vita*; she vouches herself by a strange name, and enters into the warranty, pleads and loses, so that the demandant has judgment to recover, and she over; the demandant sues execution, but she does not; then the daughter gives a moiety of other land to the son of the half blood and has issue, and dies seised of the other moiety; the son of the half blood enters in this moiety; the donor ousts him from the whole; the sister's issue brings *scire facias* against the donor and recovers by default, and then re-enfeoffs him in tail; the son of the half blood has issue a son and dies; the issue brings a writ of entry in the *quibus* and recovers by default; the sister's issue has issue and dies.'

The moot was an early example of what has become fashionable in other contexts in recent years, the rôle-play. The venue, the Old Hall in this Inn from the end of the fifteenth century onwards, was got up as a court, with bench and bar. On the bench sat senior members of the Inn – hence 'benchers' – playing the part of the judges. On forms in the body of the Hall, within the bar, sat the students or inner barristers; outside the bar or perhaps on the ends of a form, were the outer or utter barristers, whom the benchers called upon to argue the moot-case. These ranks, which originally meant something only within the Inns and then only when mooting, came to have a wider significance and eventually, in the case of barrister, to mean someone with a public function as an advocate. You became a barrister, properly an utter-barrister, when you were asked to moot: it was something you did, though you did it with permission, and not the mere acceptance of a certification. Today's barrister, still called to 'the bar', began as someone whom the benchers thought fit to moot.

In readings, the other staple of the Inns' curriculum, the statutes were expounded. Each Inn appointed a reader, one in the Lent and one in the autumn vacation, and the reader gave a reading over a series of days. These vacations, the 'learning vacations', were used because the readers had practices to attend to during term-time and the students, or the more serious of them, went to Westminster Hall to watch the courts in action. The statutes selected for readings were originally the great thirteenth-century statutes – *Quia Emptores*, for example – which had been incorporated into the fabric of the common law, and there may have been a cycle following the order of the statute-book; but later readers were free to choose. Readings were not elementary lectures but elaborate expositions. What gave the readings in their heyday their importance and their prestige was the audience they attracted and its participation. Problems

Famous readings were being reprinted long after they were given. This one was originally given at Lincoln's Inn in the Lent vacation 1530.

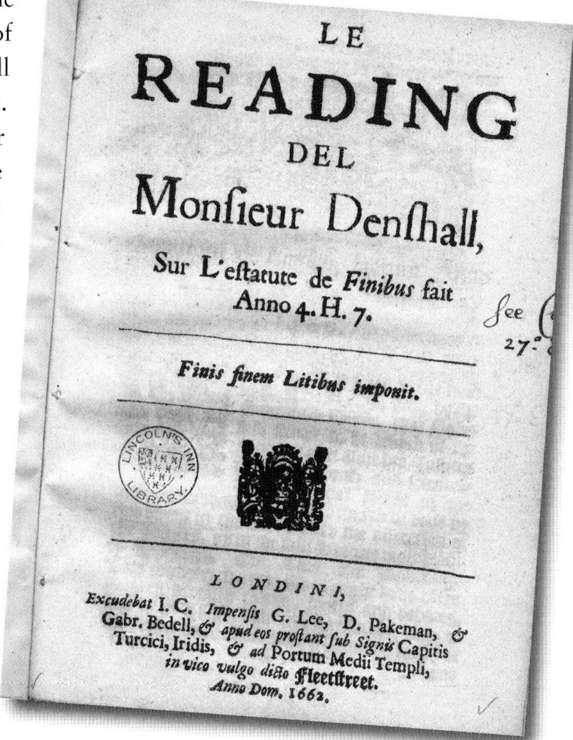
LE

READING

DEL

Monſieur Denſhall,

Sur L'eſtatute de *Finibus* fait Anno 4. H. 7.

Finis ſinem Litibus imponit.

LINCOLN'S INN LIBRARY

LONDINI,

Excudebat I. C. *Impenſis* G. Lee, D. Pakeman, *&* Gabr. Bedell, *& apud eos proſtant ſub Signis* Capitis Turcici, Iridis, *& ad* Portum Medii Templi, *in vico vulgo dicto* Fleetſtreet.

Anno Dom. 1662.

Of keeping a whole term.*

1. *(The method of keeping a whole term in the shortest compass of time).*—Attend the four days preceding grand week, and the Sunday in grand week; if the whole week in which the four days are kept form part of the term.
2. Attend the last day in grand week (Saturday), and the four succeeding days, if term continue the whole of that week.
3. Attend any two days before Wednesday, and any two days after Wednesday; with any one day in grand week, if the whole week in which the four days are kept form part of the term.
4. Attending every day in a whole week of the term, and any one day in grand week, will keep the term.
5. Attending a whole week, and every day in grand week (fourteen days), will complete the term, at the same expense as keeping it the shortest

* *Note.*—Sunday, in keeping term, is accounted the first day of the week.

A legal aptitude test? (From Thomas Lane The Student's Guide through Lincoln's Inn, *1805).*

posed by the reader were thrown open to general debate, the whole membership of the Inn taking part. Serjeants and judges, former members of the Inn who had left to join one of the two Serjeants' Inns, might attend and give their views. Not only did students hear at first hand what the leaders of the profession had to say but such debates were also an important source of law. Even now, the opinion of Lincoln's Inn may be influential on questions of property and equity, subjects traditionally associated with it. In the fifteenth and sixteenth centuries there were no rigid notions of precedent, and in a system of unwritten law what mattered was a professional consensus as to what the law was. Readings in the Inns and the discussions which they prompted generated the consensus on matters which did not or had not yet come before the court. And the students were at the heart of the process.

But readings became top-heavy. Readers began to provide showy displays of learning instead of instruction. At one time you became a bencher on completing a reading, and only benchers appeared in the central courts; but the growth of the profession made it impossible to confine the bench to former readers and so advancement within and without the Inn ceased to depend on reading. Because of their prestige, readings were attended with celebrations, to which the readers were expected to contribute largely; everyone likes a feast but no one wants to pay for it. Finding readers became troublesome and readings were suspended altogether when the Civil War began. For many years there was no reading at all. With the Restoration in 1660 there were repeated attempts to revive them, but the heart had gone out of the old system. This Inn appointed no reader after 1677. Moots continued for longer and some collections of moot-cases were published – the Library recently acquired a collection published in 1675 – but they ceased to have a central part to play. When Sir Matthew Hale of this Inn, later Chief Justice of the King's Bench, wrote in the later seventeenth century to advise law students how to study he took it for granted that the Inns had no institutional education to offer.

An eighteenth-century somnolence settled over the Inn's collegiate life. Students still had to be called to the Bar and the Inn still required 'exercises' to be performed as a condition of call, but they dwindled into a formality. As late as the middle of the nineteenth century the applicant for call mumbled a few lines of nonsense as the fossilized remnant of a moot. When Blackstone introduced the Vinerian lectures with a stately proposal for the teaching of English law in the two universities he acknowledged that, 'In the inns of court all sorts of regimen and academical superintendence, either with regard to morals or studies, are found impracticable and therefore entirely neglected….' Though the lectures, published as *Blackstone's Commentaries*, were a success, the proposal was a failure and English law remained untaught. Students had to make their own arrangements to supplement private study.

In the early eighteenth century it became common for would-be barristers to spend time in the office of an attorney and that remained true well into the nineteenth century. In 1858 Lord Bowen wrote of his pupillage:

> *I well recollect the dreary days with which my own experience of the law began, in the chambers of a once famous Lincoln's Inn conveyancer; the gloom of a London atmosphere without, the whitewashed misery of the pupil's room within – both rendered more emphatic by what appeared to us the hopeless dinginess of the occupations of its inhabitants. There stood all our dismal text-books in rows ... calculated to extinguish all desire of knowledge, even in the most thirsty soul. To use the language of the sacred text, it seemed a barren and a dry land in which no water was. And, with all this, no adequate method of study, no sound and intelligible principle upon which to collect and to assort our information.*

There were also professional lawyers who practised without being called to the Bar – 'special pleaders', whose expertise lay in converting statements of their client's cases into the highly technical formulae of the common law, and conveyancers – and a student might also spend time with them, or with a practising barrister, as a pupil. This became the standard route to practice at the Bar. By the middle of the nineteenth century the recommended course was a year in the office of a conveyancer, a year with a special pleader, and a year with a barrister in general practice. Hence the emergence of pupillage. The standard fee payable to the pupil-master became fixed at 100 guineas, where it long remained; barristers now in their fifties paid the same fee in the 1970s. Some early nineteenth-century pupil-masters took their duties very seriously and accepted numerous pupils; Joseph Chitty, prolific author and progenitor of other legal Chittys, often had more than twenty at a time, to whom he gave lectures. Students could also attend public lectures on law given by private individuals, some given in this Inn; but then the Inn merely provided the venue.

In the 1840s, however, the Inns began to bestir themselves and some thought that they might re-assume their historic responsibility for educating the Bar. The lack of any systematic education was indefensible, and the attorneys and solicitors had started to organize themselves. The indefatigable reformer and interferer Lord Brougham, who had been called to the Bar by this Inn and had become Lord Chancellor, proposed in 1845 that the Inn should establish a lectureship and invite the other Inns to follow suit. The essentials of Brougham's scheme were agreed with the other Inns the following year: each Inn would provide a lectureship on a given subject, with Lincoln's Inn taking responsibility for that on equitable jurisprudence. No student would be called to the Bar without having attended at least two of the courses of lectures. This Inn was tepid in its support for the reforms – it unilaterally dropped the requirement of attendance soon afterwards and the benchers infuriated *The Times* by putting up a placard to tell students that attendance was voluntary – but it fell into line in 1852, when the four Inns together established the Council of Legal Education.

Procedure in the Inn before call in 1846:

'The applicants went before the Bench in pairs: each was provided with a card on which was printed a proposition of Law and an argument. The one card, it might be, bore the words "I hold that A shall have the widow's estate", with an argument following. The other card bore "I hold that A shall not have the widow's estate," also with an argument following. The Bencher presiding called on one applicant to begin, who after he had read a few words was stopped by the Bencher. Then the other applicant was called on and also stopped. The next step was that of Call.'

Mr Justice Chitty 1828–99: one of the many legal Chittys.

Sir Frederick Pollock 1845–1937, Professor at the Council of Legal Education 1884–90.

FINAL AND INTERMED… WAKEHAM PURKIS, 1, Linc… Editor of "Halliday's Digest," &c. (1800 of … have been successful), assisted by Mr. J. T. B. S… LL.B., Middle Temple, has CLASSES reading f… examinations. Students can join at any time. … moderate.

EXAMINATIONS.—PRIVATE PUPILS —A Conveyancing Counsel, a public writer, PREPARES Two Resident and Two Non-resident PUPILS, without classes, for the three Law Society's Examinations; French spoken at table. Chancery-lane is within three miles of the house, and the tram fare to the City is one penny. — Address "Frondistirion," 54, Coldharbour-lane, Loughborough Junction, London.

PRELIMINARY LAW and LONDON MATRICULATION EXAMINATIONS.—Mr. JOHN GIBSON, M.A., holds Morning and Evening CLASSES for these Examinations in London, and at Bromley, Kent. The next "Matriculation Guide" will be published on 16th Jan.; the next "Preliminary Guide" on 16th Feb. During 1882, of sixty-two pupils sent up for these examinations, fifty-two were successful.—Address Bromley, Kent.

BAR and SOLICITORS' EXAMINATIONS.—An ex-Examiner will TAKE PUPILS, payment to be based on results; no failures last year.—For testimonials, &c., apply "Doctor," 44, Wellington-square, Oxford.

MR. UTTLEY, Solicitor, successfull… PREPARES CANDIDATES for Solicitors' P… liminary, Intermediate, and Final EXAMINATIO… personally or by post. Terms £1 1s. per month.—A… 5, Clarence-street, Albert-square, Manchester.

LAW EXAMINATION… BARRISTER is now forming CL… COMING EXAMINATIONS of the … ciety and the Bar; Hindoo and …

The Law Times, *1882. The burgeoning market that Gibson & Weldon was later to corner.*

The Council, which lasted until 1997, was to be funded and run by the Inns (two benchers apiece), which would provide five readerships or professorships offering lectures and tutorials to Bar students. Lincoln's Inn funded the readership on equity, and until 1964 provided premises for the Council, and the Old Hall as an exam venue for some while after that. Students would not be called unless they had either attended at least two courses of lectures or else passed a public examination. The provision of an alternative was a mistake, as the idle or untalented could qualify themselves merely by dozing unobtrusively through the lectures, and examinations eventually became compulsory in 1872. Then as now, there was a strong sentiment that a professional training was indecent unless heavily veiled with instruction of no practical use whatever. Students were expected to be familiar not only with texts of doubtless daily importance, such as *Shelford on Mortmain* and *Calvert on Parties to Suits in Equity*, but also with Montesquieu's *Esprit des Lois* and Rapin's *History of the Reigns of Elizabeth to James the Second, inclusive*. The first examination paper in Equity, in Hilary 1853, began unpromisingly with 'What is Aristotle's definition of Equity?', though it ended with the marshalling of assets. The papers on Constitutional Law and Legal History were even more remote from practice.

Although lectures and examinations were provided, aspirants to the Bar were still left in large part to shift for themselves. The serious nineteenth-century student often joined a debating society to sharpen his speaking skills, and would arrange informal moots. A revival of organized mooting by the Inn in the 1920s was short-lived and only for the last fifty years has there been continuous mooting within the Inn itself. The Council's lectures were not compulsory and it became possible, indeed usual, to prepare for the undemanding Bar examinations by attending Gibson & Weldon, crammers in Chancery Lane, where a pass was more or less certain if you wrote

PUBLIC EXAMINATION.

Michaelmas Term, 1853.

MONDAY MORNING, NOVEMBER 7th, 1853.

Half-past Nine to Half-past Twelve.

Questions on Constitutional Law and Legal History.

1. How was Henry the Seventh connected with the House of Lancaster?
2. What character does Lord Bacon give of his Legislation?
3. What act was passed affecting Land during his reign?
4. Had any act similar in its tendency been passed before, and when?
5. Had any attempt been made by persons not Members of the Legislature to accomplish the purpose of those acts? Give an account of it; of the reign when it happened, and the manner in which it was carried on.
6. What were the main securities of English freedom when Henry the Seventh ascended the throne?
7. Can you give any instances of their violation during his reign, or that of his successor?
8. Give an account of the Earl of Warwick in Henry the Seventh's time, his relation to the Crown, and his fate.
9. Who was the Mother of Cardinal Pole, and what became of her?
10. After the Children of Henry the Seventh's Queen, who was the nearest heir of the House of York in the reign of Henry the Eighth?
11. Give an account of any attempted change in the mode of holding and enjoying Landed Property during the reign of Henry the Eighth.
12. What was the effect of this attempt? How far did it succeed? Why was it thought desirable? Can you recollect Lord Bacon's opinion or expressions on this subject?
13. State any circumstance from which you would infer the influence of the Roman and Canon Law on the legislation, at the time of Henry the Seventh's accession.
14. State any Act in Edward the Sixth or Mary's time from which a similar inference might be drawn.
15. How far did Henry the Eighth carry on the Reformation?
16. What was the Law of the Six Articles?
17. What were the changes in this respect introduced under Edward the Sixth?
18. Name any sufferer for Religious Opinion in the time of Edward the Sixth.
19. For what offence was Sir Thomas More and Cardinal Fisher executed? What means were used to obtain evidence against Sir Thomas More?
20. State the insurrections in Henry the Eighth's time, with their causes and results. Did the King give way?
21. Can you name any Nobleman tried for High Treason, and acquitted, in Henry the Eighth's time?
22. What Act of Parliament in Henry the Eighth's time was most hostile to our freedom?
23. Give an account of Bills of Attainder. When were they first employed? Name some remarkable persons, in the time of Henry the Eighth, who were destroyed by means of them.
24. What was the practice of our Courts of Justice, under the reigns of the House of Tudor, with regard to the confronting of the Witnesses with the Prisoner?
25. Name any instance of persons acquitted of a charge of High Treason during the same period. What happened to the Jury in such a case?
26. Give a character of Cranmer?

1923

Trinity.

CLASS I.

The Studentship of One Hundred Gns. a year, tenable for three years, was awarded to :—

Denning, Alfred Thompson	*Lincoln's Inn*

CLASS II.

(In Order of Merit.)

Bacon, Roger Sewell	*Middle Temple*
Bicknell, Beroe Adremar	,, ,,
Bailey, Kenneth Hamilton	*Gray's Inn*
King, Archibald John	*Inner Temple*
Walton, Henry Bowyer	,, ,,
Bishop, Frank Patrick	*Gray's Inn*
Sorabji, Cornelia	*Lincoln's Inn*

Far left: Call Day 1904 when the Prince of Wales was Treasurer.

Bottom left: Bar examination results: the start of the distinguished career (in impressive company) of Cornelia Sorabji recounted by Mrs Justice Manohar on p.135.

Right: Call Day, 13 October 2005.

all you heard and learnt all you wrote – an ordeal 'boring beyond belief', according to Sir Michael Ogden. Pupillage too remained unregulated and students made their own arrangements with individual pupil-masters, a system, or lack of system, which survived until recently. Though it seems incredible now, pupillage became compulsory only in 1958, when the Inns discovered with a start that four out of ten barristers had had no pupillage when beginning practice. An undertaking was then extracted from each barrister before call not to practise without twelve months of pupillage, a reform which had the effect of deferring pupillage until after call; it had been possible, and at one time common, to undertake pupillage beforehand. The scheme thus put in place is more or less that known to today's students.

They themselves, however, are far more diverse than they were. One great change is in the geographical origin of the Inn's students. Until the middle of the nineteenth century, they were very largely English or Welsh, though the lump was leavened from Scotland – Lord Mansfield, Chief Justice of the King's Bench, was a Scot called by this Inn – and from Ireland. Occasionally natives of North America and the West Indies were also admitted and called: the first American-born member joined the Inn in 1723. Some of those from outside England and Wales had lively careers: one American-born member became Lord Chancellor, Lord Lyndhurst, and another American, Judah P. Benjamin (the Benjamin of *Benjamin on Sale*), was Attorney General and then Secretary of State of the Confederacy during the American Civil War, escaping to England when the South was defeated and being called by this Inn in 1866. But it was in the second half of the nineteenth century, with the growth of empire, that the Inns began to draw numerous students from overseas. Australasia, Canada and, especially, India sent many men to the Bar. This Inn claims to have admitted and called the first Bar student from India, Ganendra Mohan Tagore, called in 1862. In the previous year it had been agreed that someone should be appointed to teach 'the Hindoo and Mahomedan law' and the appointment was actually made 30 years later. By the early years of the twentieth century the number of Indian students studying here had greatly increased and was still increasing. Indian students did not then need to know Latin to be admitted and it is said that this Inn attracted exceptional numbers of overseas students because it was the first to do away with that requirement. The link with the Indian subcontinent and the Far East remains strong. More than a third of those currently being called are from overseas and the experiences of some of them are printed later in this book.

A still greater change within the student body, and hence the Bar, is that neither is any longer confined to men. The Inn admitted its first woman student less than a century ago. Now half of those called are women. Their contribution to the life of the Inn is also celebrated elsewhere in this book.

A subtler change lies in the social extraction of the Inns' students. Our forebears were not interested in social diversity, being more interested in maintaining barriers than breaking them down; a prohibition on admitting anyone 'in trade', which was held to disqualify the proprietor of a private lunatic asylum, was rescinded only in 1884, and there had earlier been a mysterious, though short-lived, insistence against calling anyone who had written for newspapers. But for centuries the law had been seen as providing a route to achieve social distinction and financial security for those not born to them. The difficulty lay in getting started; some help was desirable, often vital. Many private and unofficial acts of benevolence will have gone unrecorded. Ben Jonson, the playwright, was bricklaying with his stepfather on what

The Library 1947.

was then the garden wall of the Inn next to Chancery Lane and was overheard reciting Greek verse by a bencher, who was impressed and sponsored him to go to Cambridge. Christopher Tancred, who died in 1754, left a bequest to four students of the Inn to support them until call and for three years afterwards; the studentship is still paid. But the Inn as an institution was slow to wake up to the needs of poorer students. The Council of Legal Education, funded by the Inns, had been making awards since it was founded, but it was only in 1877 that this Inn decided to provide its own scholarships. In recent years, much effort has gone into raising funds. Scholarships and bursaries now exist under a variety of names commemorating both famous past members and members who have made specific gifts or bequests. The earliest name associated with a bequest is Sir Roger Cholmeley, who in his will in 1565 left the Inn the King's Grocer's House in Newgate, which was eventually sold in 1927 expressly to fund scholarships. Around a fifth of students currently being called hold at least one award, perhaps two or three. Even so, the Inn lacks the opulent endowment of some university colleges, and of the £1 million a year which it now awards less than a third comes from such funds.

That effort can be seen as part of a drive to recapture the Inn's historic role as an educational institution. The Council of Legal Education, having passed under different control, ceased to exist in 1997 and its school of law, the Inns of Court School of Law, became only one of several providers of the academic course for Bar students. That arrangement has not met with universal acclamation and it is not well adapted to teach the practical skills required at the Bar, notably advocacy. The Inns in general, and this Inn in particular, have recently taken the lead in teaching advocacy to pupils. In the nineteenth century, conservatives insisted in the teeth of demands for reform that the law could not be taught, it could only be learnt; and though that dispute is long dead the same contention is still put forward about advocacy. The Inn has taken no notice. It can and does call on the loyalty of its members to give their time and talents to the teaching of beginners, who will in due course do the same for their successors.

Nor is it only students who can benefit. The Bar has now collectively decided that it must insist on continuing professional education for barristers in practice. Partly for that reason, though only partly, there has been in recent years a mushrooming of specialist associations, lectures, seminars, and writing at the Bar, in which judges and other senior lawyers have begun to participate much as they once did. As in the days when readings and moots held sway, legal development once again does not depend solely on what happens in the courts. This Inn provides its venues and its members make their contribution, but it can do more. Readers of this book will perhaps see a pointer to the future of the Inn.

Far left: The 'Cholmeley' property at 24 Newgate Street in the mid-nineteenth century, later sold to fund scholarships.

Left: An abortive plan in the 1960s, in which Lord Denning was prominent, to build a hostel for overseas Bar students, who, according to a report by the Inns, had to 'eke out a penurious existence in lodgings' where they were 'subjected to undesirable social influences'.

Sir John Fortescue

Sir John Fortescue (c1395–1479) was admitted to Lincoln's Inn before 1420. He was Governor four times, Treasurer 1437; a Serjeant 1441; Chief Justice of the King's Bench 1442–61. He was elected MP eight times between 1421 and 1436. Politics was his downfall: he was closely associated with the Lancastrian cause in the Wars of the Roses and went into exile in France, where Henry VI made him his nominal Lord Chancellor. It was in France, probably in 1470, that he wrote what to lawyers is his lasting memorial, *De Laudibus Legum Angliae* (In Praise of English Law). The argument of the book is that the common law of England is superior to the Roman-law-based systems of continental Europe in all respects, including its institutions of legal education:

> *The Inns of Court are, besides being a school of law, a kind of academy of gentility. The students learn to sing and play music. They are taught to dance and to play every proper game. In vacation most of them apply themselves to the study of legal science, and at festivals to reading Holy Scripture and chronicles. This is indeed cultivating virtue and banishing vice. Scarcely any turbulence, quarrels or disturbance occur there, but delinquents are punished only by expulsion from communion with the Society, which is a punishment they fear more than criminals fear imprisonment and fetters.*

The painting is a nineteenth-century copy acquired by the Inn in about 1900. It was taken from an original that remained in the possession of the Fortescue family until it was destroyed in a fire in 1934.

Mark Ockelton

Sir John Glynne and Family
by Gerard Soest (c1600–81)

John Glynne (1603–1666), a Welsh lawyer and politician, entered Lincoln's Inn in 1621, was called to the Bar in 1628, and became a bencher in 1641. He was elected for Westminster in the Short Parliament of 1640, and again in the Long Parliament, becoming known aas a leading parliamentary speaker and prominent critic of the Court. In 1641 he took part in the treason trial of the Earl of Strafford, replying at the bar of the Lords to Strafford's closing speech. In 1643 he became Recorder of London, and in 1647 was one of the eleven members impeached by the Army for attempting to disband it. He was committed to the Tower, but was released and reinstated.

In 1654 Glynne was appointed Lord Protector's Serjeant, elected to the first protectorate Parliament and promoted to Chief Justice of the Upper Bench (the title by which the Chief Justice of the King's Bench was known under the Commonwealth). He was actively in favour of Cromwell accepting the Crown.

His pro-monarchical views are among those in the tract *Monarchy asserted to be the best, most ancient and legal form of government*, published at the Restoration, when he was knighted. While riding in the coronation procession in 1661 he was thrown from his horse and nearly killed, an accident in which Pepys saw 'the hand of God'. He has been described as 'a great political survivor'.

This portrait had at some time been cut in two vertically so as to separate the Chief Justice from his family. Lord Justice Harman (Treasurer 1961) is credited with having (before the purchase in 1962) prompted the reuniting of the two parts after noticing in the family part the intrusive knee from a severed-off seated judge.

George Engle

The Library:
'A Treasure not Fit for Every Man's View'

GUY HOLBORN

The death of Sir Matthew Hale in 1676 marked not only the passing of one of the Inn's greatest figures but was also a landmark in the history of the Library. In his will he provided:

> *As a testimony of my honour and respect to the Society of Lincoln's Inn, where I had the greatest part of my education, I give and bequeath to that honourable Society the several manuscripts contained in a schedule annexed to my will. They are a treasure worth the having and keeping, which I have been near forty years in gathering with very great industry and expense. My desire is that they be kept safe and all together, in remembrance of me. ... They are a treasure not fit for every man's view, nor is every man capable of making use of them.*

A fine early fifteenth-century volume of statutes with Hale's signature (Hale MS 74).

The importance and generosity of the gift were well appreciated at the time. It occasioned the first example of the Inn itself commissioning a portrait of one of its own members – it was appropriately to hang in the Library. Hale's collection reflected his deep learning in a wide range of fields, not merely the law, his assiduous and discerning purchasing, and his recognition of the need to preserve for future generations materials that otherwise might be lost. In these respects it was an exemplar for the Library as a whole.

The Library is first mentioned in the Inn's records almost exactly two hundred years before Hale's bequest, thus making it the earliest still to survive in London. Even the library at Lambeth Palace, the home of the Archbishops of Canterbury since the twelfth century, was only formally founded in 1610. The 1475 entry is somewhat ambiguous merely referring to the payment to Roger Towneshend, the Lent Reader that year, of thirty shillings 'pro bibliotheca'. A more definite record occurs

when in 1505 John Nethersole bequeathed forty marks 'that the Society might build or newly erect the Library within the Inn, to the increase of learning and the study of the law of England within the Inn'. John Nethersole, specially admitted in 1482, was an attorney of the Common Pleas, a reminder that the exclusion of attorneys and solicitors from membership of the Society was still a long way off. It is fortunate that Nethersole's name can still be invoked today in connection with such an important feature of the Inn as its library. For the other object of his bequest, that 'every Friday for ever' a requiem mass for his soul shall be celebrated by the Chaplain, despite its terms must have long since lapsed as a means of preserving his name.

The plan for the Library was acted upon, with references to plastering and wainscoting being installed appearing in the Black Books, and by 1510 there had been appointed a 'supervisor' of the Library, Thomas Willoughby, a member of eight years' standing. It is necessary to envisage the topography of the Inn before the parts to the north of the Old Hall and Gatehouse were demolished in the late nineteenth century in order to locate the position of the original Library; it was in the range of buildings extending westwards from the Old Hall to roughly where the War Memorial now stands, also containing the Council Room – on old maps, at 14 and 15 Old Buildings, or Garden Court. There are frequent mentions of chambers beneath it, so it was not on the ground floor. There was substantial refurbishment and possibly enlargement in 1602 and again in 1630. As was to happen when the Library moved to the new Stone Buildings around 1785 and then to the present building in 1845, the expansion of accommodation coincided – whether as cause or effect – with heightened attention to Library matters. The 1602 refurbishment saw the establishment of a small Library committee and some activity to secure donations of books. However, the Library had always been locked and only accessible by the benchers. Judging by the number of references to the locks having to be changed, the benchers do not seem to have been very careful with their keys. The 1630 rebuilding was thus particularly significant because it was the result of a petition of the ordinary students and barristers wanting use of the Library, also requesting

Das büech der gemeinen land
pot: Landsordnung: Satzung
und Gebreüch des Fürstem-
thumbs in Obern und Nidern
Bairn: Im fünfzehenhündert und
Sechzehendem Jar aufgericht

Above: Statham's Abridgement *(1490) – the earliest printed English law book in the Library and the first work to systematize under alphabetical subject headings the cases from the Year Books.*

Left: The Library has a surprisingly rich collection of early continental law books, such as this volume of the laws of Bavaria, printed in Ingolstadt in 1516.

improvement in the facilities it offered. Indeed the petitioners were prepared to pay for its improvement and upkeep.

The request was granted, and willingly, it would seem. It is of note that William Prynne, in dedicating in 1633 his *Histrio-Mastix* to 'his much honoured friends', the benchers of Lincoln's Inn, recognized their 'pious tender care ... of the young student's good' by building the new Library, together, equally of course, with their building of the new Chapel ten years earlier. The benchers found funds for the extensive building work, but accepted the suggestion of a termly levy and instituted the system of a payment towards the Library on admission. As with the financing of most of the Inn's activities, a complex combination of revenue-raising measures was employed. There were additional fines payable for the Library on call to the Bar, on election as a bencher, and on being created a serjeant. Failure to attend moots or exercises resulted in a further impost, and the privileges of special admission or being made an Associate of the bench were often conditional on the gift of a book (as an alternative to the equally frequently stipulated gift of wine). As late as 1857 there was still tinkering with the system of Library fines, adjustments being made variously for the sums payable on admission, on call, on a student leaving the Society, on a barrister leaving, and on call to the bench. This of course was all merely notional, bearing no relation to actual expenditure on the Library.

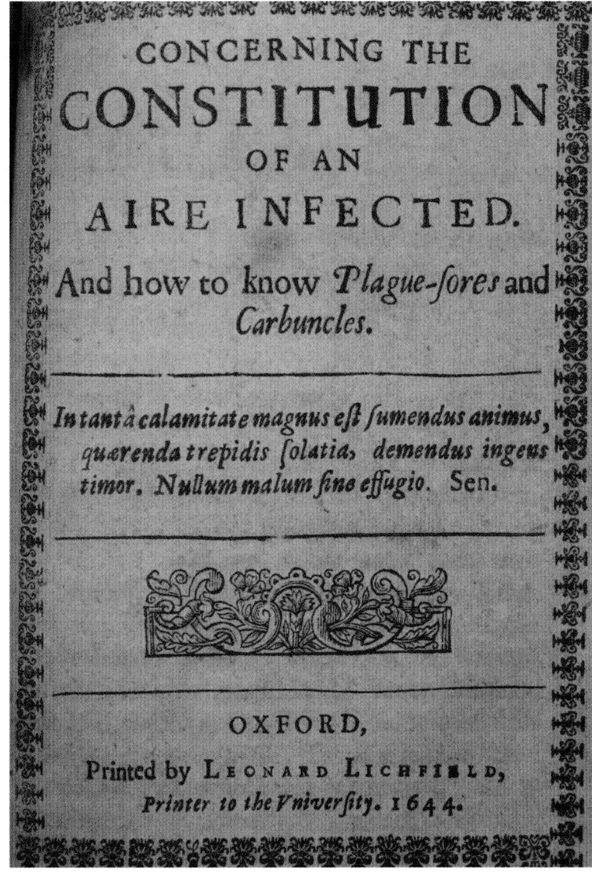
CONCERNING THE
CONSTITUTION
OF AN
AIRE INFECTED.
And how to know *Plague-ſores* and *Carbuncles.*

In tantâ calamitate magnus eſt ſumendus animus, quærenda trepidis ſolatia, demendus ingens timor. Nullum malum ſine effugio. Sen.

OXFORD,
Printed by LEONARD LICHFIELD,
Printer to the Vniverſity. 1644.

Some of the most bibliographically unusual items in the Library lie among the collections of printed pamphlets and tracts. We have over 2,000 dating from before 1700, including several where ours is the only known copy, such as this useful item.

Although the Library had an early foundation, its size and scope was for a long time extremely modest. It is true that the essentially oral tradition of medieval legal education may have meant that the literature of the common law was smaller than that of Roman and canon law, which would have occupied the shelves of the university and college libraries in considerable quantities. But books had long been the tools of the lawyer's trade. So it is perhaps surprising to discover from the first extant catalogue that in 1646, nearly 150 years after the Inn is known to have had a 'proper' library and the first law books were being printed, the Library had a mere 292 volumes of printed books, of which 214 were in fact on subjects other than the law – divinity, history, philosophy, and one book on 'Phisicke'. The personal libraries of the leading lawyers of the day, such as Coke or Selden, are known to have been much larger.

The position, however, was rapidly to improve. The problem of too many books rather than too few is first expressly referred to in 1704, following a generous gift by Baron Price, and it has remained a perennial preoccupation ever since. By 1744 the tally was almost 2,000 volumes. Relief on the pressure for space came with the erection of Stone Buildings. The Library was moved into an elegant suite of rooms designed by Robert Taylor for the purpose on the ground floor of No. 2. The rooms commanded a beautiful view of the garden and were described in Lane's *Guide* as 'very retired, and particularly well adapted for study'. According to the same source of 1805 the stock then stood at about 8,000 volumes.

The growth in the size of the membership of the Inn in the first part of the nineteenth century dictated a new Hall. Space for readers as much as for books must have also been a reason for making the Library such a prominent feature of the new building completed in 1845. The Great Hall of course attracted an enormous amount of public comment. But of the Library in particular it was written in the leading survey of libraries by Edwards published in 1859 that 'few collections in the world are more handsomely housed'.

Indeed, the mid-nineteenth century was very much the Library's heyday. With 30,000 volumes by 1859 it was the largest law library in the English-speaking world, and twice the size of the libraries at either Inner Temple or Middle Temple. That is not to say there has been a decline as such since; the position is merely that its current 175,000 volumes, now matched by Inner and Middle Temple, are sufficient to provide for most practitioners' needs without pretending to compete with the million-volume American law school libraries. A further significant change is that in 1859 the Library collected legal materials from throughout the Empire and indeed beyond, whereas now, through the specialist collections jointly funded by the four Inns, we concentrate only on certain Commonwealth jurisdictions (Inner Temple having responsibility for others).

The main alteration to the Library after 1845 was the addition of the three east bays in 1872. The slightly lighter shade of the oak bookcases at the east end is the only visible indication that there was an extension. Otherwise with the exception of the advent of photocopiers and computers and minor adjustments to the furnishings, the appearance of the Library today is very much as it was when built.

The new building also brought with it changes in how the Library was run. There had been an office of Master of the Library held by a bencher from 1608. It was not at first an annual office, but became one in 1693, and from the early eighteenth century was in fact the most senior position on the *cursus*, in the sense of being held the year following the Treasurership, rather than the year before as now, a practice only introduced in 1886. But the day-to-day running of the Library was traditionally in the hands of the butlers. In the accounts of 1565/66 there is payment to one of the butlers for writing out a catalogue of the books. In the seventeenth century it was the Second Butler who acted as library keeper, and received the termly payments stipulated in 1631. Or sometimes not: there were frequent complaints from the butler that he had not been paid, as was the case notoriously with dues generally. With the move to Stone Buildings, the Second Butler was provided with rooms underneath the Library, and so in 1795 he was in a position to avert an attempted burglary one Saturday evening. It would be nice to think that 'the large alarm bell' shown in the accounts as having been purchased shortly afterwards, is that still used today to signal closing time.

However, from 1807 direct management responsibility was removed from the Second Butler and assigned instead to the perhaps more bookish personage of the Chaplain. The first to take on the job, the Rev. William Walker, was clearly keen. In 1808 he produced a lengthy report brimming over with new ideas, among them: shelves should be numbered and the spines of the books marked with their shelf reference, the shelves themselves could be made adjustable in height, 'a contrivance which has been adopted of late in several public libraries', no bookcase to be higher than seven feet, the catalogue was to be interleaved with the British Museum catalogue (a early version of the modern concept of a union catalogue), and a book of 'desiderata' was to be maintained and inspected twice a year; he also thought it would be fitting if each bookcase were to be named after an eminent person. The reaction of the committee to which these proposals were referred is not recorded. They were possibly not greatly amenable to change: for example, the expedient of marking the spines of books has fortunately been eschewed to this day, except for the one bay containing current textbooks.

The appointment of a new Chaplain and Librarian in 1825 prompted another lengthy report from a Library Committee the following year. By this time there was an 'Under-Librarian' in post, since it was ordered that readers were not to help themselves: even the ordinary law books were to be delivered by him to the readers at their desks. In 1840, one W.H. Spilsbury was appointed to that post. He was not a university man, but he was a book man. He had previously worked for the booksellers

John Ogilby America *(1671): The Library also holds Ogilby's atlases of Africa and of Asia, all of which include printed dedications to the Inn. The remarkable geographic and cartographic printing of John Ogilby 1600–76 was an achievement that only came at the end of a varied career: dancing master (he was lame for much of his life, having injured himself performing in a masque by Jonson), courtier, theatre owner, Master of the Revels in Ireland, poet and translator before securing the title of King's Cosmographer in 1671.*

Bohn's and then for Payne & Foss of Pall Mall. He rapidly made his mark, compiling a new catalogue on his own inititiative without even the knowledge of the Library Committee. Thus in 1845 a further report noted that 'the attendance of the Librarian himself had not been requisite' since the Under-Librarian's 'ability to exercise all the duties pertaining to the office of Librarian was so manifest'. Which was just as well since the Chaplain and Librarian, by then the Rev. C.B. Dalton, was at the same time a fellow and junior bursar of Wadham College, Oxford. Spilsbury was accordingly appointed the first 'professional' librarian of the Inn, at a salary of £300, the same as that for the previous joint offices of Chaplain and Librarian. With the brand new building at his disposal, Spilsbury was to devote the next twenty-two years to the enhancement of the Library, dying in harness in 1877.

His book, *Lincoln's Inn: its Ancient and Modern Building with an Account of the Library*, went to a second edition and remains a mine of information. He also wrote verse – a very Victorian pastime. There are two slim, privately printed volumes on the shelves in the Librarian's office. Doubtless the verse is conventional, and one composition entitled 'Stanzas composed on being told that I ought not leave off writing verse' does not betray a sense of irony, but nonetheless it is quite touching that something of the personal side of the man is preserved together with the conspicuous evidence of his professional achievement.

If shelf space is one perpetual headache in any library, another is the unauthorized removal of books. It is an age-old problem. If a reference to the Library is found in the early Black Books, as likely as not it is to the difficulty of recovering books borrowed by benchers. For example one of the books known to have been in the Library from an early time was a copy of *Bracton*, but it was not one of the copies that the Library now possesses, since John Densell took it with him when he left the Inn on being created a serjeant in 1531. His widow was still being pursued for it five years later. One solution, which was used in monastic and other early libraries, was to chain the books to the shelf; on the shake-up of Library procedures at the 1602 re-building that solution was adopted here. There are several further references to the purchase of chains, until in 1777, perhaps in preparation for the removal of the books to Stone Buildings, the practice was discontinued. Some volumes still in the Library bear the evidence of their clasps on the front boards. This is also the reason why books had their titles lettered on their fore-edges rather on their spines. The books were shelved with the spine to the back of the shelf, since the chain was attached to the front top corner and necessarily hung at the front of the bookcase. Surprisingly there are no reported incidents of terrible entanglements when two or more barristers, all in a rush to resolve a point, were attempting to consult books on the same shelf.

Fecklessness of benchers in not returning books is one thing, but a much more serious incident was to occur in 1908. In the Black Books it is merely recorded that in July 1909 a complete stock-taking of the Library had been completed following the loss and recovery of a number of valuable books earlier in the year. Whether or not by conscious suppression, the Black Books tell far from the full story. Fortunately a narrative can be pieced together from papers left by the then Librarian.

In December 1908 it was discovered that a copy of Ashmole's *Antiquities of Berkshire*, a fine eighteenth-century topographical work in three volumes, was missing. A week later it was also noticed that the entries in the catalogue for several seventeenth-century editions of works by Francis Bacon had been crossed through in red ink, and the pencil shelf marks erased – the practice for books legitimately disposed of. The space on the shelves had been filled with other books to hide their disappearance. About half a dozen other early printed books were then found to be missing too. A hue and cry ensued. That very evening Whitaker, the assistant librarian, visited several second-hand bookshops in the area in case they had been offered for sale. The next day the Master of the Library was on the case and summoned Scotland Yard. Undercover detectives posing as readers were placed in the Library, cunningly observing not the shelves where valuable books were kept, nor the comings and goings at the entrance, but rather the catalogue, for anyone attempting further tampering with it. But after two weeks they had to abandon their surveillance without success.

In the meantime, lists of the missing books were circulated (more than once) to all booksellers in the metropolis and suburbs and beyond and an advertisement

One of the Library's two manuscripts of Bracton: De legibus et consuetudinibus Angliae, *the great treatise compiled around 1240, described by Maitland as 'the crown and flower of English jurisprudence'. Dating from the late thirteenth century, this copy is notable for the grotesques in the margin. Often combining human and animal forms and bearing no particular relation to the text, grotesques were the scribe's equivalent of the mason's gargoyles in Gothic architecture (MS Misc. 100, presented by Arthur Hobhouse in 1866).*

Right: A deluxe rather than a working copy of the statutes made for John Neville, Marquis of Montagu 1471 (Hale MS 194).

Below: Herbert Hardy Cozens-Hardy QC MP in 1893. Master of the Rolls and Master of the Library at the time of the 1908 thefts.

Bottom: Stolen in 1908. Fortunately the Library has retained its fine collection of topography and county histories.

placed in *The Clique* (the booksellers' trade magazine). Further visits to booksellers and auctioneers, including Messrs Sotheby, were made by Detective Sergeant Davies. The plot thickened when a man named Tinkler was arrested after a tip-off. Though he was in the possession of suspicious quantities of books they were not ours. The press got hold of the story, and a lengthy item appeared in the *Evening News* on 1 March. It was with some surprise therefore that as a result of all this publicity the Librarian received a letter from a book collector, who wished to remain anonymous, alerting him that the very same books were being offered for sale by Sotheby's at a forthcoming auction.

That day, the Master of the Library, none other than the Master of the Rolls, went round to Sotheby's, one imagines in an indignant frame of mind. He met there the Librarian, who identified the books as ours, though they had been rebound and their fore-edges coloured to disguise their provenance. The consignor of the items had unsurprisingly not delivered the books in person, but Sotheby's had two letters from him. They agreed to return the books, but declined to surrender the letters without a court order. The letters were, however, copied and photographs of them survive. They were signed, imaginatively, 'A.B. Mansfield'. The first, which requested that the books be offered without reserve, was addressed from 1 Hanbury Street, E., 'a very low class and notorious neighbourhood' according to Whitaker, who visited it with the police later in the day. It was an accommodation address at a tobacconist. The second letter asked that the proceeds of the sale be sent to the 'above address' in £5 notes and postal orders. The 'above address' was 'Post Restante, Calcutta'. Notwithstanding further elaborate measures including sending decoy letters and involving the Indian police, predictably the culprit was never caught.

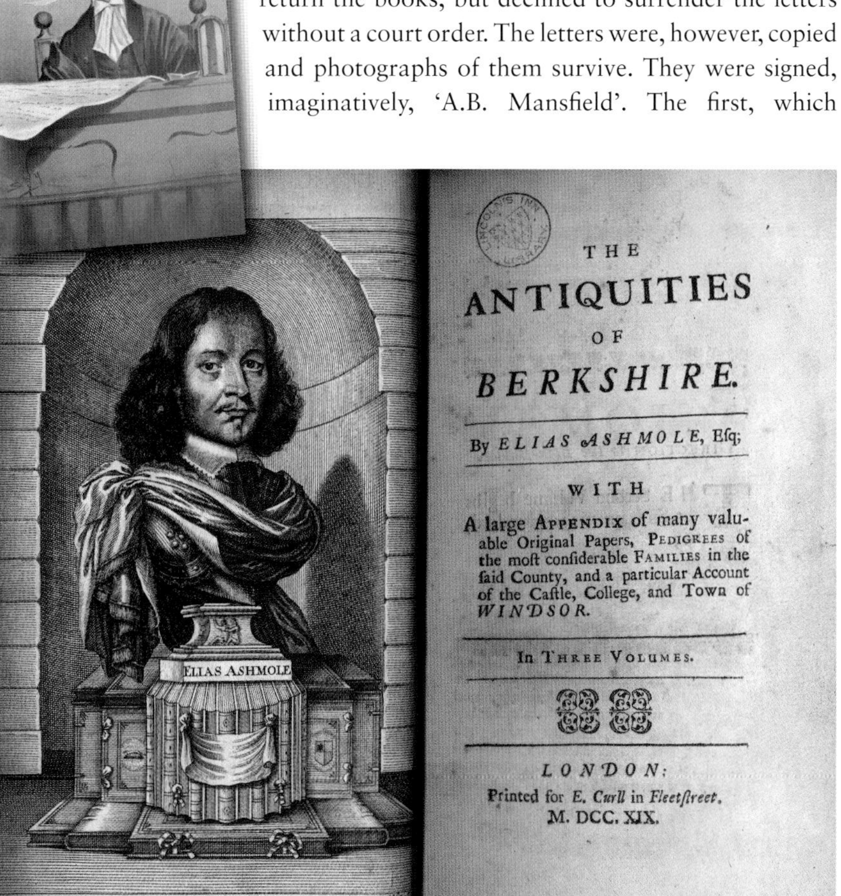

THE
ANTIQUITIES
OF
BERKSHIRE.

By ELIAS ASHMOLE, Esq;

WITH
A large APPENDIX of many valuable Original Papers, PEDIGREES of the most considerable FAMILIES in the said County, and a particular Account of the Castle, College, and Town of WINDSOR.

In THREE VOLUMES.

LONDON:
Printed for E. Curll in Fleetstreet.
M. DCC. XIX.

The Library, of course, has an outstanding collection of rare books and manuscripts, and they are not merely valuable chattels to be protected from the likes of the 1908 thief. They are used – by practitioners who are assiduously researching some historical point, by legal historians, and by outside scholars in many fields beyond the law. The Hale bequest was particularly significant for its medieval and early material. Most of the Library's seventy or so medieval manuscripts come from the collection. Year Books, statutes and other legal materials certainly feature, but it is items such as a contemporary copy of *Piers Plowman*, the cartularies of Bath, Battle, and Durham, and mathematical and alchemical treatises that equally excite scholars. But Hale was by no means alone as a benefactor. Ranulph Cholmely, serjeant-at-law and Recorder of London, who died in 1563, was the source of the first fully recorded bequest, which included *Fitzherbert's Abridgement* and early Year Books. His inscription on each volume is still preserved beneath horn covers.

Perhaps the most significant gift of a single work was the Bible presented and inscribed by John Donne following his resignation as Preacher to become Dean of St Paul's in 1621. The gift was also an occasion for a rare joke in the Black Books: by reason of his appointment 'he cannot conveniently supply the place of publick Preacher of God's Word in this House, as formerly he hath Donne' – a pun the poet himself was not averse to, telling an incandescent father-in-law of his secret marriage that it was 'irremediably donne'. And generous gifts have followed into modern times. For example the first editions of Sir Thomas More's *Utopia* and of his collected works, both exceptionally costly, were bought for the Inn by Sir Felix Cassel and Lord Russell of Killowen respectively in the twentieth century.

In making his bequest, Hale was particular to stipulate conditions as to use of the volumes. Rules and regulations generally have naturally loomed large in the affairs of the Library. A guide to the Library still being issued in 1975 puts the matter as only it could be put in an institution such as Lincoln's Inn: 'Being the Library of an Honourable and learned Society, it is not considered necessary to publish regulations. However ....' The guide then proceeds to enumerate a lengthy list of 'rules which must be observed at all times by all people using the Library'. Some are as might be expected: 'Conversation and discussion must not be carried on in the Library.' Others are not so readily explicable, nor indeed very obviously enforceable: 'The reading of newspapers should be confined to the Law Reports sections.'

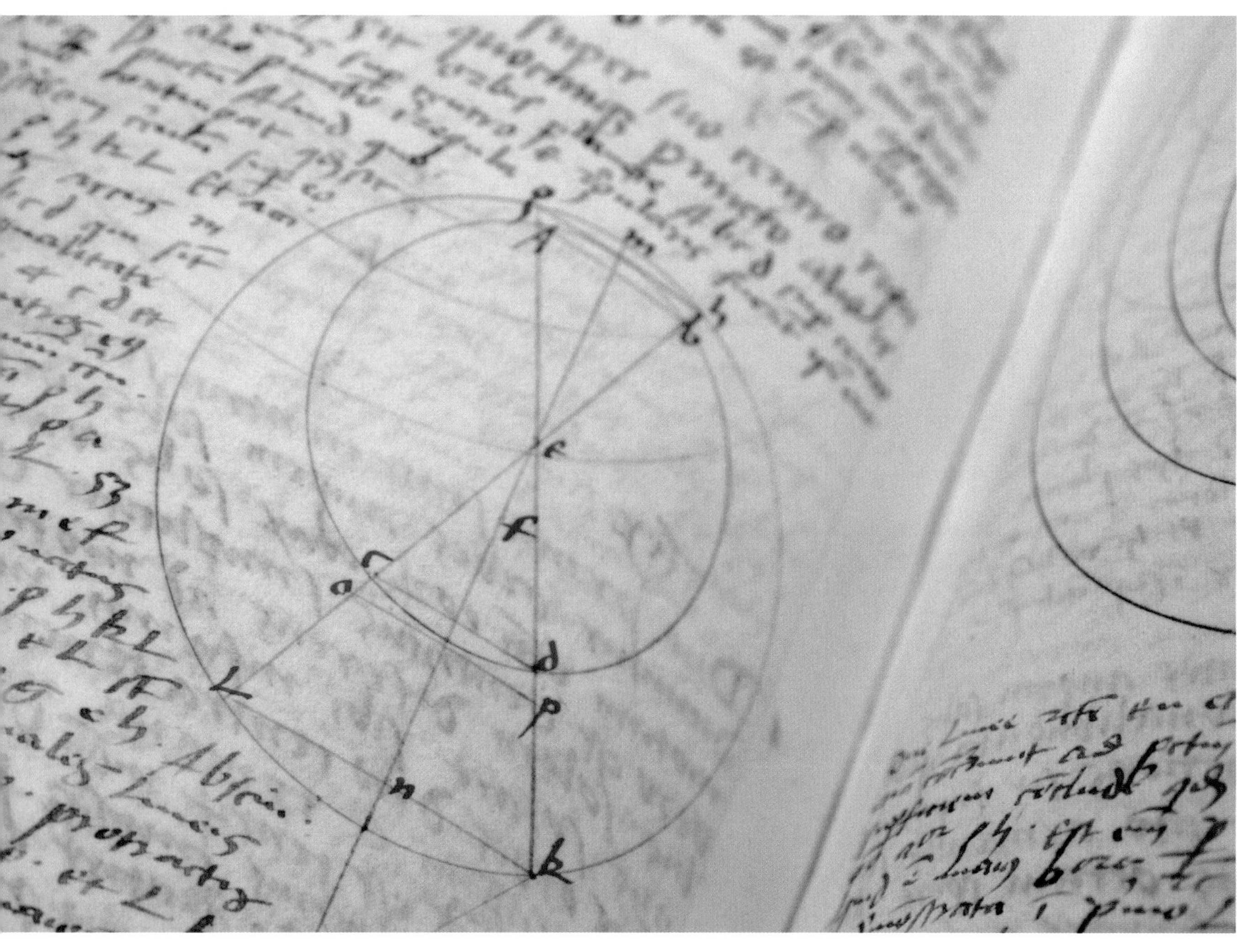

Erasmus Horicius De motibus planetarum *c1500. An unpublished work of the Renaissance mathematician, astronomer and musical theorist, also known as Erasmus of Höritz (Hale MS 105).*

Sir William Hamilton Campi phlegraei: observations on the volcanos of the two Sicilies *(1776) – a stunning survivor from the Library's non-legal collections much of which was sold in the 1960s and 1970s.*

There have always been necessary stipulations as to opening hours. These were dictated as much as by the practical consideration of lighting as by the convenience of members or the question of staffing. In 1867 the Law Society Library stole a march on us by installing gaslight enabling the library to open from 9 am to 9 pm, whereas we, as was pointedly reported in an article in the legal press, were still using candles and had to close at 4 pm in the winter months. The legal press, rather than the Black Books, is also the source for bringing to light another, rather curious, example of a stipulation as to use of the Library. The tone of the report in the *Law Journal* in May 1883 is not kind:

> *The benchers of Lincoln's Inn have shut the chief entrance into the library through the great staircase to all but their own body, the rest of the members of the Inn having to go up the narrow, dark, winding staircase in the corner turret close by the Court lately vacated by the semi-detached junior Chancery judge ... One is left to infer that the benchers are a superior order of beings ... and cannot endure that their silk gowns should come into contact with the common stuff of the inferior race of barristers of the outer bar and students. ... Even to avoid that awful contingency it was not necessary to shut the main entrance ... as they alone reserve the right of taking books from the library which others have to consult within its walls, they need never go the library at all.*

The turret entrance provided when the Library was extended in 1872 was clearly intended to be used, since in place at the foot of the turret stairs to this day is a notice:

> *Members of this Society are requested not to bring Strangers into the Library for consultations or other business purposes, as the convenience of other members using the Library for the purpose of study, is thereby interfered with.*

But the order of Council of April 1883 was quickly rescinded in July. On the other hand, the *carte blanche* afforded to benchers to borrow books, alluded to by the *Law Journal*, was a privilege that was only relinquished in 2001. This was probably not before time. Addison, somewhat rashly for a young barrister at the start of his career, berated the benchers of his Inn for the same practice in the preface to the first edition of his treatise on contracts in 1845. And the *Law Times* in 1920, more delicately than the *Law Journal*, referred to the 'keen disappointment' barristers frequently felt on finding the book they needed had been borrowed. The only remaining small privilege that benchers enjoy is use of the Benchers' Bay and the Pugin table, though anyone is of course free to admire the table (see inset).

Abolition of benchers' borrowing rights is the least of the changes seen in the Library in recent years, but none of those changes is a substitute for longevity. If one were asked to provide a recipe for establishing an outstanding library, 'splash out 40 marks and keep going for 500 years' appears to be not a bad one.

Book not sent. A.E.

Thursday
Feb 26th [1895]

3, Paper Buildings,
Temple.

Dear Sir

Would you be so kind as to give the bearer of this, my clerk, a recent copy of Davidson's Conveyancing Forms. I shall not keep it for more than an hour or so.

Yrs truly
John Galsworthy.

Pugin's Octagonal Marquetry Table

In an alcove in the appropriate setting of the Library there is to be found the most important article of furniture owned by the Inn, and probably the most important example of Gothic Revival furniture . It is the table displayed in the Medieval Court of the 1851 Great Exhibition, designed by Augustus Welby Pugin (1812–54) and manufactured in the Great Welbeck Street workshop of John Gregory Crace. It has been on display since 1924 and was the gift of Mrs Emily Hope Fellows in memory of her husband, a member of the Inn.

The fruitful but short-lived partnership of Pugin and Crace produced a number of octagonal tables; some of oak, but this table is the most richly decorated and elaborate and is made of walnut. The marquetry of the top has been set into a veneer of eight sections. It consists of sycamore, holly, boxwood and bone, with green and brown stain and penwork, set into the burr walnut veneer. There are two tones of green stain, now a darker turquoise, with a secondary stain of light olive. Pearl-like circular dots of white bone frame the outer border of rosettes and the inner eight-cusped star of the central medallion. Pugin's watercolour design for the border survives in the Victoria and Albert Museum. The walnut base is extremely interesting and is composed of ogee arches the sides of which are carved with cusped-leaf design. The feet are very striking lions' heads.

Pugin had experimented with the octagonal shape as early as 1827 and made an oak table for King Edward's Grammar School, Birmingham. Later he designed two oak tables with carved ogee stretchers similar to those he later employed in his design for the Medieval Court table, which were supplied by John Webb of Bond Street in 1847 as part of his most famous commission for the interior design and furnishings for Charles Barry's new Palace of Westminster. These tables can still be seen in the House of Lords in the Prince's Chamber, for which they were specifically designed.

The Victoria and Albert Museum has a similar table to a rather simpler design, directly inspired by the Medieval Court table, made for a Mr James Watts for his drawing room at Abney Hall, Cheshire. This is quarter veneered and the base is of carved oak. This is Crace working alone, after Pugin's premature death in 1852.

The Inn's Table is a splendid example of a great designer working with a great manufacturer, on equal terms.

Thomas Sharpe

Left: John Galsworthy not obliged by the Librarian – a mere barrister, not a bencher.

Right: The earliest manuscript in the Library – Peter Comestor Historia scholastica. *This copy of a famous work of the Middle Ages was made in France within about thirty years of the author's death in 1178. It was originally owned by the Augustinian priory of Lantony, Gloucester (Hale MS 91).*

Reverendo patri et domino suo Guillelmo dei gratia senonensi archiepiscopo Petrus servus christi presbyter trecensis vitam bonam et exitum beatum. Causa suscepti laboris fuit instans petitio sociorum. Qui cum historiam sacre scripture in serie et glosis diffusam lectitarent, brevem nimis et expositam, opus aggredi me compulerunt ad quod pro veritate historie consequenda recurrerent. In quo sic animus stilo pepercit, ut tamen a paternis non recederem. Licet et novitas favorabilis sit et mulceat aures. Porro a cosmographia moysi inchoans, rivulum historicum deduxi usque ad ascensionem salvatoris, pelagus misteriorum peritioribus relinquens. In quibus et vetera prosequi et nova cudere licet. De historiis quoque ethnicorum quedam incidentia pro ratione temporum inserui, instar rivuli, qui secus alveum diverticula que invenerit replens, preterfluere tamen non cessat. Verum quia stilo rudi opus est lima, vobis pater mi limam reservavi, ut huic operi de voluntate et correctione vestra splendorem et auctoritas prebeat perhennitatem. Benedictus deus.

Imperatorie maiestatis est tres in palatio habere mansiones. Auditorium vel consistorium, in quo iura decernit. Cenaculum in quo cibaria distribuit. Thalamum in quo quiescit. Ad hunc modum imperator noster, qui imperat ventis et mari, mundum habet pro auditorio, ubi ad nutum eius omnia disponuntur. Unde illud: Celum et terram ego impleo. Secundum hunc dicitur. Unde: Celum et terra: domini est terra et plenitudo eius. Animam vero hominis pro thalamo. Quia delicie eius esse cum filiis hominum. Secundum hanc dicitur sponsus. Sacram scripturam pro cenaculo, in quo suos inebriat, ut sobrios reddat. Unde: Ambulavimus in domo dei cum consensu. Id ipsum sapientia. Secundum hanc dicitur paterfamilias. Cenaculi huius tres sunt partes: fundamentum, paries, tectum. Hystoria fundamentum est, cuius tres sunt species: annales, kalendaria, effimera. Allegoria...

[illegible]

In principio erat verbum. De creatione mundi.

In principio erat principium in quo pater fecit celum et terram. Mundus iste quattuor modis dicitur. Quandoque empyreum mundus dicitur. Quandoque sensibilis mundus dicitur. Quandoque sola regio sublimaris mundus dicitur, quia materia nobis nota habet, de qua princeps mundi. Quandoque homo mundus dicitur, quia imaginem representat. Unde ipsum microcosmum, id est minorem mundum, vocat. Creavit, id est de nihilo fecit. Lunarem regionem creavit, id est plasmavit. De creatione hominis vero creavit, id est plasmavit. In principio illorum tamen legis lator. In principio temporis celum, id est continens et contentum, id est celum empyreum cum angelica natura. Terram, materiam omnium corporum, id est quattuor elementa, mundum sensibilem. Ex his constantem. Celum superiores partes mundi sensibilis intelligitur, terram inferiores et palpabiles. Hebreus habet Eloym, quod tam singulare quam plurale est, id est deus vel dii, quia tres persone unus deus creator est. Cum vero dicit creavit, trium errores elidit: Platonis, Aristotelis, Epicuri. Plato dixit tria fuisse ab eterno: deum, ydeas, ylem, et in principio temporis de yle mundum factum fuisse. Aristoteles duo, mundum et opificem, qui de duobus principiis, scilicet materia et forma, operatus est sine principio et operatur sine fine. Epicurus duo in principio, inane et athomos, et in principio naturam quasdam athomos solidavit in terram, alias in aquam, alias in aera, alias in ignem. Moyses vero solum deum eternum, et sine preiacenti materia mundum creatum.

Effimera febris est que durat tantum per diem. Effimera dicitur que eodem die moritur quo nascitur. Historia annalis est factum quod per annum factum est. Kalendaria historia que in uno mense facta est, id est factum aliquod insigne quod in uno mense factum est. Effimera est quod repente factum est, id est in uno die. Et per hanc similitudinem effimera est, sicut piscis qui uno die nascitur et eodem die moritur.

Great Figures

LORD MANSFIELD 1705–1793

William Murray, first Earl of Mansfield, was born on 2 March 1705 in Scone Palace in Perthshire. He graduated from Christ Church, Oxford, in 1727 and was called to the Bar by the Inn in 1730.

Mansfield was a good scholar and mixed with the best literary society, being an intimate friend of Alexander Pope, who instructed him in oratory. He quickly acquired a reputation as an advocate, earning for himself the epithet 'the silver-tongued' Murray. In 1742 he was appointed Solicitor General and in 1754 Attorney General. Two years later he was made Chief Justice of the King's Bench, being created Earl of Mansfield in 1776. He resigned at the age of 83. During thirty-two years of judicial service only six of his decisions were reversed on appeal.

Mansfield's great reputation rests chiefly on his judicial career. His decisions demonstrate a strict impartiality and a general aloofness from personal and popular prejudice. The political trials over which he presided were conducted with singular fairness and propriety, for example those involving the fiery journalist and politician, John Wilkes, and Lord George Gordon, who had led a march on Parliament to petition against the Catholic Relief Act of 1778 that led to the Gordon riots. That Gordon was tried before Mansfield, the very judge who, according to the Black Books, 'was daringly abused, and had mud thrown in his face by the rioters', as well as having had his house burnt down by them, may surprise the modern lawyer. It is a measure of Lord Mansfield's cool intellect and fairness that he ruled in the trial that Gordon had not had any treasonable intentions and he was set free.

John Wilkes Esq; before the Court of King's Bench 20 April 1768 Gent Mag

Mansfield is recognized as the founder of English commercial law. His appointment to the bench coincided with a time of rapid expansion of international trade. The common law was, up to that point, land-based, and when commercial cases arose they came before judges who still thought in terms of haystacks and horses. and decisions lacked guiding principles. Mansfield sought to make the international law of commerce an integral part of the general law of England. In the area of marine insurance, Mansfield created an entirely new discipline. The width of his education and his knowledge of Roman and foreign law, gave him a quarry for principles and illustrations, whilst his acute intellect enabled him to put his judgments in a form which almost always commanded assent.

In other branches of the common law Mansfield exerted a similar influence. His greatest contribution was to establish principle as the mainspring of the common law. He is recorded as saying, 'The law does not consist in particular cases; but in general principles which run through the cases and govern the decision of them.'

Mansfield's name is linked to the campaign for the abolition of slavery, such reputation resting upon his judgments in *Somerset's Case* and the case of the slave ship, *Zong*. In 1769 Charles Stewart, an official in British North America, brought over to England James Somerset, a slave whom he had purchased in Virginia. Somerset, or 'Somersett' in some contemporary accounts, deserted his master but was recaptured for intended re-sale as a slave. The case came before Mansfield in 1772. Previous court rulings had confirmed the treatment proposed for Somerset to be lawful. Mansfield recommended to the parties that the dispute be 'accommodated by agreement' but observed '… if the parties will have it decided, we must give our opinion. Compassion will not, on the one hand, nor inconvenience on the other, be to decide; but the law ….' In his judgment Mansfield said:

> *The state of slavery is of such a nature, that it is incapable of being introduced on any reasons, moral or political, but only by positive law … It is so odious, that nothing can be suffered to support it, but positive law. Whatever inconvenience, therefore, may follow from the decision I cannot say that this case is allowed or approved by the law of England; and therefore the black must be discharged.*

One of the Inn's two portraits of Lord Mansfield (after Sir John Reynolds)

The decision in *Somerset's Case* did not mean the end of England's involvement in slavery or that a slave on setting foot in England became free. Mansfield simply decided that the powers of a slave owner over a slave were not recognized in England so he could not be forcibly removed from England to the rigours of American slavery. To come down against slavery when the prejudices and interests of many of his countrymen were against him, together with the opinions of some eminent lawyers of the day, was no mean achievement. The decision was far-reaching and led to the release in this country of nearly 15,000 slaves.

In the case of the *Zong*, Mansfield's decision against the owners of a slave ship whose master had thrown live but diseased slaves overboard had an enormous influence on public attitudes to slavery, and from 1788 statutes began to be passed restricting the insurance of slaves.

Although the final emancipation of slaves was not achieved until 1833, these cases undoubtedly marked a turning point in the campaign for the abolition of slavery.

Lord Mansfield is buried in Westminster Abbey. On his memorial he sits in his judicial robes; to the left of him stands Justice with her scales, to his right Wisdom opening the book of the law, behind him is a youth bearing an extinguished torch. His was a light that may serve us as a beacon of the principled, fair and dispassionate application of the law.

Andrew Collender

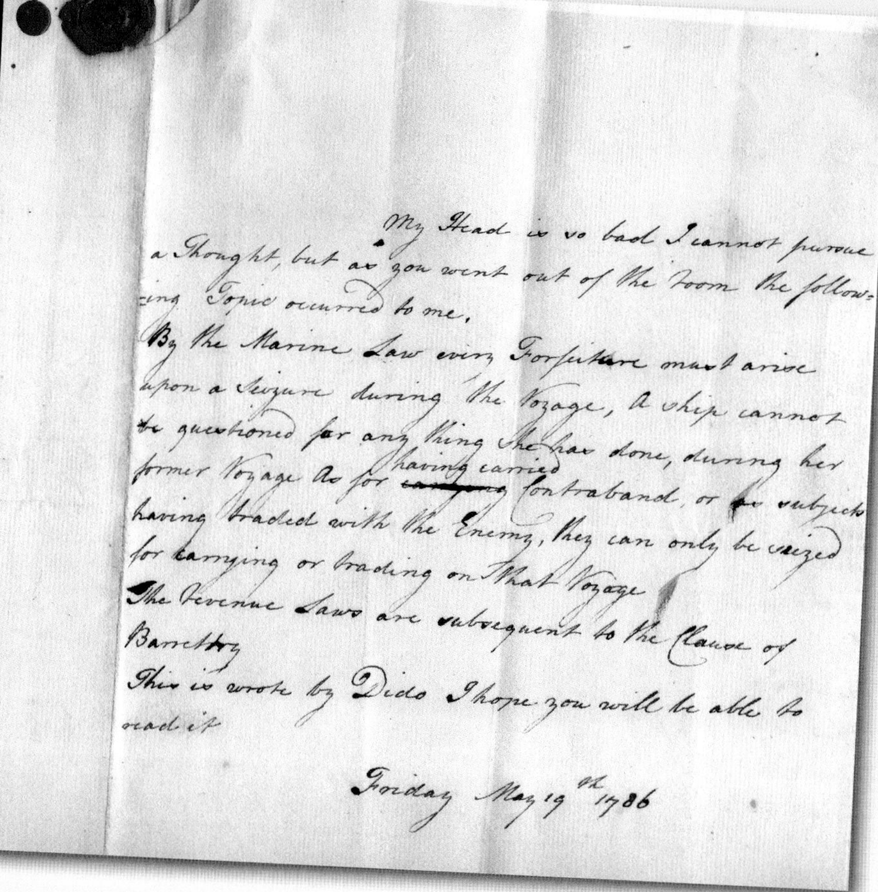

My Head is so bad I cannot pursue a Thought, but as you went out of the room the follow-ing Topic occurred to me,

By the Marine Law every Forfeiture must arise upon a Seizure during the Voyage, a ship cannot be questioned for any thing she has done, during her former Voyage As for ~~carrying~~ having carried Contraband, or ~~for~~ subjects having traded with the Enemy, they can only be seized for carrying or trading on That Voyage

The Revenue Laws are subsequent to the Clause of Barretry

This is wrote by Dido I hope you will be able to read it

Friday May 19th 1786

A letter dictated by Mansfield – 'wrote by Dido', ie Dido Belle, the daughter of a black slave and Mansfield's nephew. Her position as a protégée of Mansfield, and as a black girl living as one of the family shocked some (from the Library's Dampier Mss).

Here lies the Body
of JEREMIAH NICHOLLS Esq
Barriſter at Law and Member
of this Hon. Society who Dyed
the 1st Octor 1757 Aged 26 Years

The Chapel

MARK OCKELTON

Lincoln's Inn Chapel, raised above the bustle of legal business, is a haven of quiet out of service-time, and it is difficult now to envisage the scene on Ascension Day, 23 May 1623, when the new Chapel was consecrated. The Bishop of London led the service, and the sermon was preached by the Dean of St Paul's, Dr John Donne, who had recently been Preacher to the Inn and had laid the foundation stone with his own hands. The building was so crowded that 'two or three were taken up dead for the time'.

Left: The Undercroft.

Below: The consecration: Donne's sermon and a contemporary transcription of the liturgy for the service.

Encænia.
THE FEAST OF DEDICATION.
CELEBRATED
AT LINCOLNES INNE,
in a Sermon there vpon Ascension day, 1623.
At the Dedication of a new Chappell there, Consecrated by the Right Reuerend Father in God, the Bishop of LONDON.
Preached by IOHN DONNE, Deane of St. PAVLS.
LONDON,
Printed by AVG. MAT. for THOMAS IONES, and are to bee sold at his Shop in the Strand, at the blacke Rauen, neere vnto Saint Clements Church.
1623.

We know very little of the previous chapel, except that it stood a little southward, extending west into the Gatehouse Court. Nothing of it appears to survive save a broken alabaster sculpture discovered in 1822 and now mounted next to the pulpit stairs, and the bell, cast by Henry Bond in 1615, and still tolled at the death of a Bencher, as when it perhaps inspired Donne's injunction 'never send to know for whom the bell tolls'.

By the early seventeenth century the Chapel was in poor condition, and too small for a growing institution whose members all had to demonstrate their allegiance to the Crown by attending the worship of the Church of England. The Inn sought advice from Inigo Jones, but there is no reason to suppose he even produced a design, and of course the building is not by that English pioneer of the Palladian style. As lawyers will, the benchers chose conservatively; they apparently handed over both design and execution to an Oxford stonemason, John Clarke. He was proposed by a shadowy character called Otho Nicholson, a lawyer but not a member of the Inn, who had employed him to build the new Carfax Conduit at Oxford: but he does not seem to have been a very good choice.

His management of the work was less than satisfactory. First, he tried to claim payment from the Inn without vouchers, and then massively overspent the original budget of £2,000. He complained that the stone supplied by Nicholson was not worth what was charged for it. The Inn was involved in litigation with a joiner who had done work in duplication of that undertaken by Clarke's joiner, and when the latter died his widow had to petition the Inn for payment. Something else rather troubling must have happened during the building work,

The 1623 deed of consecration with the seal of the Bishop of London.

too, for on 18 June 1623 the benchers decided to inform the Lord Chief Justice 'touching the behaviour of John Clarke, freemason'. Clarke himself died in 1624, perhaps bankrupt: his widow approached the Inn, which gave her £20 'in commiseration of her distressed estate'.

Secondly, Clarke's work was very expensive. The Chapel cost over £2,800 in all; this may be compared with the neighbouring church of St Giles in the Fields, a substantial structure completely rebuilt in 1623–31 for £2,068. Thirdly, the building was unsound. After only sixty years it was called 'ruinous, decayed and dangerous'. Sir Christopher Wren was made a member of the Inn in 1676 and, after his advice had been taken, work was done on the east end costing again over £1,000. We can see something of the scale of that sum from the fact that many of the churches Wren was then rebuilding in the City after the fire cost between £4,000 and £6,000 in total building costs. We do not know exactly what the repairs were, but in the Undercroft it can be seen that in almost the whole of the eastern bay the bosses are of the style of the 1680s rather than matching the gothic vault, which fact, together with the large cost, suggests that the whole of the east end may have been taken down and rebuilt. After another hundred years the architect James Wyatt reported that the roof was about to fall in: the covering was too heavy for the timbers to support, and the walls

Bosses in the eastern bay of the Undercroft.

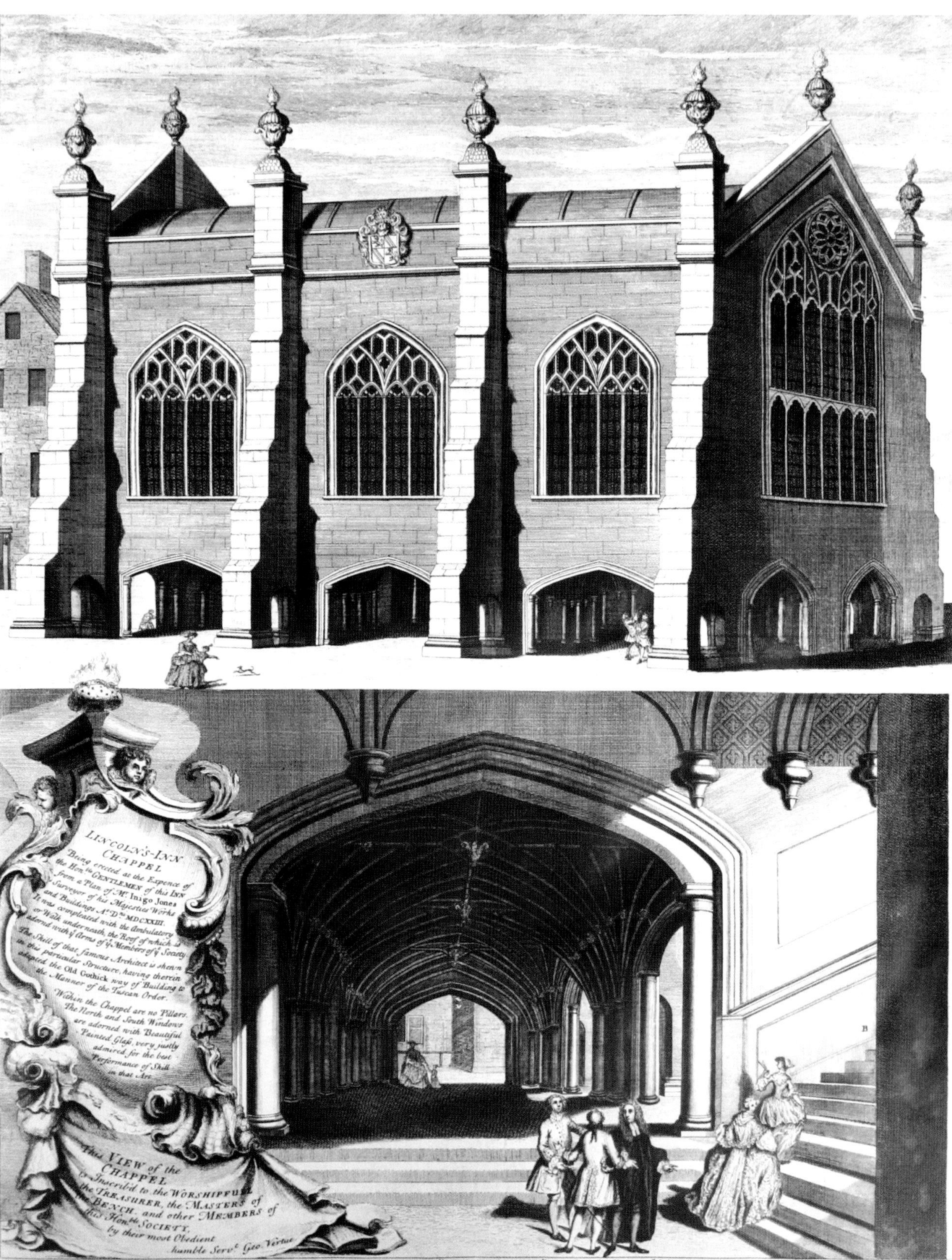

George Vertue's engraving, showing the Chapel in 1751. Artistic licence makes the staircase look quite grand.

were too thin to buttress it properly. The necessary works cost over £7,000 in the devalued money of 1795.

We do not know what the Inn expected of Clarke. The building is not in the sparse and sinuous style of gothic then being developed in Oxford, all ovals and ogees: the side windows are close copies of late fifteenth-century work, and although the rosette in the tracery of the east and west windows has an air of novelty, there was a precedent in the east window of Old St Paul's. The classical style that Inigo Jones would have recommended, and which he used at St Paul's Covent Garden in the 1630s, is here represented only by the Tuscan half-columns against the piers of the Undercroft, and the pilasters of the arches under the buttresses. That the Chapel be above ground level was a requirement of the scheme. At one stage the Inn had intended to build three sets of chambers beneath, but it was soon decided to have an open space, which became a resort of the better class of people in the seventeenth century (Pepys in his diary mentions walking there), but later was a haunt of low life, and a place for dropping unwanted babies (some of whom were raised as foundlings by the Inn and given the surname 'Lincoln') until it was railed off. There were burials there from the first.

It is fair to ask why the Chapel is raised. One suggestion has been that it enables extra use of valuable London land, but the churches of London are on the ground, and there seems little point in the exercise if the space underneath is not to be exploited. It is more likely that the Undercroft perpetuates a feature of the earlier chapel; and, for some reason, chapels in large medieval private houses and particularly bishops' palaces, seem to have been raised. The chapel of Lambeth Palace, the seat of the Archbishop of Canterbury, is on an undercroft, as is that of the medieval bishop of Ely's London house, where John of Gaunt died, which survives in Ely Place a short distance from the Inn. We may perhaps assume, therefore, that the bishop of Chichester had a chapel similarly placed in his London house and that the Inn wanted to preserve the arrangement.

Access to the Chapel was up a spiral staircase for which 1,000 bricks were supplied in 1624, and through a large door on the west side of the building at first-floor level. Sometime in the eighteenth century a wider staircase was installed, leading up out of the south-west opening of the Undercroft and returning to the Chapel door. A grander approach was inhibited by the buildings in Old Square, which ran directly in front of the Chapel, but Philip Hardwick in 1843 constructed a new staircase one bay west of the old one, that is west of the Chapel itself. His stair rose to a landing in one flight and returned in two to a lobby at the west end of the Chapel, which by then also had a gallery housing the organ. All these arrangements were swept away in 1881–2, when the Chapel was extended by one bay to its present length and the double staircase and vestries were built.

The east window with the arms of each Treasurer from 1680 to 1908.

When the Chapel was built there were three windows on each side. Soon after the building was finished they were glazed with figures of the Twelve Apostles on the south (right) side, and twelve other New and Old Testament characters on the north. After the enlargement of the Chapel in the nineteenth century some of the glass was moved, and all the windows were seriously damaged in a German air-raid in 1915. (Pock-marks from the explosion can still be seen on the outside of the building, where they are marked by a brass plaque.) The two windows on the south side are in their original position. One (St Simon) has a picture of Lincoln's Inn in the background, including the Chapel itself and Gatehouse Court. It is so accurate that we can probably trust the other backgrounds, including that to St Jude, apparently showing Westminster Abbey and Hall on the left, and the city of London with Old St Paul's Cathedral seen beyond Baynard's Castle on the right.

The Van Linge window showing St Simon with a contemporary depiction of the Inn in the background.

Richard Butler, a London glass-painter who was at the time based in Chancery Lane, was paid for two of the apostle windows; the third apostle window is by Bernard van Linge, and the other windows by Abraham van Linge. The project may, however, have been a real collaboration, because the windows with the London backgrounds are amongst those signed 'Bernard', whilst those with the initials 'RB' have backgrounds of imaginary churches in the Netherlandish gothic style of the van Linge brothers' homeland. The shields of benefactors beneath the figures, sometimes continued by crests in the tracery, include those of the Earl of Southampton, Shakespeare's patron, and the Earl of Pembroke, to whom the First Folio was dedicated. A tiny inscription at the foot of the figure of St John reveals that John Donne gave this light.

The other windows have the coats of arms of Treasurers since 1680, continuing a tradition that may have started in the glass of the old chapel. The east window alone represents 228 years of the Inn's history in this way. In the tracery at the top of that window are some of the 'gothic ornaments' inserted by William Egington of Birmingham in 1818. The old glass in the west window, including some coats of arms painted 'by a Dutchman' (presumably one of the van Linges) in 1624 was largely destroyed by the bomb in 1915. At the outbreak of the Second War much of the stained glass had been stored in the wine cellars, but what was left went in the Blitz.

The benches and pews are largely those supplied by Hugh Pryce in 1623. His detailed accounts show that at that time there was also a screen, marking off the east end as a separate chancel. There were two pulpits, one no doubt for use as a lectern, the other possibly transferred from the old chapel and newly carved to bring it up to date. The likelihood is that the arrangements at the east end were

The interior in 1808.

greatly changed in the work of 1685: certainly the altar rails are of about that date and it was probably then that a bench for communicants, going round three sides of the chancel, was removed. The present pulpit, however, is a replacement following a decision and a legacy in 1730, and the early seventeenth century Communion table came as recently as 1938. The arrangement of the pews in a central block appears to have been a deliberate and original decision, although the benchers were advised that a middle aisle was more fitting; evidently the usual collegiate plan of inward-facing seating did not attract them either. There were complex rules for the allocation of seats amongst members of the congregation, from 'Noblemen, Judges, Serjeants at Law and other persons of eminent quality' down to 'clerks and ordinary servants'.

The arms of previous Preachers who have become bishops or deans are displayed on the corbels and walls of the Chapel but there are few other monuments. One is to the assassinated Prime Minister Spencer Perceval (see p.63). An earlier Perceval, Robert, was buried in the Undercroft after being murdered in the Strand in 1677. His brother, Sir John, planned a monument by Grinling Gibbons in his memory, but the sculptor was at the time involved in a partnership dispute and could not oblige. So the Inn was deprived of what might have been a notable work of art.

Why do we maintain a Chapel in the Inn? Our recently retired Preacher, Canon Bill Norman, used to suggest three main reasons. First, because everyone needs to consider, even if they cannot answer, the great questions of life, who we are, why we are here, to whom if anyone we are responsible, and so on. What is done in Chapel may help us to think about these questions, and to point in the direction of answers. Secondly, because the very existence of such a place reminds us, whether or not we believe in God, that there is more to life than work, and more to work than making a living; there is in fact a spiritual (or at least a non-material) dimension to our existence. Thirdly, because we are a community and the Chapel is a worthy place for the prayer and praise of the community to be offered to Almighty God.

Why should the Chapel be Anglican, rather than multi-denominational or multi-faith? What may be called (without any derogatory implication) 'formal' worship needs some form or other. The Church of England's form is the one for which the Chapel was built and intended. However, much of what we do is not specifically Anglican and we hope that all our services, formal or informal, may be found helpful and positive by any believer in God or seeker after truth. It is also found to be a convenient place for quiet meditation, and the high pews are well suited to those who wish to pray undisturbed.

Top: The arms of William Warburton, Preacher 1746–57. Later when Bishop of Gloucester he founded the lectures in his name given in the Chapel.

Far left: One of a pair of communion chalices (1708).

Left: F.D. Maurice 1805–72 (after Samuel Lawrence). From the earliest times until 1917 (with a brief resuscitation 1935–9) there was separate from the Preacher the office of Chaplain, who took daily services (held until 1872) and preached on Sunday afternoons. Maurice, who held the office 1846–60, was perhaps the most famous. His afternoon sermons attracted a huge congregation and during his tenure Lincoln's Inn became the centre of the religious revival known as Christian Socialism.

Music

There is no record of any music-making in the pre-Reformation Chapel of the Inn, although one can assume that as in most wealthy establishments the Mass was sung by a choir. During the seventeenth and eighteenth centuries very little music would have been heard in the Chapel. Without an organ, a 'Psalm Raiser' was employed to lead the singing of the hymns; he chose his own tune, pitch and speed for each hymn, usually at the moment that he started it. Contemporary accounts from other London churches describe this singing as being extremely slow (a hymn might take as long as ten minutes to perform) and often no more than a 'groaning' from within the church.

This situation was obviously of some concern to the Inn, as an organ was offered as a gift to the Chapel on more than one occasion. Finally in 1820 an organ was purchased from the firm of Flight & Robson and a relation of one of the owners of the firm was appointed as the first organist. The musical team now consisted of an organist and two singers but this was increased to six (including three boy choristers) in 1841. It appears that the standard of music-making was poor because in 1852, the music publisher J. Alfred Novello was employed to provide music for the Chapel. Not an organist himself, he was obliged to employ someone to play for him whilst he conducted the choir. Novello had originally approached one of the virtuosi of the day, W.T. Best, but illness prevented Best from accepting the position and Josiah Pittman was employed in his place. By 1855 it is clear that not all was harmonious between the choirmaster and the organist. Novello dismissed Pittman for his 'intention of playing in a different time from that which I, as the choirmaster, directed'. W.T. Best finally replaced Pittman in the spring of 1855, but his appointment lasted a matter of months as he was appointed organist to St George's Hall in Liverpool that summer.

Once again the Inn sought to revitalise its music. Novello's contract was not renewed and Pittman was reappointed. A school was set up jointly with the Inner Temple for the education of the choristers and a new organ purchased. Pittman remained until Advent Sunday 1863 when he disagreed with the Chaplain's choice of the tune Helmsley due to its secular origins and so played it 'in what he deemed to be the original tempo for dancing purposes … till the whole exercise ended in confusion'. He was dismissed by the Inn the next day. Under Pittman's successor, Charles Steggall, standards improved greatly, The Times describing a memorial service for the death of Queen Victoria as containing 'solemn, inspiring music'.

The twentieth century saw the gradual phasing out of boy choristers. They had evidently become a cause of concern as by 1907, the organist was being instructed to 'do his best to better the class of boys in the choir'. By 1937 they had been entirely replaced by a professional adult choir by C.H. Trevor, laying the foundations for the current musical tradition.

Nicholas Shaw

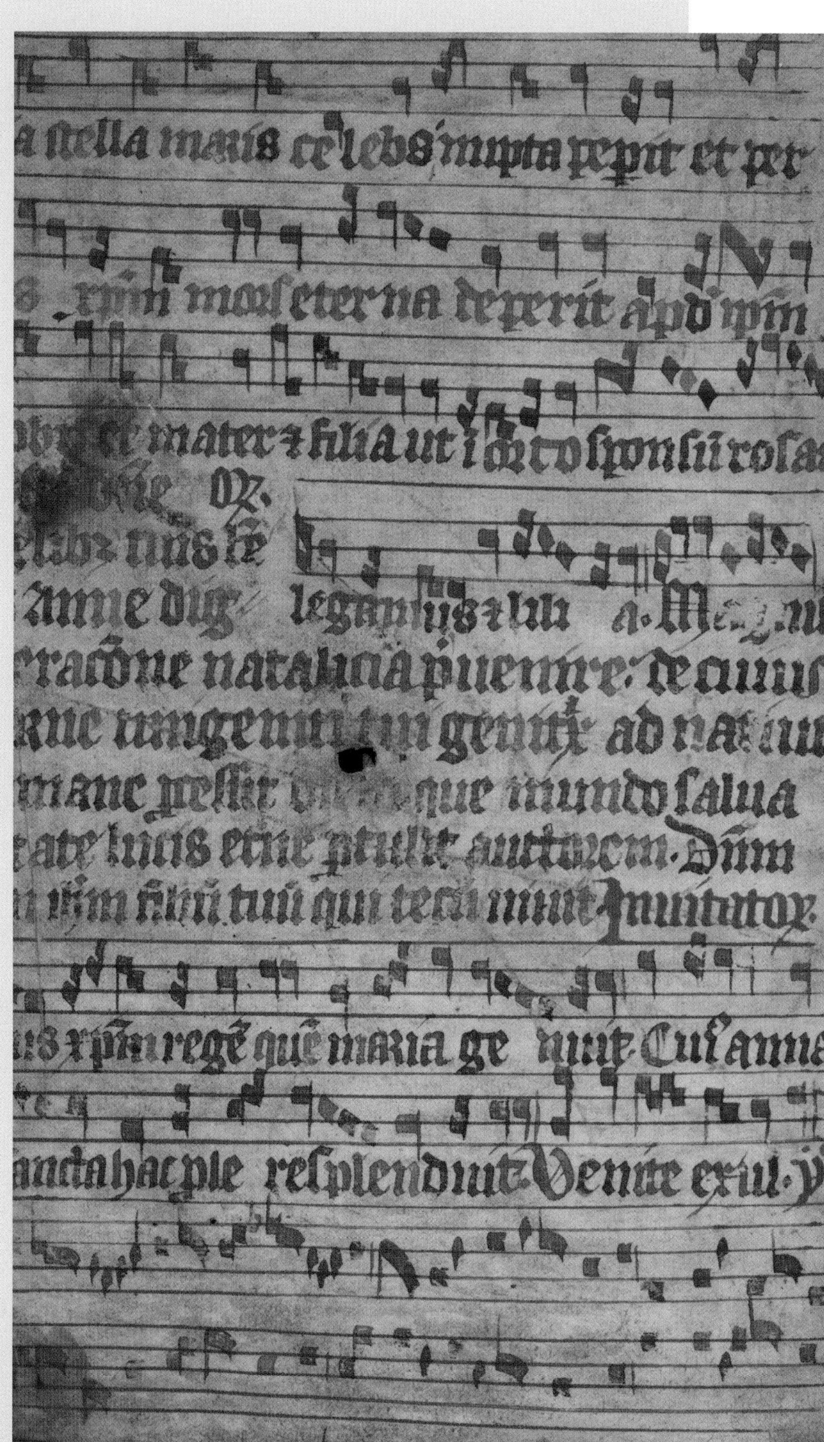

A fragment of liturgical music c1400 used as a pastedown in the binding of the Library's MS Misc. 1 which is otherwise a legal volume.

Great Figures

LORD ERSKINE 1750–1823

The dead of Culloden had been buried not four years when this glittering alumnus of Lincoln's Inn, Thomas, the third son of the tenth Earl of Buchan, was born in Edinburgh. Lauded by Lord Birkett as 'the very greatest advocate who ever practised at the English Bar', he showed a desire from the earliest age to enter one of the learned professions. But life was hard in Scotland after the 1745 rebellion. Reluctantly at the age of thirteen, due to the straitened circumstances of his family, he joined the Navy, serving four years as a midshipman in the *Tartar*.

Erskine first set his foot on the ladder of fame when he came to the attention of Lord Mansfield, with whose encouragement he was admitted to the Inn in 1775 and called in 1778, having eaten, as was the obligation of the day, seventy-two dinners. The following rungs scaled were silk in 1783 (at the age of only 33), bencher in 1785, Treasurer in 1795 and appointment as Lord Chancellor in 1806.

Erskine lived in a troubled and turbulent era. Resonating with our own times, the ministry of William Pitt responded to the insecurity engendered by the French Revolution by restrictions on long-cherished freedoms.

Erskine's first brief was to defend Captain Thomas Baillie, lieutenant governor of the Naval Hospital at Greenwich, on a charge of criminal libel. Baillie had published accusations of abuse in the management of the Hospital against Lord Sandwich, the First Lord of the Admiralty. In the face of reproof from Lord Mansfield, Erskine named Lord Sandwich as the author and prime mover of the prosecution. In simple and direct language, delivered in a clear and firm voice, Erskine attacked Lord Sandwich. His speech was described by Lord Campbell as the most wonderful forensic effort of which we have any account in our annals. The prosecution was routed, Baillie remained free, and Erskine's fortune was made. When asked how he had had the courage to stand up to Lord Mansfield, Erskine answered, 'I thought I heard my little children plucking at my robe and crying out to me, "Now father is the time to get us bread".'

Thomas Erskine aged 52 (Sir Thomas Lawrence).

Erskine secured notable victories in defence of our right to agitate by lawful means for the causes in which we believe. In 1781 he defended Lord George Gordon on a charge of high treason for instigating the anti-Catholic riots of 1780, and in 1794 he defended against the same charge of treason, Hardy, Horne Took, and Thelwall, members of a society formed to advance the cause of reform. These successful defences delivered the death blow to the doctrine of constructive treason.

But perhaps his most famous case was his defence of Tom Paine, whom William Pitt had caused to be indicted for treason for publishing the republican pamphlet, *The Rights of Man*. The courtroom hushed as Erskine rose to address the jury. He argued that the charge of seditious libel violated a key principle of the British constitution – the liberty of the press. Erskine attacked the view, defended by Blackstone, Mansfield, and Tory writers such as Swift and Dr Johnson, that Parliament is always the sovereign power. Erskine argued that in matters of publishing, Parliament's power is limited by the right of individuals freely to speak and publish their views. Liberty of the press is a natural right that cannot be infringed by any earthly power: 'Every man,' Erskine emphasized, 'may analyze the principles of its constitution, point out its errors and defects, examine and publish its corruptions, warn his fellow citizens against their ruinous consequences.' So, says Erskine, in the redolent language of the 1792 edition of his speech (a passage oddly diluted in the *State Trials*): 'Let men communicate their thoughts with freedom, and their indignation fly off like a fire spread on the surface; like gunpowder scattered, they kindle, they communicate; but the explosion is neither loud nor dangerous: keep them under restraint, it is subterranean fire, whose agitation is unseen till it bursts into earthquake or volcano.'

Erskine exercised his calling however unpopular the cause. His name will for ever be associated with his fearless advocacy for the freedom of the press, the independence of the Bar and of juries. It is no surprise that when he obtained a grant of arms he took the motto 'Trial by Jury'. His defence of politicians and reformers was a salutary check on repressive government and a buttress to our personal liberties.

In response to widespread criticism for accepting the defence of Tom Paine, Erskine splendidly justified the independence of the Bar and the cab rank principle:

I will for ever, at all hazards, assert the dignity, independence and integrity of the English Bar , without which impartial justice, the most valuable part of the English Constitution, can have no existence. From the moment that any advocate can be permitted to say that he will, or will not, stand between the Crown and the subject arraigned, from that moment the liberties of England are at an end. If the advocate refuses to defend, from what he may think of the charge or of the defence, he assumes the character of the Judge; nay, he assumes it before the hour of judgment; and, in proportion to his rank and reputation, puts the heavy influence of, perhaps, a mistaken opinion into the scale against the accused, in whose favour the benevolent principle of English law makes all presumptions and which commands the very Judge to be his counsel.

Andrew Collender

The Gordon riots: the resulting trial before Lord Mansfield (whose house had been burnt down) afforded Erskine one of his notable cases for the defence (engraving by H. Roberts).

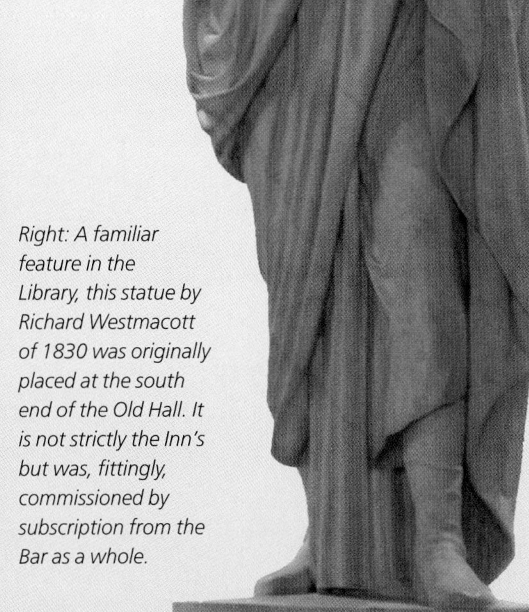

Right: A familiar feature in the Library, this statue by Richard Westmacott of 1830 was originally placed at the south end of the Old Hall. It is not strictly the Inn's but was, fittingly, commissioned by subscription from the Bar as a whole.

Food, Drink, and Merriment

THESE, THY CREATURES, TO OUR USE

David Harris

The first ringing testimony to the quality of life in Lincoln's Inn is provided by Sir Thomas More, who reflects, having given up the Lord Chancellorship in 1532, that, 'But, by my counsel, it shall not be best for us to fall to the lowest fare first. We will not therefore descend to Oxford fare, nor to the fare of New Inn, but we will begin with Lincoln's Inn diet, where many right worshipful and of good years do live full well.'

Some 150 years later, on 29 February 1672, King Charles II dined at the Inn. Whether or not it is the case that wine flowed so freely that when the Loyal Toast came to be drunk, the ability of his hosts to assume the perpendicular was questionable (the Black Books are silent on the point), it may well be true that His Majesty granted us at that time the privilege of drinking his health seated, a privilege shared only by the Royal Navy. Also, His Majesty, always a man to appreciate the good things of life, admitted himself a member of the Inn, as the Black Books proudly record 'itt being an example not presidented by any former King of this Realm' (or Queen, for that matter). In 1972, a dinner was held in Hall to celebrate the tercentenary of this occasion, and as far as possible the original menu was replicated.

Things, however, fluctuated, particularly while the Inn effectively subcontracted its catering. In 1616, members complained of meat which was 'ill-rosted dry and burnt, for the profit of the Chief Cooke, and not looked to by himself or the second Cooke, but by the turne spitte and boyes'. The benchers declared in response that 'yf the loynes be not soe well rosted as at the gate [sic], the Chief Cooke shall be punished for yt'. 'Bad and unwholesome' meat was the subject of another complaint in 1753, with a prayer that the cook be dismissed.

In 1710 a regimen of 'boyled beef', roast loins of mutton (making their first appearance in the Inn's records) and fish on Fridays was laid down. Later in the eighteenth century, the following commons were specifically provided for both benchers and other members of Hall, 'to be varied by the Masters of the Bench in commons according to the season, keeping however as near as may be to things of the same value as are undermentioned':

The Wandesford Basin and Ewer

Like many other institutions the Inn seems to have sold all its plate in the Civil War effort: this fine ensemble is the first silver acquired by the Inn thereafter. Philip Lord Wharton gave it in 1652 in memory of Sir Rowland Wandesford, his father-in-law, a bencher from 1613 and very active in the Inn's affairs until well into his seventies. Despite having been active in the Parliamentary cause, the donor can have had little sympathy with the Puritan ways of the Commonwealth, for these pieces are clearly meant to create a sumptuous display at dinner.

The Watts Cup

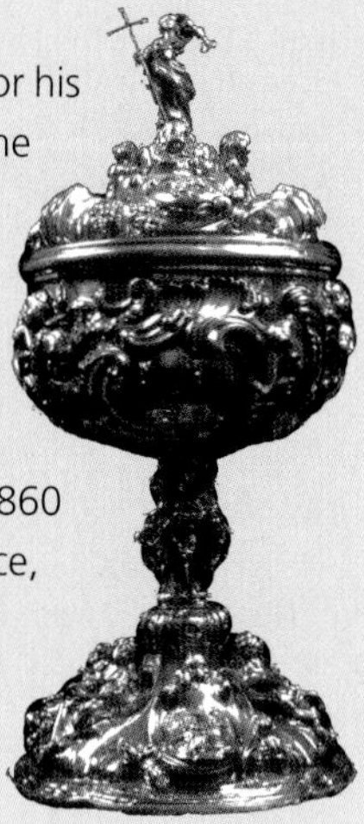

Presented by the Inn to G.F. Watts for his fresco (see p129), his widow gave the cup back to the Inn in 1925. A silver-gilt ciborium (for holding the wafers at Mass), it is one of the Inn's most impressive and interesting pieces of plate. It bears no hallmarks. The Inn bought it in 1860 as an eighteenth-century Italian piece, but the vendors have subsequently described it as seventeenth-century and Spanish.

Easter Term 1748:

Sunday: *sirloin of beef, roasted, 7lbs to a mess undrest, with pickles and horse raddish; and baked plumb pudding.*

Monday: *a neck of mutton, boyled, with proper roots and greens; a fowl, roasted, with gravy and egg sauce.*

Tuesday: *necks of veal, roasted with 100 of asparagus.*

Wednesday: *boyled brisquets of beef, with roots and greens, 7lb weight; 4 pidgeons, roasted.*

Thursday: *roast beef, as on Sundays; with pudding or asparagus.*

Friday: *fresh fish in season, with proper sauce; a loin of mutton, roasted, with pickles and horse-raddish.*

Saturday: *boiled tongues, roots and greens; a couple of rabbits* (probably not by this time still home-produced. Like many medieval establishments, the Inn had a coneygarth, a rabbit warren, which was a source of food and fur. It was where the North Gardens are, forming a boundary to the Inn. Students were forbidden from hunting the rabbits either with bows and arrows or, after the arrival of gunpowder, shooting them).

The Friday and Saturday diet did not change for Trinity term, and Sunday was the same, except that cucumbers were served instead of pickles. Only one neck of veal was allowed for Tuesday, with a 'dish of pease' instead of asparagus; and horseradish and cucumbers and a dish of peas replaced the pudding or asparagus on Thursdays. On Monday beans and bacon were offered with a neck of mutton, roasted, with pickles and horse-radish; on Wednesday, bacon and a fowl, with greens and a shoulder of mutton, roasted. In Michaelmas term, the Sunday roast beef was not specified to be sirloin, and brisket was no longer required on Wednesdays, when a couple of rabbits replaced the four pigeons of Easter term. Thursday's pudding or asparagus became pickles with a hot apple pie, and Saturday's rabbits gave place to a breast of mutton, roasted, with pickles. This was also allowed on Fridays, accompanied by 12d-worth (5p-worth) of oysters and fresh fish in season. On Tuesday, a boiled fowl with oyster sauce was required, plus a shoulder of

Below: Kitchen accounts 1745.

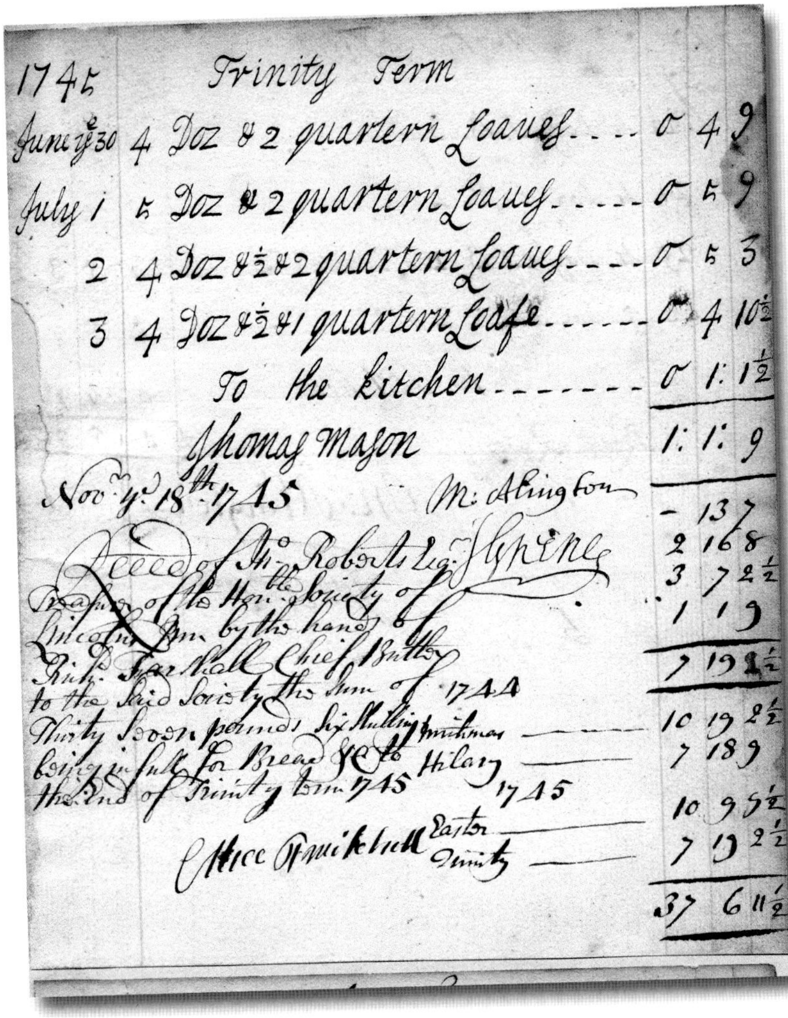

1745 Trinity Term

June ye 30 4 Doz & 2 quartern Loaves 0 4 9

July 1 5 Doz & 2 quartern Loaves 0 5 9

2 4 Doz & ½ & 2 quartern Loaves 0 5 3

3 4 Doz & ½ & 1 quartern Loafe 0 4 10½

To the Kitchen 0 1 1½

Thomas Mason 1 1 9

Nov ye 18th 1745 Mr Alington

Rec'd of Mr Roberts Esq Treasurer of the Honble Society of Lincolns Inn by the hands of Richd Farhall Chief Butler to the said Society the Sum of Thirty Seven pounds Six Shillings being in full for Bread &c to the End of Trinity term 1745

1744 Michaelmas — 10 19 2½
Hilary — 7 18 9
1745 Easter — 10 9 5½
Trinity — 7 19 2½

Alice Rmickell

37 6 11½

PREMIER SERVICE.

La Tortue.
Le Saûmon de Severn.
Les Ris de Veau piqués à la Toulouse. Le Salmi de Cailles au Vin de Bourdeaux.
La Tortue Liée. La Tortue Claire.
Les Cailles à la Jardinière. Les Cotelettes de Mouton à la Macédoine.
Le Saûmon de Severn. Le St. Pierre Sce Hollandaise.
Les Boudins de Levraut à la Périgord. Le Turban de Lapéreaux à la Financière.
La Tortue Claire. La Tortue Liée.
Le Suprême de Volailles conté aux Truffes. La Casserole de Ris à la nesle à l'Allemande.
Les Rougets à l'Italienne. Le Turbot Sce aux Homards.
Les Cotelettes d'Agneau aux Concombres. Les Filets de Canetons à la Bigarrade.
Le St. Pierre Sce. Hollandaise. Le Saûmon de Severn.
Les Filets de Poulets sautés aux petits Pois. Les Filets de Pigeons à la St. Ménéhould.
La Tortue Liée. La Tortue Claire.
Le Pâté chaud de Mouton à l'Italienne. Les Boudins de Poulets à la Royale.
Le Saûmon de Severn. Les Rougets à l'Italienne.
Les Filets de Pigeons sautés, Sauce Bohémienne. Les Ris de Veau piqués au petits Pois.
La Tortue Claire. La Tortue Liée.
La Chartreuse de Légûmes en surprise. Les Tendrons de Veau à la Villeroi.

LES RELEVÉES.

2 Les Poulardes à la Montmorenci.
2 Les petits Poulets en Macédoine.
2 Les petits Poulets au Langue de Mouton.
2 Les Grénadins de Veau piqués aux Pois.
2 Le Jambon et la Langue.
Le Pâté chaud à la Périgord.
Le Filet de Bœuf piqué au Vin de Madère.
2 Les Poulets rôtis aux cressons.
2 Les Canards braisés aux Navets.
Le Serpent de Veau en Macédoine.

BUFFET.

Le Potage Printanier.
Le Venaison.
Le Bœuf rôti.
Le Mouton rôti.
Les petits Pâtés.
Les Légûmes.
La Langue de Bœuf.

Above and top right: The banquet for the opening of the Great Hall by Queen Victoria 30 October 1845.

Right: The Kitchen 1952.

mutton, roasted, with pickles etc. Hilary term was the same as for Michaelmas, but with a baked plum pudding, instead of rabbits, on Wednesday.

Varied combinations of the same dishes were provided for in 1762, but with the addition of gooseberry pie on Thursdays in Easter term and Sundays in Trinity (with a basin of cream on the latter day), fruit pie on Thursdays in Trinity and 'country pork' and 'bouilli' respectively on Mondays and Wednesdays in both Michaelmas and Hilary terms. In 1792, the fare also comprised a garnish of butter sauce and parsley, spinach and capers; marrow pudding; and salmon. By 1832, benchers were enjoying mulligatawny soup, grapes, French plums, 'confectionary', figs, almonds, raisins and turtle. The Bar were allowed (inter alia) three haunches of venison (but no necks or pasties) and salmon.

In 1986, not long after he had joined the Inn, John Tomaschek, the present catering manager, at the suggestion of the Bar Representation Committee, devised a replacement for the now moribund Bar Ladies' Night. The result was the very successful and popular Gourmet Dinner, where the collective resources of kitchen and cellar are concentrated to produce the finest of food and wine, with dancing or entertainment to follow, thereby continuing the Inn's long-standing and honourable tradition of good living.

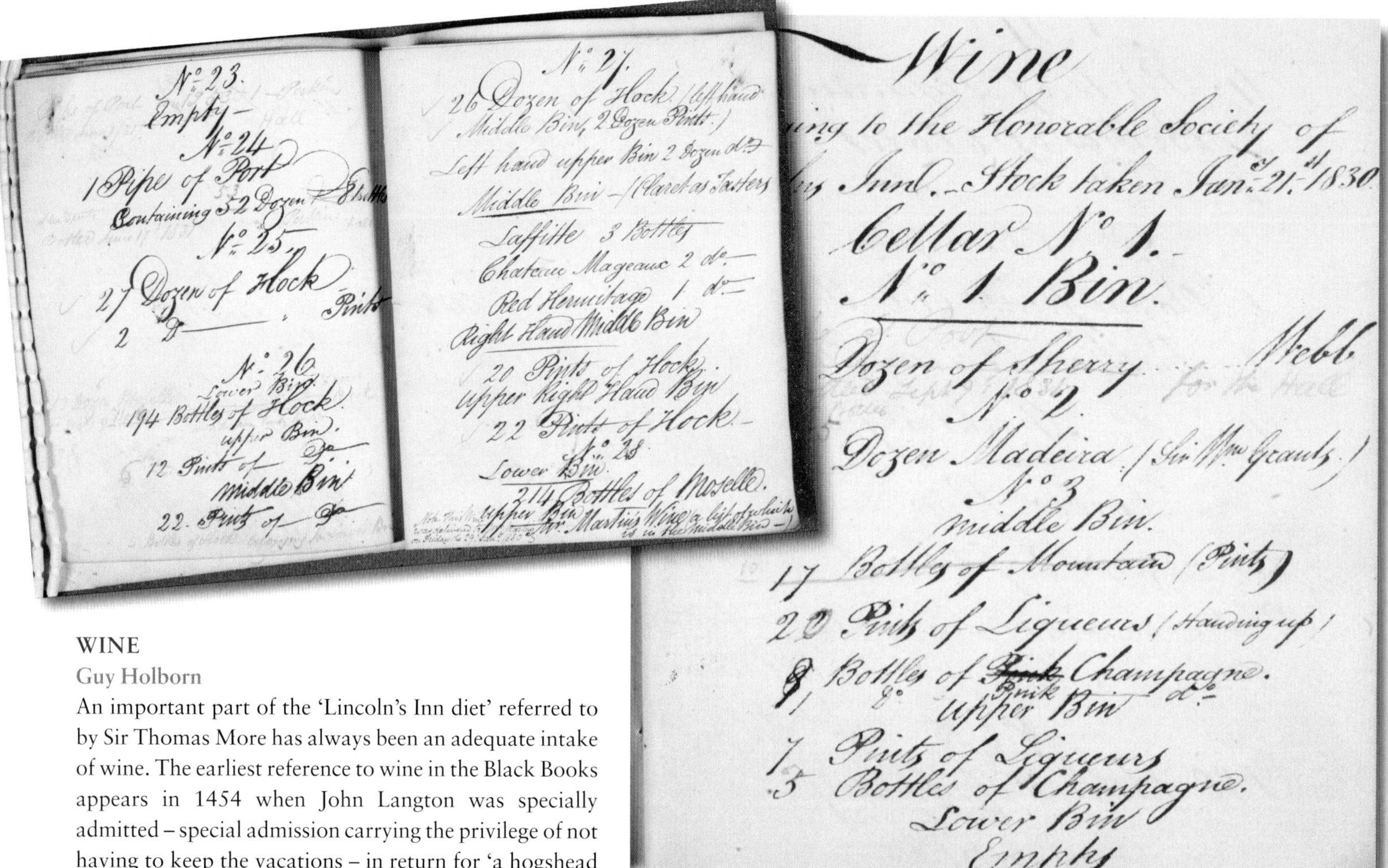

No. 23.
Empty –
No. 24
1 Pipe of Port
Containing 52 Dozen Bottles
No. 25.
27 Dozen of Hock
2 D° – Pints
No. 26
Lower Bin
194 Bottles of Hock
upper Bin
12 Pints of D°
middle Bin
22 Pints of D°

No. 27.
26 Dozen of Hock (left hand Middle Bin, 2 Dozen Pints)
Left hand upper Bin 2 Dozen d°
Middle Bin –
Laffitte 3 Bottles
Chateau Margeaux 2 d°
Red Hermitage 1 d°
Right Hand Middle Bin
20 Pints of Hock
upper Right Hand Bin
22 Pints of Hock
No. 28
Lower Bin
214 Bottles of Moselle.
upper Bin

Wine
…ing to the Honorable Society of
…s Inn. Stock taken Jan. 21. 1830
Cellar No. 1.
No. 1 Bin.
Dozen of Sherry … Webb
No. 2
Dozen Madeira (Sir Wm Grant's)
No. 3
Middle Bin.
17 Bottles of Mountain (Pints)
20 Pints of Liqueurs (Hanging up)
8 Bottles of Pink Champagne.
1 d° upper Bin d°
1 Pints of Liqueurs
3 Bottles of Champagne.
Lower Bin
Empty

The cellar book 1830.

WINE

Guy Holborn

An important part of the 'Lincoln's Inn diet' referred to by Sir Thomas More has always been an adequate intake of wine. The earliest reference to wine in the Black Books appears in 1454 when John Langton was specially admitted – special admission carrying the privilege of not having to keep the vacations – in return for 'a hogshead of red Gascon wine'. This sensible form of levy was quite common right through to the end of the sixteenth century. The Society must have accumulated quite substantial stocks by this means. John Langton's 'hogshead' was the usual quantity, which by a statute of 1483 (1 Ric. III c.13) was standardized as 63 gallons, that is old wine gallons, or 52½ imperial gallons, which is about 318 modern bottles. It is difficult to judge consumption, because we do not have accurate figures of how many members were in residence, but in 1471 a pipe – two hogsheads – was deemed sufficient for use at Christmas. We have a slightly better idea of bench consumption since in 1609 they rationed themselves to one hogshead during the Easter and Michaelmas terms, and a 'terse' – a third of a pipe, so two-thirds of a hogshead – during the Hilary and Trinity terms. Except during the slightly longer Michaelmas term, the termly ration had to last about three weeks. Given that there were fewer than twenty active benchers in 1609 – average attendance at Council was about fifteen – a rough calculation could theoretically be made. That is not counting of course special occasions such as revels, for which separate supplies were laid in.

It is not at all clear how arrangements for dining were run during vacations for those who remained in residence. But a possible inference from a deplorable incident in 1530 is that provision of drink was less generous, if not absent. For during the summer vacation 'certeyn personz of the Company vnknown' were driven to break the window of the buttery 'and brake the seler dore, and lett out the wynne'. It was agreed 'that all the hoolle Comapnye shalbe sworne vppon the Euangeliste to tell what they knowe concerning that acte'. In the Black Books a list of thirteen names follows – 'mostly benchers', the editor drily notes. Eight stood firm against this 'own up or else' tactic, neither admitting guilt nor pointing the finger. They were all 'banished for ever', only to be re-admitted a week later on the personal intervention of both of the King's Serjeants, which was as well since their number included four future Treasurers and a future Chief Justice of the Common Pleas.

The wine drunk at this time was confined to 'Gascon' or 'claret' or simply 'red'. By the eighteenth century taste and refinement in choice of wine had developed. 'Burgundy' first makes an appearance in the records in 1732. White wine also starts to appear. In 1705 two dozen 'white Lisbourne' were ordered, and it seems that white wine was specifically used for the grace cup. Punch also became fashionable – it was served particularly at Adjourned Councils, ie Council meetings out of term, when the benchers made a point of treating themselves. 'White Lisbourne' is not the only unfamiliarly named wine. In 1727 7s 6d was paid for six pints of 'Canary' and in 1750 six gallons of 'Mountain' were ordered. A footnote by the 1899 editor of the Black Books that the latter was a form of 'Malaga' does not greatly enlighten the modern wine-drinker. Port, surprisingly, is only specifically recorded for the first time in 1727, but was soon being ordered in substantial quantities. For example in 1745 of the Inn's entire annual expenditure of £2,927, £43 4s was accounted for by buying port. And that would have only been for the needs of the bench and Bar – students were not provided with port until 1826. A special committee in that year noted that all three of the other Inns gave students one bottle of port per mess. Wishing, as always, to maintain the Inn's reputation and alert to the 'probable increase of students who may be induced to dine in the Hall', the benchers readily acceded to the recommendation to follow suit. The luxury of 'Champain' does not seem to have been indulged in until 1775, when four dozen were

Lincoln's Inn.

GRAND DAY,
EASTER TERM, 1903.

TUESDAY, APRIL 28th.

Wines.

CHABLIS.
MADEIRA, vin. 1845.
SHERRY.
HOCK, Marcobruner Cabinet, 1865.
CHAMPAGNE, Ve. Clicquot ... 1889.
CLARET, Ch. Latour ... ... 1887.

Dessert.

PORT, ... Vin. 1863.
CLARET, Ch. Lafite ... ... 1870.

ordered. It was indeed a luxury even then – the modest-seeming cost of £19 4s for the four dozen works out at about £36 a bottle in today's money. Thereafter orders were limited to one dozen for Grand Days only.

Today we have a Wine Committee, and judging by the number of glasses set out in the Council Room for their meetings, a conspicuously conscientious one. The beginning of delegation of decisions relating to wine may be traced to 1805 when a bencher was nominated 'to take upon him the trouble of ordering the wine of such person as he shall think proper', the task hitherto having been performed personally by each Treasurer. The minutes of the Wine Committee are extant from 1870, making it, if precedence is taken from longevity, the third most senior of the current nineteen principal standing committees of Council, after the Finance and Library Committees. Discernment sometimes necessitates acknowledging that a wrong decision has been made – after all, predicting how wine will develop after long laying down is not an exact science. When in 1902 no less than thirty-seven dozen of 1870 port had to be condemned, the Committee may not have been aware that their decision was by no means unprecedented. In 1573 a whole hogshead of claret had to be sold at a loss of 15s, and the Treasurer who had bought it compensated, because it 'was not well tasted'. It is a fortunate fact that few who dine in the Inn today can complain that the wine they are served does not taste very well indeed.

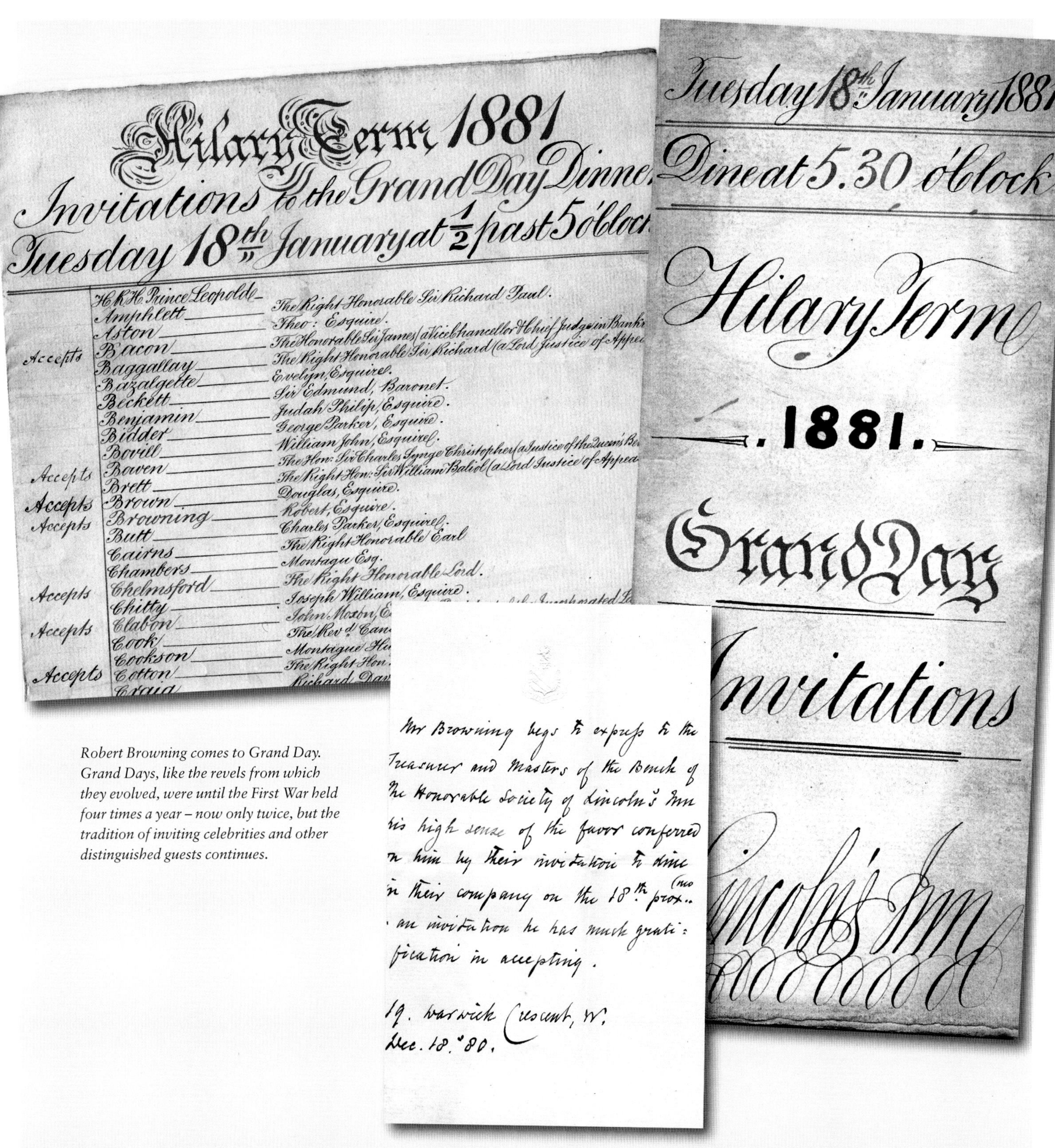

Hilary Term 1881
Invitations to the Grand Day Dinner
Tuesday 18th January at ½ past 5 o'clock

	H.R.H. Prince Leopold	
	Amphlett	The Right Honorable Sir Richard Paul.
	Aston	Theo: Esquire.
Accepts	Bacon	The Honorable Sir James (a Vice Chancellor & Chief Judge in Bankr...
	Baggallay	The Right Honorable Sir Richard (a Lord Justice of Appe...
	Bazalgette	Evelyn Esquire.
	Beckett	Sir Edmund, Baronet.
	Benjamin	Judah Philip, Esquire.
	Bidder	George Parker, Esquire.
	Bovill	William John, Esquire.
Accepts	Bowen	The Hon: Sir Charles Synge Christopher (a Justice of the Queen's Be...
	Brett	The Right Hon: Sir William Baliol (a Lord Justice of Appea...
Accepts	Brown	Douglas, Esquire.
Accepts	Browning	Robert, Esquire.
	Butt	Charles Parker, Esquire.
	Cairns	The Right Honorable Earl
	Chambers	Montagu Esq.
Accepts	Chelmsford	The Right Honorable Lord.
	Chitty	Joseph William, Esquire.
Accepts	Clabon	John Moxon, E...
	Cook	The Revd Can...
	Cookson	Montague H...
Accepts	Cotton	The Right Hon...
	Craig	Richard Dav...

Tuesday 18th January 1881
Dine at 5.30 o'clock
Hilary Term
. 1881 .
Grand Day
...nvitations
...incoln's Inn

Mr Browning begs to express to the Treasurer and Masters of the Bench of the Honorable Society of Lincoln's Inn his high sense of the favor conferred on him by their invitation to dine in their company on the 18th prox. (mo... an invitation he has much gratification in accepting.

19. Warwick Crescent, W.
Dec. 18. '80.

Robert Browning comes to Grand Day. Grand Days, like the revels from which they evolved, were until the First War held four times a year – now only twice, but the tradition of inviting celebrities and other distinguished guests continues.

MERRIMENT

Alan Nelson

The four Inns of Court in London were famous from the fifteenth through the seventeenth century for the high spirits in which they celebrated their holidays, particularly the Christmas season, which lasted from All Saints' (1 November) to Candlemas (2 February). Festivities included drinking, banquets, and games of chance, particularly dice; music, dancing, plays, and masques; and the shooting of cannon, equestrian ridings, and mock martial combat. Participants here were primarily gentlemen of Lincoln's Inn itself, but also included visitors from other Inns, and outsiders. Dancing sometimes required women as partners for the gentlemen, and dramatic or quasi-dramatic activities might include women in the audience.

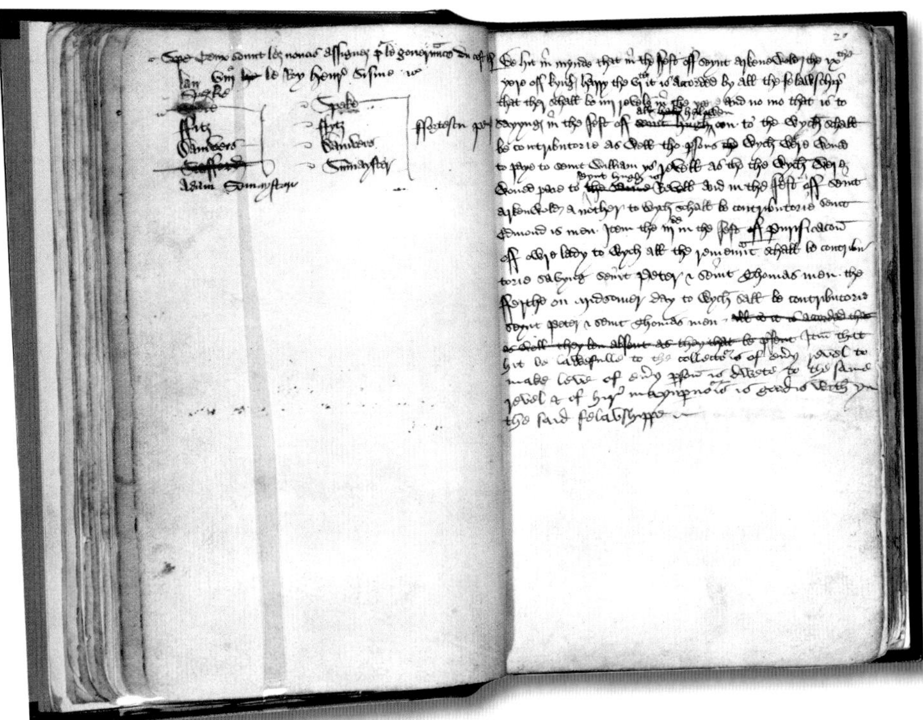

The entry in the Black Books in 1431 (the first in English rather than Latin) ordering 'that ther schall be iiii revels in the yeere and no mo'.

A torchbearer in American Indian costume – one of the costumes designed by Inigo Jones for the Memorable Maske *of 1614.*

Contemporary and antiquarian documents alike took particular note of entertainments which involved royalty, like the Smithfield jousts of 1467-68, for which Lincoln's Inn supplied four armed men, or the coronation of Henry VIII in 1509, for which the Inn supplied a hogshead of claret and £5 in money 'in making of Scaffolds at Westminster to stand on, for view of the Justs and Tiltings'. The historian and antiquary William Dugdale (1605–86), who had family connections to Lincoln's Inn and who wrote an account of all four Inns in *Origines Juridiciales* (1666), noted both of the older royal events, and added three of more recent date: a masque 'presented by this Society before the King, at the marriage of the Lady Elizabeth, his daughter, to the Prince Elector Palatine of the Rhene' on 15 February 1614; 'the performances at the Barriers' for the creation of Prince Charles as Prince of Wales on 4 November 1616; and 'that famous Mask' presented to King Charles and Queen Henrietta Maria on 3 and 13 February 1634. Theatre historians recognize these events as George Chapman's *The Memorable Maske of the Two Honorable Houses or Innes of Court; the Middle Temple, and Lyncolns Inne* (1613/14); a display of military and equestrian prowess in tournament lists supplied with a median fence or 'barrier'; and James Shirley's *Triumph of Peace* (1633/34), a demonstration of loyalty by all four Inns in reaction to William Prynne's attack on players and by implication on the Queen in his

[Masque. From Strutt's Royal Antiquities.]

notorious *Histrio-Mastix* published earlier the same year. Its dedication to his 'much honoured friends', the benchers of Lincoln's Inn, did not prevent Prynne's expulsion from the Inn.

The subtitle of Chapman's *Memorable Maske* of 1614 hints at the splendour and variety of the event:

> *With a description of their whole show; in the manner of their march on horse-backe to the Court from the Maister of the Rolls his house: with all their right noble consorts, and most showfull attendants. Invented, and fashioned, with the ground, and speciall structure of the whole worke: by our kingdomes most artfull and ingenious architect Innigo Iones.*

Unsurprisingly, the entertainments of 1614 and 1634 reverberate in the Black Books principally in the form of assessments which ran on for many years, so huge was the debt incurred on each occasion. Indeed, *The Triumph of Peace*, which cost the four Inns a total of some £21,000, may have been the most expensive English masque ever.

Dugdale ascribes two rather more generic occasions of merriment to Lincoln's Inn: 'Revells', which he defines as 'Dancings for their recreation and delight'; and 'Grand Christmasses', which he defines as 'splendid Shews, notable pastimes, and costly feastings'. Revels were probably annual events, except in plague year, while a

HISTRIO-MASTIX.
THE
PLAYERS SCOVRGE,
OR,
ACTORS TRAGÆDIE,
Divided into Two Parts.

Wherein it is largely evidenced, by divers *Arguments*, by the concurring Authorities and Resolutions of *sundry texts of Scripture*; of the *whole Primitive Church*, both under the *Law and Gospell*; of 55 *Synodes and Councels*; of 71 *Fathers and Christian Writers*, before the yeare of our Lord 1200; of above 150 *foraigne and domestique Protestant and Popish Authors*, since; of 40 *Heathen Philosophers, Historians, Poets*; of many *Heathen*, many *Christian Nations, Republiques, Emperors, Princes, Magistrates*; of sundry *Apostolicall, Canonicall, Imperiall Constitutions*; and of our owne *English Statutes, Magistrates, Universities, Writers, Preachers.*

That popular Stage-playes (the very Pompes of the Divell which we renounce in Baptisme, if we beleeve the Fathers) *are sinfull, heathenish, lewde, ungodly Spectacles, and most pernicious Corruptions; condemned in all ages, as intolerable Mischiefes to Churches, to Republickes, to the manners, mindes and soules of men. And that the Profession of Play-poets, of Stage players; together with the penning, acting, and frequenting of Stage-playes, are unlawfull, infamous and misbeseeming Christians.* All pretences to the contrary are here likewise fully answered; and the unlawfulnes of acting, of beholding Academicall Enterludes, briefly discussed; besides sundry other particulars concerning *Dancing, Dicing, Health-drinking, &c.* of which the *Table* will informe you.

By WILLIAM PRYNNE, *an Utter-Barrester of* Lincolnes Inne.

Cyprian. De Spectaculis lib. p. 244.
Fugienda sunt ista Christianis fidelibus, ut iam frequenter diximus, tàm vana, tàm perniciosa, tàm sacrilega Spectacula: quæ, etsi non haberent crimen, habent in se et maximam, et parum congruentē fidelibus vanitatē.
Lactantius de Verò Cultu cap. 20.
Vitenda ergo Spectacula omnia, non solum ne quid vitiorum pectoribus insideat, &c. sed ne cuius nos voluptatis consuetudo delineat, atque à Deo et à bonis operibus avertat.
Chrysost. Hom. 38. in Matth. Tom. 2. Col. 299. B & Hom. 8. De Pœnitentia, Tom. 5. Col. 750.
Immo vero, his Theatralibus ludis eversis, non leges, sed iniquitatem evertetis, ac omnem civitatis pestem extinguetis: Etenim Theatrum, communis luxuriæ officina, publicum incontinentiæ gymnasium; cathedra pestilentiæ; pessimus locus; plurimorumque morborum plena Babylonica fornax, &c.
Augustinus De Civit. Dei, l. 4. c. 1.
Si tantummodo boni et honesti homines in civitate essent, nec in rebus humanis Ludi scenici esse debuissent.

LONDON,
Printed by *E. A.* and *W. I.* for *Michael Sparke*, and are to be sold at the Blue Bible, in Greene Arbour, in little Old Bayly. 1633.

Grand Christmas might occur only upon the election of a 'Christmas Prince' willing to stand a considerable personal outlay. It is a virtual certainty that all intramural merriment took place in the Inn's Old Hall.

Absent from Dugdale's description of Lincoln's Inn, and very sparse in the historical record, are the kinds of plays associated so prominently with the other three inns. While Lincoln's Inn sponsored 'disguisings' in the 1530s, and plays by the Children of the Chapel under the direction of the minor theatrical entrepreneurs Richard Edwards and Richard Ferrant in the early years of Elizabeth, nothing approaches the cultural significance of Shakespeare's *Comedy of Errors* at Gray's Inn in 1594, or his *Twelfth Night* at Middle Temple in 1602. Indeed, the

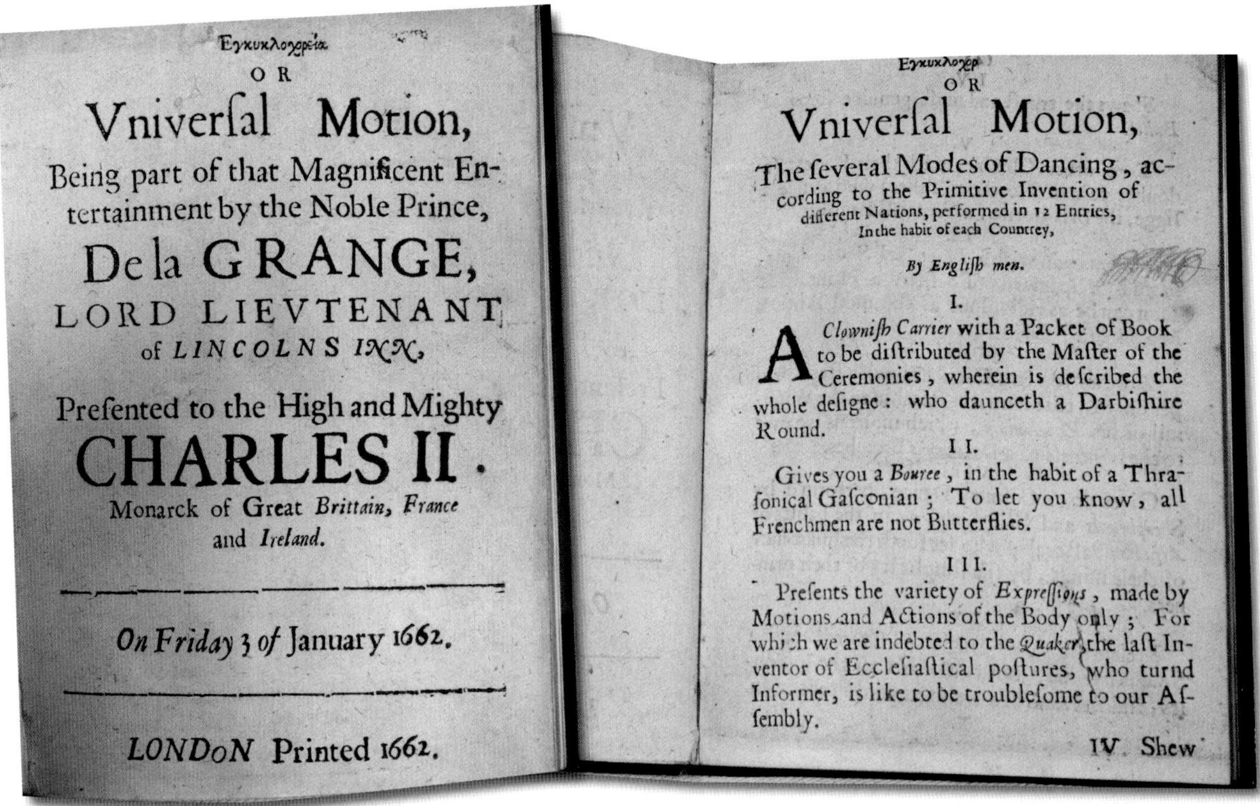

Εγκυκλοχορεία
OR
Vniverſal Motion,
Being part of that Magnificent Entertainment by the Noble Prince,
De la GRANGE,
LORD LIEVTENANT
of LINCOLNS INN,
Preſented to the High and Mighty
CHARLES II.
Monarck of Great *Brittain, France* and *Ireland.*

On Friday 3 *of* January 1662.

LONDON Printed 1662.

Εγκυκλοχορ
OR
Vniverſal Motion,
The ſeveral Modes of Dancing, according to the Primitive Invention of different Nations, performed in 12 Entries, In the habit of each Countrey,

By Engliſh men.

I.

A *Clowniſh Carrier* with a Packet of Book to be diſtributed by the Maſter of the Ceremonies, wherein is deſcribed the whole deſigne: who daunceth a Darbiſhire Round.

II.

Gives you a *Bouree*, in the habit of a Thraſonical Gaſconian; To let you know, all Frenchmen are not Butterflies.

III.

Preſents the variety of *Expreſſions*, made by Motions and Actions of the Body only; For which we are indebted to the *Quaker*, the laſt Inventor of Eccleſiaſtical poſtures, who turnd Informer, is like to be troubleſome to our Aſſembly.

IV. Shew

three semi-dramatic or non-dramatic entertainments from the reigns of James I and Charles I were joint ventures, in which Lincoln's Inn apparently served as junior partner.

The notoriety of the few entertainments for royalty and the relative paucity of dramatic plays at Lincoln's Inn must not divert attention from the Christmas festivities, which were far more characteristic of life at the Inns over the years. In early autumn, each Inn appointed mock officers in imitation of the royal court, always including a Master of the Revels, a Christmas Steward, and a Christmas Marshall. The antiquity of the Lincoln's Inn Black Books, which date from 1422, permit reconstruction of Christmas festivities and Christmas officers back to the reign of Henry VI. It is pleasant to think that the 'Mr Donne' appointed Christmas Steward in 1594–5 was John Donne the poet and divine, admitted to Lincoln's Inn 6 May 1592.

Evidence of merriment during the Civil War is naturally sparse, but the Restoration brought some attempts at reviving old traditions. In January 1662/3 an entertainment organized by the Prince 'De la Grange', *alias* Lord Lieutenant of Lincoln's Inn, was presented to Charles II; a description complete with text was published almost simultaneously under the title *Enkyklochoreia*, or *Universal Motion* (illustrated above). Despite this revival, and though Christmas officers continued to be appointed into the eighteenth century, nothing again would match the merriment of the reigns of the Tudors and early Stuarts.

Below: Bar Theatrical Society performing Much Ado About Nothing *in the Great Hall December 1964.*

Before the Dinner
by William Dring RA (1900–90)

In 1979, Lincoln's Inn could boast a particularly impressive array of members holding high public office: Mrs (later Lady) Thatcher (Prime Minister 1979–90), Lord Hailsham (Lord Chancellor 1979–87), Lord Widgery (Lord Chief Justice 1971–80), Lord Denning (Master of the Rolls 1962–82), and Sir Robert Megarry (Vice-Chancellor 1976–85).

William Dring RA painted a portrait of the group. The picture now hangs towards the southern end of the east wall of the Great Hall. Echoing *The Short Adjournment*, it shows the group members in the Benchers' Drawing Room attending a black-tie guest night before Gainsborough's painting of William Pitt the Younger.

The painting was commissioned by and presented to the Inn by the Treasurer, Lord Renton. He was called to the Bar by the Inn in 1933 and has served in Parliament for more than sixty years, having sat in the House of Commons as the member for Huntingdon for thirty-four years until his elevation to the House of Lords by Mrs Thatcher in 1979. At 98, he is the Inn's oldest bencher. It is particularly fitting that he presented this painting to the Inn, being closely acquainted with all represented. Quintin Hogg (Lord Hailsham) was a firm friend from student days. and Lord Renton had sponsored Mrs Thatcher's admission to Lincoln's Inn and has remained a staunch friend and admirer.

Andrew Collender

From left to right: standing: Lord Widgery, Sir Robert Megarry, Lord Denning; seated: Mrs Thatcher, Lord Hailsham.

A Hemicycle of Lawgivers
by George Frederic Watts (1817–1904)

Watts's fresco, painted 1854–60, carries the perspective of the Great Hall into an imaginary realm where the lawgivers of history meet in a 'hemicycle' or semicircle. Evidently inspired by Raphael's *School of Athens* in the Vatican, the composition has a particular effect here, where the circle is completed at dinner by the barristers and students of Lincoln's Inn, the lawgivers of the future, who with their predecessors encircle the bench as lawgivers of the present.

The artist was not yet 30 when he proposed the project. He wanted the opportunity of painting a 'true' fresco, in which the colours are laid onto the wall mixed with egg in fresh plaster, and so offered his services free, and used his friends as models. The fact that he was not being paid may have affected the speed of progress on the work, and the Inn had frequently to press him. When it was finished, however, he was warmly entertained, presented with an antique cup containing 500 sovereigns and told by the Treasurer that 'no time had been too extended' for this so satisfactory conclusion. Like many similar experiments it is somewhat unstable chemically and has required several exercises in conservation.

Watts rapidly developed his career in other fields, especially portraiture; the Inn has his superb portrait of Lord Selborne (1891). His appointment as one of the original members of the Order of Merit gives some indication of the stature during his lifetime of this largely forgotten Victorian artistic giant.

Mark Ockelton

Alumni Around the World

OVERSEAS CONNECTIONS

Michael Wright

Lincoln's Inn has been accepting students from overseas jurisdictions for many years. The first reference to an 'overseas member' in the records of the Society appears to be on 4 March 1681, when an entry in the Black Books records that the Moroccan Ambassador '...was pleased to enter his own name in the book, as a member thereof ...'.

The Inn's influence overseas was extended by its members' participation in the colonization of America and in particular the founding settlement at Jamestown, celebrating 400 years in 2007. Although the settlement was largely financed by members of the Middle Temple, one of the founding members, and the first elected president, was Edward-Maria Wingfield of Lincoln's Inn.

With the growth of Empire, the Inns became a leading provider of education to colonial lawyers who were expected to return to practise in their own countries. Their distinctive contribution comes from the thousands of barristers who have been called to the Bar of England and Wales and have contributed enormously to the spread and influence of the common law abroad. Most of these have quietly passed into history, but they have left an indelible mark on the development of jurisprudence in their countries. The following pages have space for only a small sample of contributions from former students. But the influence of the Inn is clear, both on them and the countries of which they write.

Lincoln's Inn has always attracted large numbers of overseas students and there are over 2,000 members now practising in a wide range of jurisdictions from Australia to Zambia within the Commonwealth and beyond it to from America to Taiwan.

In 2006 there were over 200 new students from overseas jurisdictions. The majority each year are from Malaysia, Bangladesh, Pakistan, and the Caribbean. In recent years Finnish, Russian, Chinese, Bahraini, Jordanian, Polish, South Korean, and Brazilian students have all studied at the Inn, neatly circumnavigating the globe. The importance of these links to spreading the common law tradition cannot be overestimated, and the Inn will do its best to ensure that they continue to be nurtured into the future.

GENTLEMEN THINKING

Bola Ajibola

I began my struggle for admission to Lincoln's Inn as a student at the tail end of December 1958 but did not succeed until Michaelmas term 1959.

Curiously, at that time I had observed some eminent gentlemen walking on the grass where signboards were plainly and openly pegged to 'keep off the grass'. I was always wondering why these gentlemen should claim exemption from this warning while others obeyed it. One day I asked an elderly barrister why they were walking on the lawn. He replied: 'Those gentlemen are exempted from the rule, they are having some serious and confidential discussion and thinking about legal matters which require a lot of serious attention but above all they are benchers of Lincoln's Inn.'

Over forty years thereafter, when I was honoured with the membership of the bench as an honorary member, a friend then asked me about my feeling concerning my noble elevation. I replied that my first delight, which I considered to be the foremost achievement, was to walk on the grass so that others too may look upon me as 'a gentleman thinking' while walking on the grass at Lincoln's Inn. It is a status that cost me about thirty-eight years of my life to achieve. My gratitude must go to the late Sir Michael Kerr of blessed memory, who introduced me to our Inns of Court as a suitable, 'fit and proper' person to be given the great honour of a bencher.

THE AMERICAN INNS OF COURT

Randy J. Holland

The idea for the American Inns of Court originated with Warren E. Burger, former Chief Justice of the United States and a friend of Lord Denning. In 1977, Chief Justice Burger led a delegation of lawyers and judges on a visit to the English Inns of Court as part of an Anglo-American exchange. He was fascinated by how the English Inns trained barristers and instilled high standards of excellence, ethics and civility. He was so impressed he decided to explore ways of adopting the English Inns' training methods in the United States.

A proposal was refined over the next two years. Chief Justice Burger with Judge Wallace and Judge Christensen concluded that, while there was much to be learned from the English system, there were significant differences in American legal education which would require the American Inns of Court to develop their own distinct pedagogy.

The first American Inn of Court was chartered on 12 February 1980, and met in Provo, Utah, under the leadership of Judge Christensen. Later that year, Judge Christensen met leading British lawyers including Lord Elwyn-Jones, then Treasurer of Gray's Inn and former Lord Chancellor. His subsequent article, 'The Concept and Organization of an American Inn of Court: Putting a Little More "English" on American Legal Education', was published in *Federal Rules Decisions* in 1982. Although many American Inns of Court are affiliated with law schools and have law student members, their focus is on lawyers who have already been admitted to the Bar. As Justice Sandra Day O'Connor wrote in her Foreword to their history: 'The typical American Inn of Court includes judges, experienced lawyers, law professors, and new lawyers as well as law students.' The American Inns of Court meet each month and conduct a skit or moot that, in the English tradition, is either preceded or followed by a meal.

Today nearly half the federal judges in the United States and over one-fourth of all state judges are active or alumni members of an American Inn of Court. Over 28,000 practising lawyers are currently active members and another 65,000 are alumni. There are 400 chartered American Inns of Court throughout all of the United States.

A significant factor in the success of the American Inns of Court has been its relations with the four English Inns of Court, and specifically with Lincoln's Inn. There has often been a speaker from the English Bar or bench at

William Penn 1644–1718

William Penn, Quaker founder of the English Province of Pennsylvania, trained for a legal career at Lincoln's Inn, which at the time (1660) was described as 'the most prestigious law school in England'.

Penn was the son of Admiral Penn of the English Navy and Margaret Jasper of Rotterdam. At the age of 16 he went up to Christ Church, Oxford, where he acquired a reputation as a 'hard student, a skilful oarsman, an adventurous sportsman'. He had an exceptional memory, an excellent knowledge of history and theology, read Greek and Latin, and was fluent in French, German, Dutch, and Italian. However, Penn ran up against the conformist atmosphere of Restoration Oxford. He absented himself from chapel but attended meetings of Thomas Lee, a follower of the Quaker George Fox. Penn was fined by the College authorities. This aroused the young non-conformists to open rebellion. They paraded the streets, refused to wear the gown, and tore off the vestments of those who did. Penn was soon expelled from university.

Penn plainly had an attractive personality and genuine humour. Within his wide circle of friends was the King himself. Charles II enjoyed Penn's company, and would allow their meetings to go on for hours, irritating the courtiers who were kept waiting. His close friendship with the the royal family gave rise to totally unfounded rumours that Penn was a Papist and Jesuit in disguise. Indeed, Penn was arrested for suspected treason after James II (another of his close friends) fled London in 1688. The Privy Council examined him as to his association with James, but Penn made it clear that, while he was, and remained, a friend of James, he did not agree with his policy or views.

In 1670, Penn took part in a meeting at Gracechurch Street and was arrested on a trumped-up charge of 'tumultuous assembly against the peace of the King'. Questioned as to the legal ground for his arrest, the Recorder broadly asserted 'upon the Common Law'. Penn asked for 'clarification' and was told roundly that it was based on 'many adjudged cases'. Penn ridiculed the Recorder in front of the jury by saying 'if it be common, it should not be so hard to produce.' The result was an acquittal, not accepted by the trial judges, who imprisoned both Penn and the jury! The transcript was on the streets of London the next morning becoming an instant 'bestseller'.

Penn became convinced that Parliament would never permit religious toleration in England and approached the King with a petition for a charter to establish an English province in America. On 24 February 1681, he was granted about 40,000 square miles of North America, the largest English land grant ever made, in exchange for two beaver skins to be given annually to the King.

Charles II asked Penn to name the new province. Penn suggested New Wales which the King rejected. Penn tried 'Sylvania' next. The King accepted this but, to the embarrassment of Penn, prefixed in his own handwriting 'Penn' to 'Sylvania'. Penn was so embarrassed that he petitioned the King to have the annotation removed. He even proffered 20 guineas to the secretary of the Privy Council. Penn himself later suggested in a letter, not wholly convincingly, that the King's annotation was actually in honour of his father.

Penn drafted the first constitution for the province and granted toleration for all faiths; in advance of his time, he included provision by the state for education, marriages, legal proceedings, registers, bail, and dispute resolution through mediation and arbitration. At independence, it was Penn's constitution that became the model for the Constitution of the United States.

Penn's enlightened attitude extended to native Americans. Notwithstanding his grant from the King, he reached an amicable and lasting agreement with the Lenni Lenape tribe for the purchase of lands from them.

In 1693 Penn wrote a treatise on peace between nations advocating an international parliament for the discussion of international issues rather than war and bloodshed. His parliament was even to include the Sultan of Turkey and the Czar of Russia. In memory of Penn's contribution to international peace, United Nations Day is celebrated on Penn's birthday.

Peter Castle

William Penn buying off the claims of the Lenni Lenape (Delaware) Indians 1683.

the American Inns of Court annual meeting. In 1990 Lord Goff of Chieveley issued a challenge: the British Inns would indict George Washington for treason, if the American Inns would defend him. The trial was held in the Great Hall of Lincoln's Inn. Witnesses included George Washington, Thomas Jefferson, Benjamin Franklin, and Lord North. At the conclusion of the trial, a bench of three distinguished jurists, two from England and one from the United States, voted unanimously to acquit President Washington.

The American Inns of Court participate in the Pegasus Scholarship Trust exchange programme. Young British barristers come to the United States each year to visit American Inns of Court and learn about the American legal system. Conversely, young American Inns of Court members visit Great Britain to learn about the English legal system. Since 1996, the American Inns of Court have overseen a legal exchange programme in cooperation with the Commercial Bar Association, which arranges placements of Temple Bar scholars in barristers' chambers each year. The scholars also meet the most senior law officers, visit Lincoln's Inn and meet the Treasurer, Under Treasurer and distinguished members of the bench and Bar. The first international American Inn of Court was chartered in April 2006 in London. Its founders included Peter Castle, a bencher of Lincoln's Inn, and Janie Castle, both of whom reside in the Inn.

In 2007 the four English Inns will commemorate the 400th anniversary of the first British settlement in the New World, in Jamestown, Virginia, by dedicating a plaque in recognition of the Anglo-American common law heritage.

Chief Justice Burger summarized his pride in the organization he inspired and worked to create in the words: 'The American Inns of Court will remain the greatest legacy of my tenure as the Chief Justice of the United States.' Lincoln's Inn, renowned for its international efforts to promote the rule of law, helped make Chief Justice Burger's dream a reality.

INSPIRING ROLE MODELS

Sujata V. Manohar

A decade after the end of the Second World War, when I joined Lincoln's Inn in 1954 as a student from Oxford, there were two distinguishing features of the Inn. It had, among all the Inns of Court, the best library because it escaped bombing, and it had a conspicuous presence of overseas students, mostly from the Commonwealth. An Indian from Lincoln's Inn, Kuldeep Singh, was the President of the Inns of Court Students' Union. He later became a Judge of the Supreme Court of India. I was the editor of the Inns of Court students' magazine, *GLIM* (an acronym for the four Inns of Court). Ashok Desai, the former Attorney General of India; Milon Banerji, the current Attorney General of India, and Dipankar Gupta, former Solicitor General of India are from Lincoln's Inn. Dipankar Ghosh and S.B. Mukerjee became distinguished lawyers. Of the first generation of women

Cornelia Sorabji, one of the first women to practise law in India and a champion of women's rights.

High Court judges in India appointed in the late 1970s, Manjula Bose (Calcutta) and Leila Seth (Delhi) were members of the Inn. Leila Seth later became the Chief Justice of Himachal Pradesh. Shankar Dayal Sharma, former President of India, was the only Indian honorary bencher of Lincoln's Inn when I became one in 1997. Now Milon Banerji has joined me.

There is an interesting photograph in Lincoln's Inn of an Indian woman in a typical Parsee Gujarati saree. She is Cornelia Sorabji (1866–1954), who shared the same call as Lord Denning. She came from a Parsee family in Bombay, and later converted to Christianity. In 1889 she sought admission to Bombay University. In the application form there was no column for a female student, and the university had to amend its rules and its form to accommodate her. Sorabji became the first woman graduate in India. She went on to Oxford and was the first woman to study civil law there. She qualified in 1894, although she was not called to the Bar (Lincoln's Inn), until 1921, having had to wait for legislation to enable women to be admitted.

Back in India, Cornelia Sorabji was only allowed to practise on condition that she would not appear in court and would confine her practice to advising pardanashin ladies. After the Indian Legal Practitioners Act was amended in 1923, she was enrolled as an advocate in the Calcutta High Court on 24 November 1924. She appeared occasionally in court, but became an active champion of women's rights and a social reformer. At a time when a woman was associated with the law only figuratively – as a blindfolded emblem holding the scales of justice – Cornelia brought the figurine down from the tallest spire of the court building and breathed life into her in the courtroom. It was a remarkable achievement, considering that even now women judges and lawyers constitute less than one per cent of the profession in India. Cornelia Sorabji's photograph at Lincoln's Inn should inspire all women who aspire for a career in law.

The Supreme Court of Madras in session (early nineteenth century).

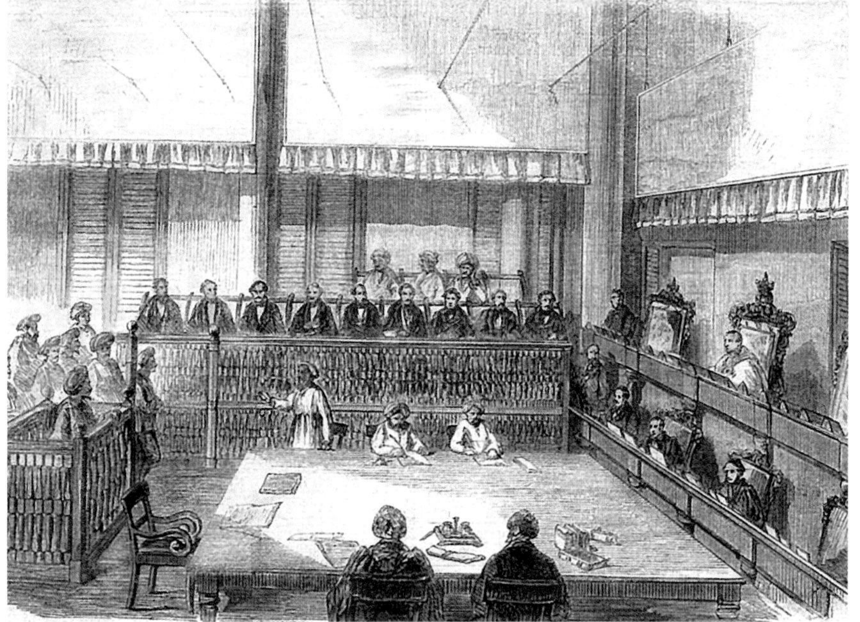

K.P. Jayaswal

The stamp issued in India to commemorate the centenary of the birth of K.P. Jayaswal (1881–1937), distinguished lawyer, historian of India, and Sanksrit scholar, called to the Bar by Lincoln's Inn in 1910. His daughter, Dharamshila Lal (1910-1976), was also called to the Bar by Lincoln's Inn, in 1935, and in 1937 was enrolled in the Patna High Court becoming the first woman barrister to practise in Bihar, where she became one of the foremost advocates.

THE INN AND THE AUSTRALIAN BENCH

Kenneth Handley

The impact of members of the Inn on Australian law has been considerable. Members of the Inn made a particularly significant contribution to the development of the Australian legal system in the nineteenth century. They include the first and third Chief Justices of New South Wales, who held office for forty-one years between 1825 and 1873. It is even more remarkable that the first three Chief Justices of Victoria, who held office between 1852 and 1892, were also members. Other members have made and are making contributions in Australia but nothing can compare with those made by these early Chief Justices.

The first Chief Justice of New South Wales (1825–37) was Sir Francis Forbes, who had been called in 1812 and read with Edward Sugden, later Lord St Leonards. Forbes was a civil libertarian who established trial by jury in criminal cases and upheld the freedom of the press against the Governor's attempts to control it. He was described as 'the model of an excellent judge'.

Far left: Sir Francis Forbes, Chief Justice of New South Wales 1825–37.

Left: Sir Alfred Stephen, Chief Justice of New South Wales 1845–72.

The third Chief Justice of New South Wales (1845–72) was Sir Alfred Stephen, who was called in 1823 and emigrated to Tasmania in 1825 to become its Solicitor General and Crown Solicitor. He was appointed a puisne judge of the Supreme Court of New South Wales in 1839 and its Chief Justice in 1845. He was an exceptional judge.

The first Chief Justice of Victoria (1852–7), Sir William à Beckett, was called in 1829 and emigrated to Sydney in 1837. His progress at the Bar was rapid and he was appointed Solicitor General with a right of private practice in 1841. He became an acting judge of the Supreme Court of New South Wales in 1844 and its resident judge in Melbourne in 1846. When Victoria became a separate colony he became Chief Justice. His conduct as a judge was greatly admired.

Sir William Stawell, the second Chief Justice of Victoria (1857–86), was called at Lincoln's Inn in 1839. He practised on the Munster Circuit until 1842, when he saw forty hats on the Circuit and not enough work for twenty, and emigrated. He was admitted to the Victorian Bar in 1843, became Attorney General in 1852, and Chief Justice in 1857. He held office with great distinction.

The third Chief Justice (1886-92), George Higginbotham, who refused a knighthood, was called in 1853 and admitted to the Victorian Bar in 1854. He was Attorney General for the Colony between 1863 and 1868, and then returned to the Bar. He was appointed a puisne judge of the Supreme Court in 1880, and its Chief Justice in 1886. His judgments were lucid, elegant and concise.

Direct contributions of this kind declined at the end of the nineteenth century because most members of the Australian Bar now had their legal education in Australia, and English and Irish members of the Inn no longer sought fame and fortune in this country.

In more recent times links have been maintained through members of the Inn who have been called to one of the Australian Bars, the appointment of Australian judges as honorary benchers, and the Inns of Court Fellowship at the Institute of Advanced Legal Studies.

Wu Ting-fang, diplomat and law reformer

The earliest Chinese name entered in the Black Books was Ng Achoy, on 26 January 1877. Better known as Wu Ting-fang, a more carefully selected and more intellectual name, he was one of a handful of men who played a vital role in the legal and political changes in the transition of modern China.

Wu Ting-fang was called to the English Bar by Lincoln's Inn on 26 January 1877, and returned to Hong Kong to practise as a barrister. Like many other members of the Inn, his main interest later diverted to politics. In 1880, he was appointed Hong Kong's first Chinese legislative councillor by a controversial liberal Governor, Pope-Hennessy, and played a significant part in the early social and economic changes of Hong Kong.

Wu was later run out of town by the stuffy colonial society of the time. In 1882 he joined the Chinese service as a Legal Advisor and was involved in the drafting and negotiations of the Sino-French Treaty 1885 and the Treaty of Shimonoseki 1895, under which Taiwan was ceded to Japan.

From 1896 to 1910 he served as Minister of Imperial China to the United States, Spain, Cuba, Mexico, Peru, and Japan. His readiness to look at international affairs from a Western point of view helped persuade many Westerners in turn to take an occasional glance at things from the Chinese point of view. When he was recalled from the US by the Emperor, a newspaper article regretted his parting: 'We shall miss the clever pointed saying with which his subtle wit enlivened the monotony of after dinner speeches; and we can only hope that his government has given him "something better", and us a successor who is something like him.'

The emperor not only entrusted 'something better' to him, but also something of greater importance. Wu was appointed Minister of Law Reform and assumed the task of reforming Chinese laws. He recommended the opening of the ports for trading, the state regulation of foreign trade, and the abolition of harsh laws and cruel punishment to achieve the abolition of extraterritoriality, so hated by the Chinese people. Having been trained in England, he also made attempts to introduce the jury system.

His efforts brought, among other things, the new Criminal Code of Great Ching, with the abrogation of certain cruel corporal punishments, the first ever Commercial Code, and modern civil and criminal procedures. This reform represented a new era in Chinese legal history because of its foreign elements: for some 3,000 years prior the Chinese legal system had maintained its heritage with virtually no foreign influence.

In 1911, Wu Ting-fang, as representative of anti-Ching revolutionaries, held successful peace talks in Shanghai with Tang Chao-yi, representative of the Ching government. After the foundation of the Republic of China in 1912, he held prominent civil, judicial and diplomatic posts in the government, such as Minister of Justice, Minister of Foreign Affairs, until his death in 1922.

Huijian Zhu

Wu Ting-fang, when Minister of Imperial China to the United States.

A DISTINGUISHED LINE

Frank Stock

Wu Ting-fang (profiled on the previous page) was amongst the first in a long line of Hong Kong practitioners called by the Inn who accumulated considerable distinction. In 1882, a few years after Wu, Dr Ho Kai was also called to both Bars. He became a Member of the Royal College of Surgeons and Senior Equity Scholar and Senior Scholar in Real and Personal Property, Lincoln's Inn, and he too made his way in due course to the Hong Kong Legislative Council. He was knighted in 1912, the first Chinese to have been accorded that honour.

It is invidious to choose names from more recent history, but no Hong Kong/Lincoln's Inn history would be a worthy one without mentioning Sir Oswald Cheung SC, Patrick Yu Shuk-shiu, and Martin Lee SC. Sir Oswald was called to the Bar in England in 1950 and returned to Hong Kong, where he sat first as a magistrate and then enjoyed considerable success at the Bar. He was a Legislative Councillor and later a member of the Executive Council, and when he died in 2003 the Chief Justice described him as 'the doyen of the Bar and ... one of the most distinguished Hong Kong citizens in the second half of the twentieth century'. Patrick Yu read PPE at Oxford and was called to the Bar on the same day as Sir Oswald, with whom he later shared chambers. His reputation was that of an outstanding advocate and mentor to many, among them Martin Lee, who later rose to the top of the professional tree. Martin Lee was called in 1965 and to the Inner Bar in Hong Kong in 1979. He was Chairman of the Bar here from 1980 to 1983 and has been a member of the Legislative Council since 1985, later founding Chairman of the Democratic Party.

The Lincoln's Inn Society of Hong Kong was established by Gerald Godfrey QC, who was a Vice-President of the Court of Appeal. The Society is strong, boasting seventy-six practising members, plus eighteen members of the judiciary. In June 2004 it held a dinner in honour of Lord Millett, then Treasurer. Among those attending were the Chief Justice and the Under Treasurer. In 2005 there was a dinner in honour of Sir Anthony Mason, formerly Chief Justice of Australia, who is an honorary bencher as well as a non-permanent member of the Hong Kong Court of Final Appeal. The musical interlude included a staged piece from *Trial by Jury*, with words suitably adapted for the occasion.

Above: The Old Court House, Singapore, completed in 1827. Today, altered beyond all recognition, it forms the core of Singapore's old Parliament House.

DOWNING THE DELIGHTS

Sukhwant Singh

I was enrolled in 1980 as an overseas student from Singapore. For homesick students, the warm Library was somehow reassuring; everything we imagined a good old library to be. Besides, it was the best place to get to know the girls. And we enjoyed our dinners. On Fridays, when fish was served in small portions, we jostled to sit next to a Malaysian Muslim who brought his own delicious home-cooked food, which the kitchen heated and solemnly served him. He always had far too much, so we undertook the joyous task of properly disposing of the excess, then downed the delights with a good red wine. When I was called to the Bar in July 1981, who should turn up at the admissions ceremony but Lord Denning himself. I still cherish the photo I have of the two of us.

I learnt (and enjoyed) a lot – lessons which still are dear to me as a senior partner in Friedman Lurie Singh & D'Angelo, Western Australia's largest 'plaintiff' law firm, which I helped found in March 1996.

THE INN AND THE FOUNDING OF UPPER CANADA

Guy Holborn

In 1991 the Inn co-operated with the Law Society of Upper Canada to mount a major exhibition on the Inn's heritage in the Society's museum at Osgoode Hall in Toronto. The Inn has from time to time lent pictures and other items for exhibitions, but this venture was unusual in the range and number of items made available for loan and for it being, probably uniquely, an exhibition overseas. A splendid opening ceremony was attended by the Treasurer, Sir Michael Davies, and myself.

The exhibition was to mark the 200th anniversary of the Constitution Act of 1791, which established the colony of Upper Canada (now Ontario) and granted it its system of government and justice on the British model. Lincoln's Inn can trace connections to every corner of the world. But there can be few other overseas jurisdictions where the Inn can claim such an intimate connection with the very founding of a new country as Canada.

The Act of 1791 was introduced by one of the Inn's most distinguished members, William Pitt, actively supported by two of his Lincoln's Inn colleagues, Henry Addington, who was then Speaker of the House of Commons, and William Grant, a former Attorney General of Quebec with a thorough knowledge of Canada, and newly elected to Parliament under Pitt's patronage the previous year. (Pitt and Addington of course also feature in the roll of Prime Ministers.) Sir William Grant's reputation among lawyers is as a highly distinguished equity judge, being Master of the Rolls for nearly seventeen years (while remaining for much of the period an MP, as was then permitted).

Below: Model of The Golden Hind *presented in 1931 by Viscount Bennett, Prime Minister of Canada and Honorary Bencher.*

The two members of the Inn central to the story, however, were John Graves Simcoe, admitted in 1773, and William Osgoode, called to the Bar in 1779. Simcoe, a protégé of Addington, was appointed the first Lieutenant-Governor of Upper Canada in 1791, and he picked his former Inn associate Osgoode as his first Chief Justice and key advisor. These energetic figures were in large measure responsible for establishing the political, social and judicial structures of the province. Simcoe vowed to bring to Ontario a constitution 'which is the very image and transcript of that of Great Britain'. Simcoe and Osgoode also had the development of a legal profession in the colony as one of their earliest concerns. What emerged in the establishment of the Law Society of Upper Canada in 1797 was a self-governing body with high standards both for admission and for conduct, very much modelled on the ethos of the Inns of Court. To this day the members of its governing body are known as 'benchers', though the fact that they are all freshly elected every four years by a vote of the whole membership perhaps indicates a less deferential approach to tradition than that to which we are accustomed.

So began a long and fruitful connection between the Inn and Canada. The most remarkable Chief Justice to follow in the steps of Osgoode was John Bevereley Robinson (1791–1863) who was to hold the post for thirty-three years. He was already Solicitor General for the province when at the age of 24 he was admitted to Lincoln's Inn in 1815. His diaries survive, though apparently their record of his time at the Inn is mainly confined to assessments of the daily menus, such as 'I dined again at the Hall on boiled chicken and roast mutton'. In the twentieth century, Supreme Court Chief Justices Laskin, Dickson and Lamer all accepted invitations to become honorary benchers. The appointment of Beverley McLachlin, the current Chief Justice of Canada, as an honorary bencher in 2000 represents the latest link in the chain of continuity.

FAMOUS SONS

Collin Sequerah

I was called to the Bar on 26 November 1985. I still remember how hard it was to study for Bar Finals in the Library when surrounded with so many literary riches, coupled with its impressive architecture. My attention was too easily absorbed inspecting numerous treasures, particularly the ancient Black Books. I shall also never forget the excellent dinners served at the Inn in the awesome ambience of the Great Hall, especially at my Call Day. I still retain the menu served that night. I am truly proud to belong to such an ancient heritage.

The Inn's influence is widespread in my country. Malaysia's second Prime Minister was the late Tun Abdul Razak, while our third Prime Minister was the late Tun Hussien Onn. Both were called as barristers at Lincoln's Inn. The title of Tun preceding their names is the highest title that is bestowed upon Malaysians.

I should also mention, among the many famous sons of Lincoln's Inn, Sultan Azlan Shah, the present ruler of the State of Perak and formerly the Yang Di Pertuan Agung or King of Malaysia. He has also held the office of Lord President and thus the head of the Malaysian judiciary. He is a bencher of the Inn, as is Justice Gopal Sri Ram, a Court of Appeal judge and the President of the Inn's Alumni Association in Malaysia. Justice Gopal Sri Ram holds the distinction of being the only judge who was elevated straight to the Court of Appeal without first having to serve in the High Court.

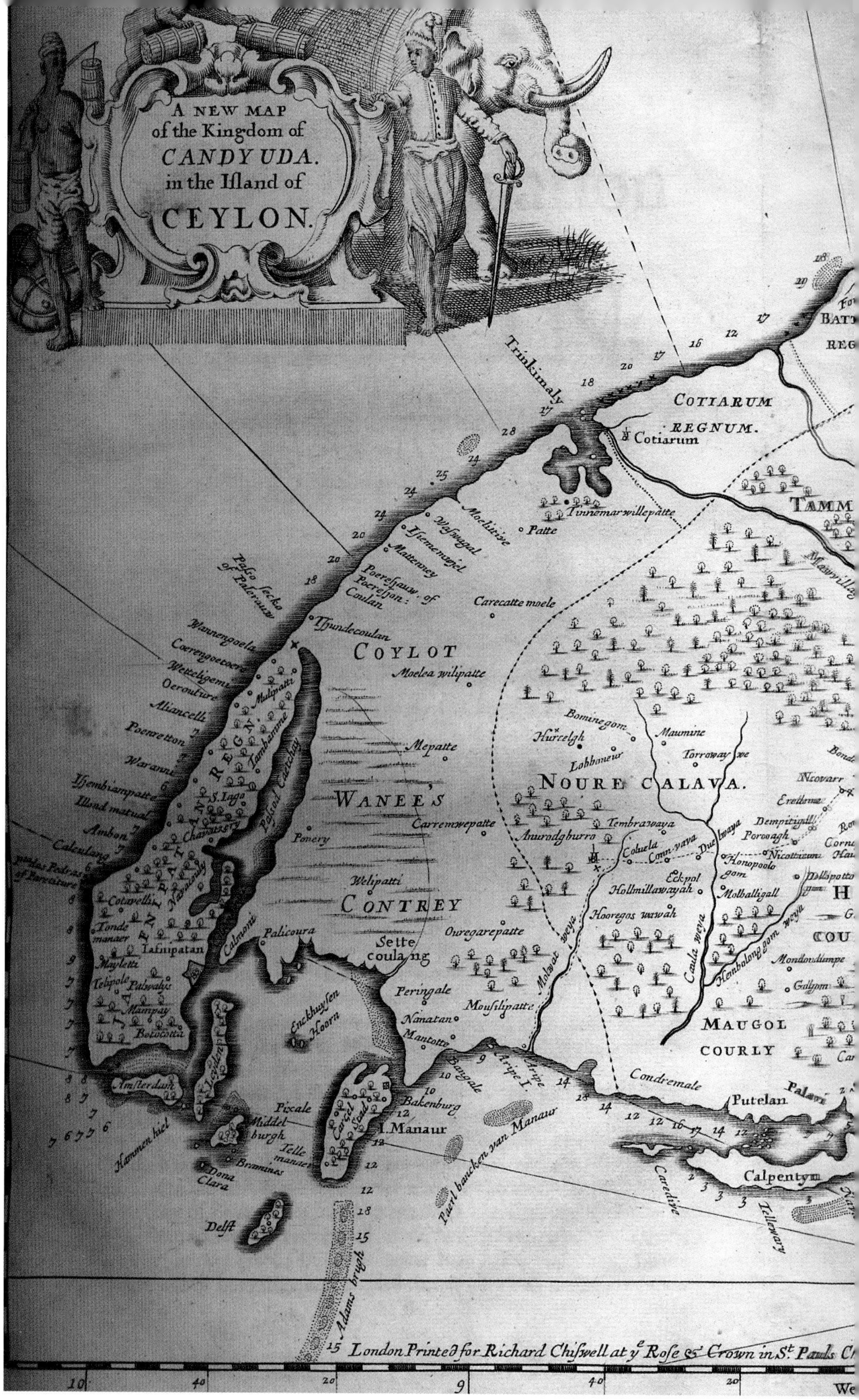

THE SRI LANKAN CONNECTION

Desmond Fernando

Lincoln's Inn has been a very popular Inn for Sri Lankans. The late Sir Lalitha Rajapakse was called to the Bar in 1925. He returned to Sri Lanka and practised as an advocate of the Supreme Court, and was appointed Queen's Counsel in 1944. He was the first Minister of Justice of independent Sri Lanka and held this Office from 1947 to 1953. He returned to practice at the Bar when he left office. Subsequently, he was appointed Ambassador to

Above: From the Library's copy of Robert Knox An Historical Relation of the Island Ceylon *(1681).*

France in 1967 and from 1968 to 1970 he was High Commissioner for Sri Lanka in the United Kingdom.

Another highly distinguished member of Lincoln's Inn was called in in 1944) was the late Professor T. Nadaraja. After achieving first class honours in both parts of the Law Tripos at Cambridge and winning the Bond Prize for Roman Law and the Davies Prize for English Law, he went on to be awarded the Buchannan Prize for his performance in the Bar Finals. He was Professor of Law at the University of Colombo from 1951 to 1968, when the Department of Law was made a Faculty, and he served as Dean of the Faculty until his retirement, when he became Emeritus Professor. He was an expert in the field of Roman-Dutch law.

In more recent times, Mr L.C. Seneviratne was called to the Bar by the Inn in 1958 and is in active practice, having become a President's Counsel in 1987. He was a member of Sri Lanka's delegation to the Indo-Sri Lankan Talks in Thimpu in 1987. He enjoys an outstanding career as a lawyer, in both the original court and the appellate court. He has twice served as Deputy President of the Bar Association, most recently in 2005–6, He has also served with distinction as a member of the Law Commission, and has been a member of the Council of Legal Education, which administers the professional educational institution of the legal profession in Sri Lanka, the Law College.

A number of young people have recently returned to Sri Lanka after being called to the Bar by Lincoln's Inn.

EUROPE: SOME SHARED HISTORY

Nicolas Bratza and Edite Ligere

Europe is, of course, a relatively modern idea. At the Inn's founding there was little concept of Europe; rather, there was an appreciation of 'Christendom'. However, in the early years of the Inn the principle that secular learning had value was beginning to spread across Europe. The fourteenth century saw the foundation of more universities than had occurred in the previous three centuries. Ideas thrive in places of learning and ideas were the lifeblood of the 'new learning' of the fifteenth century; the Inn played its part in that process.

Humanist circles sprang up from Oxford to Cracow and from Salamanca to Lvov. All paid homage to the greatest of their number – Erasmus, whose close friend was Sir Thomas More, barrister and bencher of Lincoln's Inn. Erasmus wrote *Moriae Encomium* (In Praise of Folly, published 1511) in More's house. and dedicated it to him.

In the twentieth century, the Inn played a key role in the creation of the single most important instrument of the Council of Europe, the European Convention on Human Rights. Drafting of the Convention is generally acknowledged, correctly, to be a British effort. The name usually associated with it is that of David Maxwell Fyfe, later Lord Kilmuir, who was indeed heavily involved. But the starting point for the drafting of the Convention by the nascent Council of Europe was in fact an earlier draft convention produced by the British section of the

International Council of the European Movement, in which Maxwell Fyfe was also a leading light. Brian Simpson, in *Human Rights and the End of Empire: Britain and the Genesis of the European Convention*, fixes the authorship of the first draft: 'Maxwell Fyfe did not himself undertake any drafting. Instead, John Harcourt Barrington was hired for this purpose at a fee of one hundred guineas, which was, in accordance with British legal tradition, paid to him after prolonged delay.' Barrington was called to the Bar by the Inn in 1930 so we can say with some justification that the ECHR turns out to be the product of 100 guineas' worth of honest Lincoln's Inn effort.

The Inn has been represented for over twenty-five years at the European Court of Human Rights. Like the present incumbent (Nicolas Bratza), his two immediate predecessors, Sir John Freeland and Sir Vincent Evans were members and benchers.

The Inn has for some time run a successful European law educational programme, founded by Paul Heim CMG, another member and bencher. Paul Heim had a distinguished career at the heart of a number of European law institutions, as Administrator at the Commission and Court of Human Rights and the Council of Europe and as the Registrar of the European Court of Justice. Lectures are given by distinguished speakers on topical 'Euro' subjects; a high point of the year is the annual Sir Thomas More lecture. There are annual trips to the European Court of Human Rights in Strasbourg, the European Court of Justice in Luxembourg, and the International Criminal Court in The Hague. The Inn attracts a significant number of European students and offers European scholarships and exchange programmes with European students.

The Inn's history coincides with the history of modern Europe. We can be confident that the Inn will continue to play a full part within European legal institutions.

A YEAR OF MEMORIES

Danish Iftikhar

Lincoln's is the most widely recognized Inn in Pakistan, largely because Muhammad Ali Jinnah, the first Governor General of Pakistan, was a member of this Inn when he was called to the Bar. Since that date if not before, Lincoln's Inn has been popular amongst Asians, particularly Malaysians and Pakistanis.

Delighted as I was to come to this historic society, which has so many prominent politicians, judges, leaders and the like from all over the world, I was particularly happy to discover that the people I met here were friendly, sociable, and warm. This was true not only of students and barrister members but also of the staff. The Treasury Office and catering staff were always sensitive and helpful, despite dealing with a daunting number of enquiries.

The diversity of the members of the Inn, perhaps greater than all the other Inns combined, was reflected by its policy of catering for all needs, even serving Halal meat from time to time. I took the opportunity of attending eighteen dinners in all, comfortably in excess of the compulsory number. The dinners provided an opportunity to meet friends, some old, some new, and the atmosphere of the Inn took me by surprise every time I attended.

The Call Day was the biggest experience of all. As the day got closer, I was overtaken by excitement whenever I thought about the transformation that was about to take place. I was happy that my family was present to witness this event. One by one the names were called and when mine was announced, my face, which had been beaming all day, was filled with a nice, wide smile, showing feelings of both joy and satisfaction. I could not let go of the call certificate even when I was out of the Hall, and kept looking at my name in the list out of sheer joy. This was just the start, I thought to myself, yet the end of a year of memories I would cherish for a long time to come.

Danish Iftikhar with his mother, Parveen.

Muhammad Ali Jinnah

The future founder and first Governor General of Pakistan was admitted to the Inn on 5 June 1893 having passed the Preliminary Examination. His name had appeared in the admission register as Jinnahbhai. His request to the Inn to change its records (on the right) was granted in 1895 and he was called to the Bar on 29 April 1896, when he returned to practise in Karachi. He came back to England many times in pursuit of independence for his country. In the 1930s he also practised in London on Indian appeals before the Privy Council.

His life-time ambition came to fruition on 14 August 1947 – Independence Day of Pakistan.

Muhammad Ali Jinnah 1876–1948 (Howard Barron) presented to the Inn by the Pakistan High Commission in 1965.

35 Russell Rd
Kensington
W

30th March 96.

To
The Steward
Lincoln's Inn

Sir, I beg to inform you that I am desirous of dropping the ending of my name namely bhai – meaning Mr. As I explained to you. It being customary in India, at the time of my admission I happen to give the name after that fashion. I shall feel much obliged if you can and will alter it without its causing you any great inconvenience the name should be M. A. Jinnah or in full Mahomed Alli Jinnah

Hoping you will see that it is altered at any rate before my call.

Yours faithfully
M. A. Jinnah

254 No. 31.

Lincoln's Inn – Mahomedalli Jinnahbhai of Karachi, India, Aged 19 years, the First Son of Jinnahbhai of Karachi, Sind, India, aforesaid, Merchant, was Admitted into the Society of this Inn on the Fifth of June in the Fifty sixth year of the Reign of our Sovereign Lady Victoria by the Grace of God of the United Kingdom of Great Britain and Ireland Queen Defender of the Faith and in the year of our Lord 1893, and hath thereupon paid to the use of the said Society the sum of Eight pounds seven shillings and six pence.

Admitted by

Certificate of having passed Preliminary Examination.

Dated 25th May 1893.

Deposit £100.

+ Name altered to "Mahomed Alli Jinnah" by Order of Council 14th Apl 1896

HENRY PETER BROUGHAM, FIRST BARON BROUGHAM AND VAUX 1778–1868

Nowadays the name 'Brougham' is perhaps most widely associated with a peculiar form of closed four-wheeled carriage, drawn by one horse, which Lord Brougham himself designed when he was about sixty. He better deserves to be remembered as one of the most colourful members Lincoln's Inn has ever known, who combined the roles of lawyer, politician, educationalist, philanthropist, and polymath.

The son of a Westmorland squire, he spent his childhood and early youth in Edinburgh, where he had a brilliant academic career, first at the High School and then at the University, which he entered at the age of 13, to read Humanity and Philosophy. But his precocious thirst for knowledge soon led him into wider fields. A year later he formed the Juvenile Literary Society. He developed an intense interest in experimental science and at 17 published two papers describing experiments upon light and colour in the journals of the Royal Society. Such was his reputation that he was elected a Fellow of the Society at the age of only 25. In 1802 he played a leading part in launching the highly influential *Edinburgh Review*, to which in the course of the next ten years he contributed about a hundred articles.

Brougham was called to the Scottish Bar in 1800, but his political ambitions soon led him to London. In November 1803 he was admitted to Lincoln's Inn, and in 1808 was called to the English Bar. Thereafter he conducted a lucrative practice on the Northern Circuit, where he tormented weak judges, and, though not so strong in legal argument, could mesmerize juries by his eloquence. In 1820 he was elected a bencher of Lincoln's Inn, following his appointment as Attorney General to Queen Caroline. Thereafter his brilliant defence against the bill of divorce brought against her won him great fame and popularity with the public. In cross-examination he made rings round her livery servant, who had been called to give evidence as to her supposed adultery; the servant's evasive refrain 'Non mi ricordo' became a byword. The King and his supporters were less pleased by his performance. Only on his third application was Brougham made a King's Counsel in 1827.

In 1810 he had at last succeeded in obtaining a seat in Parliament, where, on and off, he remained a member over the next twenty years and achieved a matchless predominance by his personality, wit, and fearless oratory. During that period provisions for the extension of education owed much to his initiative. He played a crucial role in the establishment of London University in 1826. He was also a leading figure in the anti-slavery campaign.

Lord Brougham by Spiridone Gambardella, presented in 1934 by Mrs Heelis (Beatrix Potter), whose father was a member of the Inn.

His commanding influence greatly assisted the return of the Whigs to power in 1830. He then reluctantly accepted the office of Lord Chancellor. Lincoln's Inn elected him Treasurer for 1831 and Master of the Library for 1832. As Chancellor, he did much to improve the legal system. He reformed the Old Bailey and was responsible for the creation of the Judicial Committee of the Privy Council. He remedied many of the abuses of the old Court of Chancery. He also played a leading part in the passing of the Reform Bill in 1832 and the Slavery Abolition Act of 1833.

By today's standards, Brougham's oratory would be regarded as somewhat extravagant. During the course of one debate on the Reform

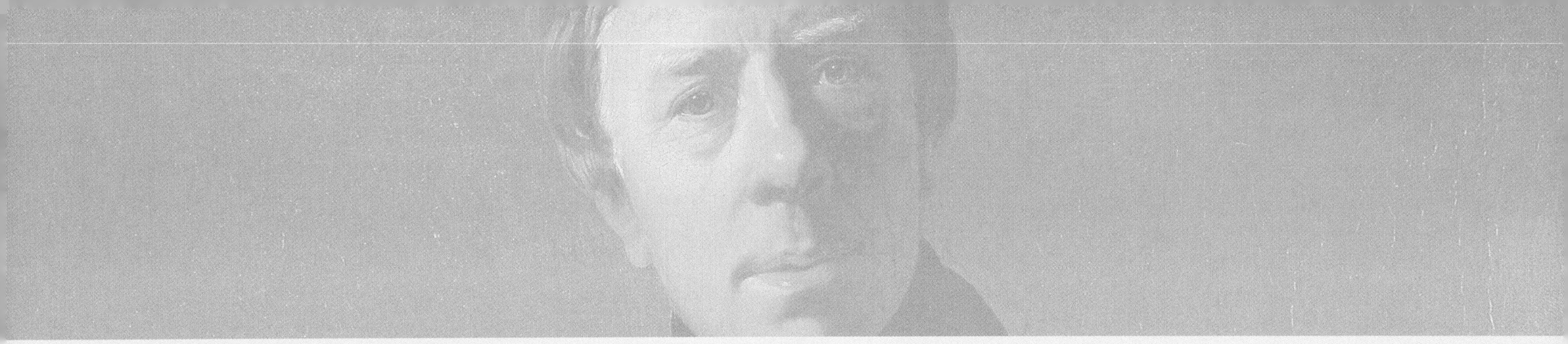

Bill, having refreshed himself by drinking three tumblers of unwatered negus, he ended on his knees, with his arms outstretched above his head, and only restored himself to the Woolsack with great difficulty. His conduct was never predictable. One flamboyant tour of the North did nothing to improve his reputation: quite improperly, he took the Great Seal with him, and then played games with it in the evening. He turned up at the Edinburgh races in the full regalia of Lord Chancellor's wig and gown.

The fall of Lord Grey's government in November 1834 effectively ended Brougham's political career. While he was a good-natured and congenial man, his obsessive vanity, self-advertisement, sharp tongue, and tactlessness had left him with too many enemies; his loyalty to his colleagues was also in doubt. He was never again offered office in government. He continued to introduce bills in the Lords on all manner of topics, particularly law reform. He remained a most active supporter of countless liberal causes. He wrote copiously and, to the end, maintained his interest in literature and experimental science.

'That very eccentric Lord Brougham', as Queen Victoria once described him, died in 1868 in his ninetieth year. Though he may not have wholly fulfilled himself, he had certainly lived life to the full.

Christopher Slade

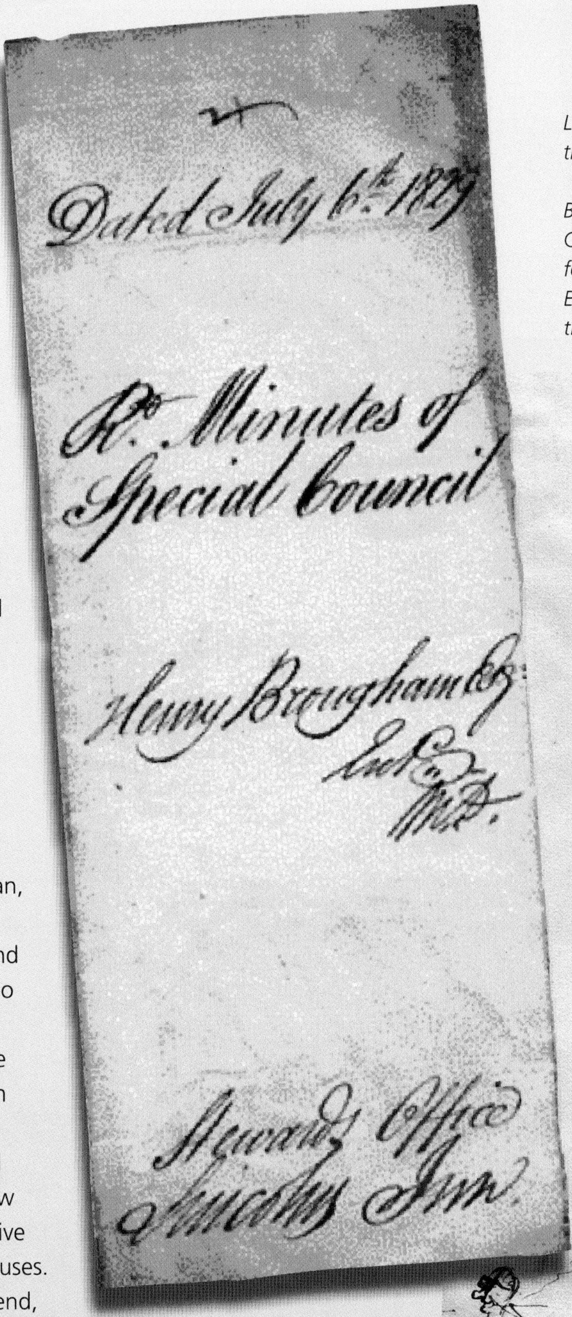

Dated July 6th 1829

Minutes of Special Council

Henry Brougham Esq

Stewards Office Lincolns Inn

Left: Council minutes July 1829, when Brougham was Keeper of the Black Book.

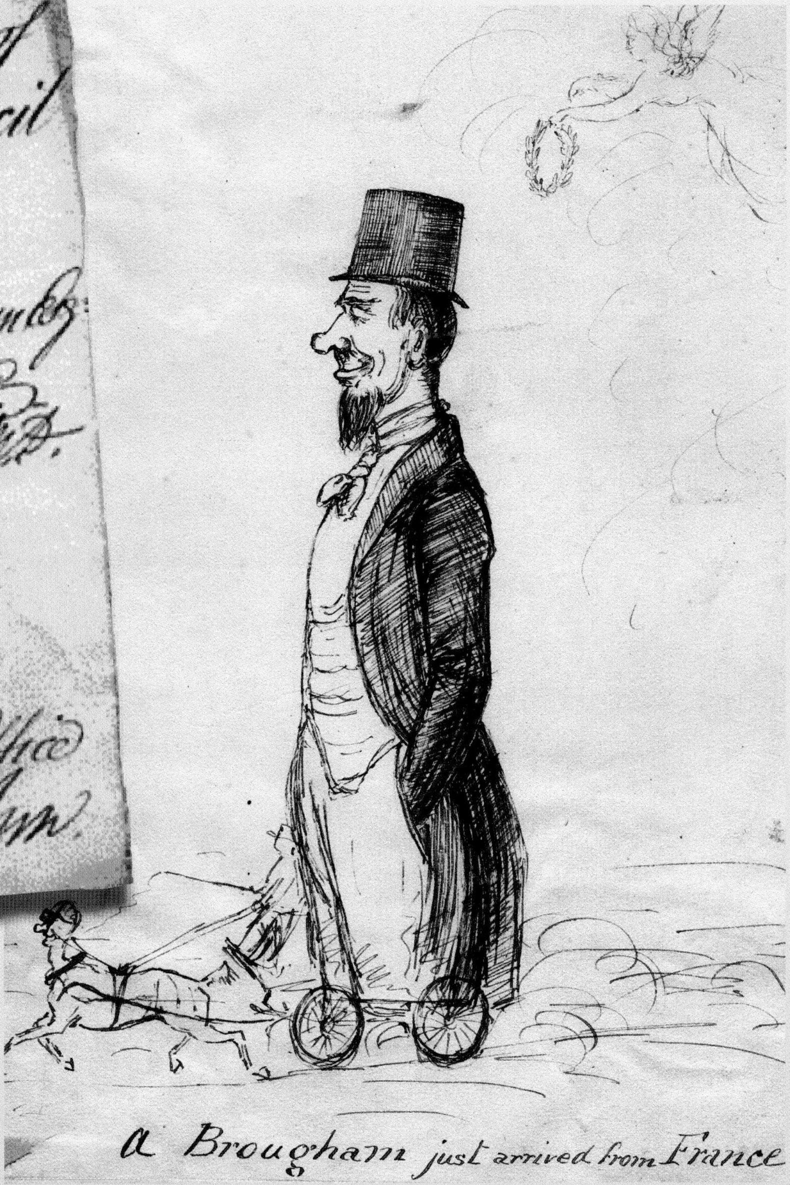

Below: Brougham spent much of the last thirty years of his life at Cannes. His French tendency, culminating in his attempt to qualify for the French National Assembly in 1848, evoked much ridicule in England, as in this caricature (an original pen and ink cartoon from the Library's Romain Collection).

Lifting the Bar:
The Women's Story

THE TRAILBLAZERS

Angela Holdsworth

'It was exhilarating. We had broken into a closed society. Mind you they weren't ready for us. On my application form each "his" had been crossed out by hand and replaced with "her".' Speaking to me in the 1980s, Theodora Llewellyn Davies, the second woman to be admitted to an Inn, remembered the culmination in 1920 of the long battle women had fought for admission. Ninety-two women had unsuccessfully petitioned Lincoln's Inn as far back as 1873, asking to be allowed to attend lectures. Christabel Pankhurst's application was similarly turned down thirty-one years later. In 1911 Gwynneth Bebb, an Oxford graduate with a first in jurisprudence, applied to sit the preliminary solicitors' exams. The Law Society refused because a woman was not a 'person' within the meaning of the Solicitors Act of 1843. Miss Bebb took the Law Society to court but both the High Court and the Court of Appeal dismissed the claim.

It took the First World War to shake traditional attitudes. By the end of the war women had shown themselves competent in all sorts of spheres previously thought unsuitable or beyond their abilities. Gwynneth Bebb, by then Thomson, was running the Legal Department of the Ministry of Food in the Midlands and had ambitions to practise as a barrister. In 1918 and again in 1919 she applied to join the Inn as a student. Her first application (referred to as 'a communication from a Lady') was denied, but the Inns set up a Joint Committee to report on the whole vexed issue of admitting women. One possibility mooted was for a separate Inn but, apart from the problems of financing, the Committee felt it to be 'in the interests of men and women alike that women should take their place with the least possible friction in the existing well-established order of the profession ...'. It was recommended that in all aspects of education, dining

Christabel Pankhurst's father, Richard, was a member of the Inn. Her petition to be admitted to the Inn was turned down in 1904.

and pupillage, men and women should be treated the same. The matter of dress was postponed, but rules devised later encouraged the perfect lady barrister to look as indistinguishable as possible from her male colleagues. All the Inns adopted the Report and awaited the Royal Assent of the Sex Disqualification (Removal) Act in December 1919.

Unfortunately Gwynneth Thomson was ill and unable to be admitted, as planned, on the 7 January 1920. The first woman to be a student at the Inn was Marjorie Powell, a lecturer in Political Economy at Manchester University. Gwynneth Thomson was admitted ten days later. Sadly she died the following year, never achieving her ambition to be called to the Bar. The first to be called by the Inn, in 1923, were Mithan Ardeshir Tata from Bombay, who had come to London four years earlier at the age of 20 to further the cause of women's franchise in India and Mercy Ashworth, a former schools inspector, who was 53 at the time of her call.

Mercy, typically of the first women at the Bar, seems barely to have practised at all. Interviewed at the time of her call by the *Daily Chronicle*, she was clearly aware of the difficulties ahead: 'None of us knows yet what the future of women barristers is likely to be. It depends so much on the attitude of solicitors.' As Patrick Polden puts it in his excellent piece, 'Portia's Progress: women at the Bar in England 1919–39' (*International Journal of the Legal Profession*, November 2005), the successes of getting there 'stand out in high relief from the melancholy fate of most of those who set out on the route in the early days'. His research shows that once the enthusiasm of breaking through the barrier had died down, few women were called to the Bar between the wars. The dropout rate before call was high, finding chambers was difficult, and few who practised were noticeably successful.

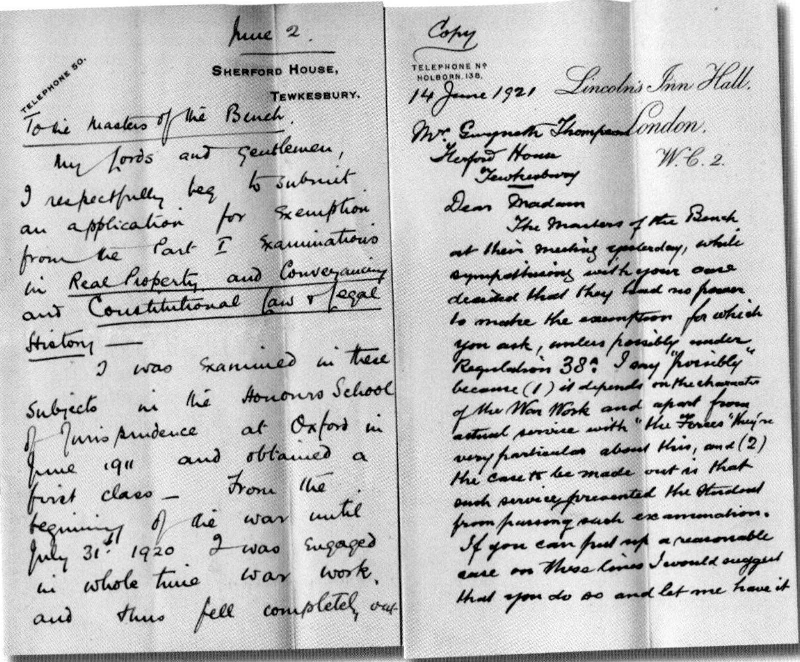

June 2.

TELEPHONE 50.

SHERFORD HOUSE,
TEWKESBURY.

To the Masters of the Bench.

My Lords and Gentlemen,
I respectfully beg to submit an application for exemption from the Part I Examinations in Real Property and Conveyancing and Constitutional Law & Legal History —

I was examined in these subjects in the Honours School of Jurisprudence at Oxford in June 1911 and obtained a first class – From the beginning of the war until July 31st 1920 I was engaged in whole time war work, and thus fell completely out

Copy

TELEPHONE Nº HOLBORN. 138.

14 June 1921

Lincoln's Inn Hall,
London,
W.C. 2.

Mrs. Gwyneth Thompson
Sherford House
Tewkesbury

Dear Madam
The Masters of the Bench at their meeting yesterday, while sympathising with your case decided that they had no power to make the exemption for which you ask, unless possibly under Regulation 38a. I say "possibly" because (1) it depends on the character of the War Work and apart from actual service with "the Forces" they're very particular about this, and (2) the case to be made out is that such service prevented the Student from passing such examination. If you can put up a reasonable case on these lines I would suggest that you do so and let me have it

Correspondance between the Inn and Gwynneth Thomson in which she unsuccessfully requests exemption from Part I Examinations.

Theodora Llewellyn Davies hung up her wig and gown within two years of being called: 'I decided that I'd rather devote my time and interest to joining my husband and the work he was doing. In those days it wasn't very customary for married women to work, apart from domestic duties, and it didn't really occur to me that it would be possible to combine the two.' With a marriage bar operating in most professions, Theodora's decision was not unusual. Others such as Alix Kilroy, who joined the Inn as a student in 1925, abandoned law, attracted by the more secure life and expanding opportunities in the Civil Service, where she later became the first woman principal.

For those who persisted at the Bar, life was not easy. In the lean inter-war years competition for work was intense

Mercy Ashworth 1868–1943: called to the bar on 26 January 1923 together with Mithan Tata, though it was Tata, having been admitted as a student three days before Ashworth, who would have walked onto the dais in Hall in front, to become our first woman barrister.

Helena Normanton and Rose Heilbron, the first women KCs 1949

and women faced additional obstacles in the shape of clerks and solicitors, used to working with male barristers, who thought women too risky. Some chambers operated an open 'no women' policy, but others found convenient excuses. Hannah Cross, called by the Inn in 1931, applied to several sets for pupillage. The pattern was the same. She was welcomed by the head of chambers but would later be told that after discussion with the clerk it was impossible to take her on because of the lavatory facilities. Eventually she was given a place at 1 New Square on the understanding she would use the public lavatories in Lincoln's Inn Fields.

Lincoln's Inn, in common with the other three, had a policy of equality, but Hannah Cross found members chilly and learned not to sit at some of the more popular tables at lunch. In his biography, Sir Arthur Underhill, then a bencher, recalls the first night a girl student dined in the Inn. He comments that she was very pretty and he and a fellow bencher decided to be friendly. His colleague, having told all the young men to be nice to her, ended up by saying, 'I certainly have never seen anyone better qualified to pervert the ends of justice.' Underhill goes on to profess surprise that women, often successful as litigants in person, were not more successful at the Bar but notes that 'the solicitor branch will not venture to employ them, lest, if anything should go amiss, the beneficial client should blame them. A considerable majority of our girl barristers have married fellow members and have given up attempting to practise, rightly, considering marriage a whole-time job.'

Daily Mirror *June 1921.*

The exceptional successes of the early years – Helena Normanton, Rose Heilbron (in 1949 the first women KCs), and Elizabeth Lane (appointed to the High Court in 1965), were not members of Lincoln's Inn. Perhaps not surprising, as for several decades the Inn had the fewest women of all the Inns and the Chancery Bar proved one of the hardest places for a women to succeed. Patrick Polden suggests that since it lacked any equivalent to the poor persons' procedure and dock brief, it was harder to make a start.

Reading for the Bar had its attractions. Leila Seth, the mother of the author Vikram Seth, found it compatible with running her house and raising her children because the only attendance required was to take her dinners at the Inn. She was first in her Bar exams, earning plaudits in the press (she later became the first woman Chief Justice in India). But despite such triumphs, the number of women practising scarcely increased in the post-war years. In 1955, 3.2 per cent of barristers were women. Twenty years later they comprised only seven per cent of the profession. Helena Kennedy, writing in 1978 (*The Bar on Trial*), found the same obstacles continuing to block progress. 'At a meeting of Heads of Chambers in 1975, attended by about eighty men and two women, one of the elder statesmen said, "Our prime concern must be for those young men with wives and mortgages." Few will ever accept that a woman is not merely working to pass the time until she has children, or else to provide a second salary in a male-provider's household.'

Cherie Booth's feelings that had she known the obstacles she might have chosen a different career (see below) are shared by many of her contemporaries and perhaps account for the small percentage of women barristers in the 1970s. There were still chambers with a 'no women' policy. (Until it was amended in 1990, the 1975 Sex Discrimination Act did not apply to barristers and chambers.) Women were understandably reluctant to join a profession which was perceived as unfriendly. In 1976 there were only two women High Court judges, none in the two higher courts, and only four practising silks out of a total of 366. The Inn's first QC was Patricia Coles in 1974 and its first bencher, Mary MacMurray QC, was elected in 1986.

Even with equal numbers entering the profession, roughly the case today, it may well take a couple of decades (as in other spheres such as the BBC) for a critical number to rise through the system and become a significant force at the top of the profession. But, as Tessa Hetherington points out below, while the position of women at the Bar has vastly improved, many leave mid-career. They need encouragement from role models to stay the course. All the more important that the Inn today has two Lady Justices of Appeal, two High Court judges, twenty-five women benchers (including seven honorary) and expects Elizabeth Appleby QC to be our first woman Treasurer (as an ordinary bencher) in 2008.

STARTING IN THE 1970S

Cherie Booth

I sometimes wonder whether I would ever have chosen the Bar as a career if I had known how badly the odds were stacked against women at the time. When I was called to the Bar in July 1976, women made up only sixteen per cent of entrants – and this was the first year that the figure had crept into double figures. The group picture of the eighty-one members called to Lincoln's Inn that day illustrates the point perfectly. There we are at the front – a dozen females in a sea of men, just behind the all-male benchers. But it wasn't just the numbers against women. It was also the culture of the time.

No less an authority than Professor Glanville Williams QC warned how difficult it was for women to

Cherie Booth's Call Day July 1976.

succeed at the bar. In the 1973 – not 1903 – edition of his classic text *Learning the Law*, he stated, 'Practice at the Bar is a demanding task for a man; it is even more difficult for a woman ... It is not easy for a young man to get up and face the court; many women find it harder still ... A woman's voice also, does not carry as well as a man's.'

Fortunately, the scholarship committee of the Inn had a more enlightened view and granted me both a Hardwicke Entrance Scholarship and then the Kennedy Scholarship. I am very grateful to them. Without this help, I doubt whether I could have afforded to go to the Bar at all. And without the support and friendship of many colleagues here, it would have been much more of a struggle.

For there were plenty more obstacles for aspiring women barristers to overcome. Finding pupillage was difficult in an era when chambers would quite happily declare that they had a policy of no women at all or restrict women tenants to one in case, they said, of a double pregnancy problem.

Nor could you escape the male-dominated world when you finally qualified. It is etched into my memory how an entire circuit robing room fell silent in shock and horror when it dawned on them that I intended to change there as well.

I remember, too, being warned that unless I wore a long-sleeved white shirt, a black knee-length skirt and a black jacket so I looked like a nun, I would be thrown out of the tiny women's robing room that is now the disabled toilet on the first floor of the Royal Courts of Justice.

It is no wonder that the attrition rate amongst women barristers was much higher than that of men. By 2002, the Inn's records show that I was the only one of those female entrants still in full-time practice, while nineteen of our male counterparts are still colleagues at the Inn.

The position, thankfully, has been transformed. Today, women make up roughly a third of the practising Bar and almost 50 per cent of entrants to the profession. The excellent Bar Equality and Diversity Code, which treats discrimination of all kinds as professional misconduct, means that those old robing room attitudes have long gone (or at least been driven deep underground).

What remains the same, however, is the Inn itself, which still provides valuable scholarships on merit to ensure the profession remains open to all and continues to provide a community based on friendship. It is why my experiences at Lincoln's Inn, both then and now, have been overwhelmingly positive.

Many of the friends I made back in 1976 have gone on to become leaders of the Bar (and indeed our country!). They were never infected by the old-fashioned attitudes of the time; never saw women as inferior. They helped ensure that these out-dated views belong in the past to the benefit of not just our profession but the system of justice as a whole.

The Rt Hon Dame Mary Arden (left) and the Rt Hon Dame Janet Smith (right): the Inn's first women in the Court of Appeal.

WOMEN AT THE BAR TODAY

Tessa Hetherington

I was called to the Bar in 2004, in an intake which was 48.7 per cent female – a stark contrast to 1976 when Cherie Booth joined. Certainly as a student on the Bar Vocational Course, a participant in the various excellent training activities organized by the Inn, a pupil, and in my relatively brief time as a practising barrister, I have had little cause to feel that my gender has put me at a disadvantage. I am on the management committee in chambers, which is also headed by a woman, and certainly have no qualms about the ability of my voice to carry, both in chambers and in court.

That said, I am aware that my positive experience as a young female barrister working in public and employment law from a progressive set of chambers may not be shared by all those working in the more traditional settings of the Bar, where life as a young woman may be a much more isolated experience. The old robing room attitudes described by Cherie still live on in some spheres; one of my contemporaries was taken aside during a mini-pupillage and told that it was inappropriate for her to be wearing a trouser suit.

Equally, I am aware that as a woman without children or other family commitments, I am able to cope with the long hours and financial insecurity that goes with life at the Bar. Women may now make up roughly a third of the practising Bar, but many leave midway through their

career, and women make up a smaller proportion of self-employed barristers than of employed barristers – testament, perhaps, to the difficulties of juggling family responsibilities with the unpredictable demands and precarious financial rewards of the self-employed Bar. It was certainly a factor that weighed in my mind when choosing my career path. The work of the Inn in providing scholarships to assist young barristers is invaluable in enabling progress to be made, as is the increasing acceptance by at least some sets of chambers of more 'family-friendly' ways of working and the need to protect the position of women during maternity leave and beyond. Combining motherhood and the Bar is still, however, undoubtedly fraught with difficulty.

Furthermore, those aspiring to the senior ranks of the profession and the judiciary are still faced with an extremely male-dominated picture. Less than ten per cent of senior judges are women. As a barrister practising in public law, it is still fairly unlikely that I will appear in front of a female judge. The chances would be even slimmer were I to be appearing in the Chancery Division. The appointment of the first female judge to the House of Lords was long overdue, and the outcome of the recent QC appointments process, in which thirty-three women (forty-nine per cent of female applicants) were successful, is encouraging. The reform of the appointments process for both QCs and judges and the concurrent abolition of 'secret soundings' is extremely important, but until the numbers of women in the judiciary and senior Bar reach a 'critical mass' and it becomes clear that the concepts of 'merit' being applied are not such as to disadvantage women, female barristers may still be reticent about seeking such positions.

I would certainly agree with Cherie that the position has been transformed since 1976. I hope that there is more transformation to come.

Life in the Inn

IN CHAMBERS

David Ainger

The French origin of the word 'chamber' suggests that for centuries chambers were used both as places for work and rest, rather like rooms in a hall of residence or Oxbridge college. Indeed, in 1571 the Inn had licensed 'bedmakers'. Women servants were acceptable, but in 1657 benchers ordered that it was 'against the ancient orders and customs' of the Inn that any women 'lodge' in the Inn at night time. There had been a ban on fornication in the Inn since the late fifteenth century, with a hefty fine of 100 shillings if committed in chambers but the smaller sum of 20 shillings if discovered in the gardens or Chancery Lane. Chambers then were not numbered but given names such as 'Le Horsmill' or 'Le Douffhouse' (dovecote). An Order of the Privy Council of 1574 imposed a maximum of two barristers for every set in Lincoln's Inn and the two Temples.

It seems that successful barristers did not share their chambers. Thus, James Bacon who became Vice-Chancellor in 1870 describes in his *Recollections* a visit to Sir Charles Wetherell's chambers in 5 Stone Buildings as:

> *A sight not to be forgotten. One of the largest rooms on the ground floor – they had once been handsomely furnished – large mirrors – gilded arm chairs, console table, etc. But the chambers had not been painted nor even whitewashed for many years – all was dirty and in decay. Upon the marble top of the gilded table lay Wetherell's Court suit – velvet coat and breeches – shoes and buckles an inch thick in dust – papers, letters, books, scattered in heedless profusion. At the end of the room a partition formed by folding doors within which lay his bed – a deplorable little four-poster with hangings which once had been white ...*
>
> *I was once summoned to a consultation with him. It was during [a] debate on the (1830/2) Reform Bill. His faithful clerk showed us into the large room – and told us (in confidence) that his master had come in very late – or early – and was in bed, but would soon be with us. We waited (that is I and the Client ...) for at least a quarter of an hour when, after we had proposed to the Clerk that we should come at some more convenient opportunity, the doors were suddenly thrown open and Wetherell came out in his night shirt. He – nothing abashed – said 'Oh! It is you – Come in'*

Old Buildings 1906 (Alan Stewart).

> *– and threw himself back on his bed – decently drawing the sheet over him. We approached – not without some awe – and then and there we had our consultation. That he had read his brief there could be no doubt – for he knew the case perfectly … He dismissed the Attorney but asked me to wait a few minutes while he dressed. He immediately put on a dressing gown and proceeded to shave. His toilet apparatus was of the simplest kind – upon the shelf of a very handsome mantelpiece of carved Carrara marble stood a small pot with soap in it – and a well-worn brush. Against the wall was a piece of broken looking glass and a dilapidated razor lay behind it. With this he shaved himself rapidly, certainly and steadily – not at all like a man who had been up the greater part of the night – and without any other preparation (washing was out of the question) he huddled on his clothes and we went together to the V-C's Court where in a very short time we utterly demolished [the opposition].*

Sir Charles Wetherell was able to shave but 'washing was out of the question'. It is not clear whether this was because there was insufficient water available or because time was short. The Black Books give only a patchy picture as to plumbing or mod-cons; though when the subject is referred to, it is not always for the squeamish. A mid-seventeenth-century entry in the Black Books noted that pedestrians in Chancery Lane had been 'annoyed with Chamber [*note the word*] Pots [*or presumably the contents*] thrown out of the windows …'. Punishment for future conduct of the same kind was, if the offender was tenant of the chambers, to be debarred from dining (cooking of food was not, I suspect, allowed in chambers) or if a 'laundress' that she be expelled. In 1771 the tenant of chambers in Gatehouse Court was permitted at his own expense to make a 'water closet' and to 'lay on New River Water' for it.

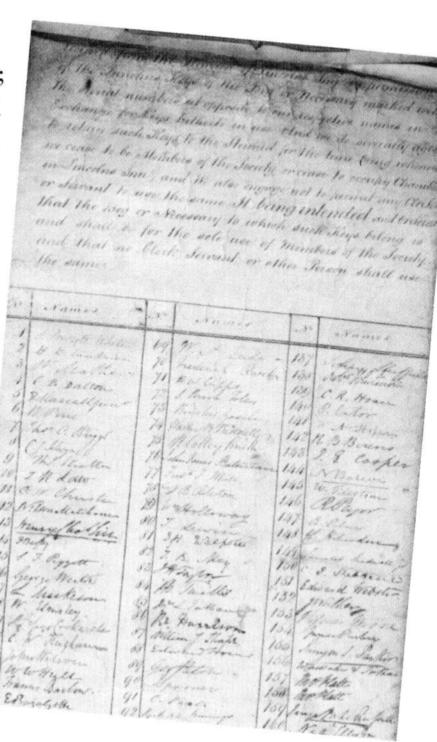

The Black Books contain several references to wells and pumps, and it looks as though by 1784 Stone Buildings had available a supply of water from the New River Company, which brought water by aqueduct from Chadwell and Amwell (near Ware) to large open-air cisterns near Sadlers Wells. From there it was diverted, as required, into mains formed by hollowed-out, abutting elm tree trunks and surrounded by puddle clay, to flow by gravity towards the City and Holborn (hence Lamb's Conduit Street). (I once had a pupil who had a lavatory seat made from a section of such a main.) The Black Books record that in 1814 wooden pipes in the Inn were to be replaced by iron pipes. At a Council in 1866 there are references to two pumps in the Inn, one supplied with hard water from a well and the other from a tank holding soft New River Water. Only the latter was found to be wholesome so the handle of the former was removed.

It is not clear when the Inn first installed a water closet. There are numerous references in the Black Books to a (communal) 'House of Office'. Council was so concerned with control of its use at the time of the Plague in 1665 that it ordered that the locks on the various doors be changed. It was moved when Serle was developing New Square and concern was expressed that it should not be too near the Kitchen Garden; its location was fixed with care in April 1692. This is recorded by the cornerstone set into the north-west corner of what is now

Above: The Boghouse key book c1840.

Left: Serjeant Snubbin's Chambers in Old Square, Pickwick Papers *(1901 edn).*

A tenant in 1927 sought permission to install an Elsan in chambers. Despite this persuasive advertisement, preserved in the tenancy files, permission was declined.

A QUIET HOME IN OLD SQUARE

This charming flat is situated in one of the oldest portions of Lincoln's Inn, of which the original buildings date from 1518, and although so near London's busiest centres, it is secluded and restful, as if the peace of bygone centuries still lingered for a while. No. 18, Old Square, is approximately the same age as the historic Gatehouse. John Thurloe, Cromwell's Secretary of State, had chambers in adjacent buildings and in this square Disraeli was a student

The long-case clock seen in the entrance hall belonged at one time to the Duchess of Cleveland and came from Battle Abbey. There is a letter-box here that was in the possession of Queen Alexandra

A feature of the library is the unique collection of first editions, many of them signed by their authors and exceedingly valuable. There is also a collection of rare antique boxes. The large bookcase is a Georgian example in mahogany. The candle sconces in carved and gilt wood, came from Hawarden Castle and once belonged to Mr. Gladstone. The modern upholstered settee and easy chairs provide comfort and a note of informality. Antique Oriental rugs are used as floor coverings over parquet

A Japanese screen of exceptional charm, another piece of furniture that once belonged to Queen Alexandra and came from Marlborough House, conceals the fireplace and harmonises admirably with the mantel surround. An antique bronze Renaissance candlestick has been converted into a floor standard for use with the electric light

38

Feature on 18 Old Buildings, then known as 18 Old Square, Good Housekeeping *April 1932.*

16 New Square in 1989. It records that, 'On this site from 1693 to 1987 stood successive communal privies always known as The Boghouse'.

My recollection is that (as in 1665) the Boghouse had a number of locked doors with labels such as 'Benchers', 'Barristers', and 'Clerks'. That as recently as 1873 chambers were designed with little or no internal plumbing is suggested by the plan of the ground floor of the west side of Old Square published in *The Builder* for 29 November 1873. It shows five sets of chambers – two with two barristers' rooms with another for pupils and a fourth for the clerk (9 Old Square), and three with three rooms, one each for the barrister, his pupil(s) and clerk. Only one cupboard is shown serving 10 Old Square. On every floor of each staircase there was one long slim room with an entrance from the 'common parts' (possibly with a pan under the window). No wash basins are shown.

As to plumbing and heating, generally things do not appear to have changed much for the next eighty years. Sir Christopher Slade, who in 1952 became a pupil in chambers on the second floor of 8 New Square (where the 'resurrected' chambers of his father 'Pen' Slade QC had reopened after World War II), describes the situation thus:

> *The chambers were rough and ready ... They had no central heating or running water. China basins, in which people could wash their hands, were to be found secreted in cupboards with buckets below. More accurately, buckets were intended to sit below. On one particularly unfortunate occasion they were not there. At a drinks party ... the distinguished visitors were greeted by a stream of water running over the floor and down the stairs ...*
>
> *I sat by the coal fire in [my pupil-master's] room and one of my jobs was to transfer to the fire his cigarette ends when he misdirected them. Since he was a chain smoker and his direction was not particularly good, this was a boring chore. But he was ... very kind and entertaining ...*
>
> *My first conference of any importance took place on a bitterly cold winter's day, when a thick carpet of snow covered the Inn. An industrial magnate travelling down from the North with a team of henchmen, was to seek my advice on his financial affairs. I had prepared myself to the last degree for this encounter, but had not anticipated its preface. I heard a muttered question as the team assembled outside the door of my room, which was followed by*

> *[my clerk's] answer: 'No, I am very sorry, we haven't got one here. We are a bit primitive'. To which I heard the bellowed reply: 'Primitive! Pre-ice age, I would say'. So the very elderly magnate had to be directed to trudge over the snow to the Boghouse at the other side of New Square.*

Sir Christopher confesses that one of his less worthy motives for joining Lincoln's Inn *ad eundem* was to acquire legitimate access for himself to rather more civilized 'Members' facilities'.

Heating and lighting were of course amenities as important as sanitation. In 1817 the Treasurer entered into a lengthy agreement with the Gas Light & Coke Company 'for lighting the ground and buildings ... by means of a combustion of inflammable air usually called gas light'. Gas lighting seems to have been first installed in Stone and Old Buildings in 1862. Electrical lighting only came to the Great Hall and Library in 1885. In chambers, coals and candles were long the order of the day – so much so that whereas brief fees were quoted as say 2 guineas plus 2/6 for the clerk, the equivalent fee for a conference was instead augmented by 5 shillings, the extra 2/6 for the clerk being supposedly attributable to the cost of candles and coals necessitated by a visitor, a position that survived until the demise of guineas and separately quoted clerks' fees on decimalization in 1971.

Another significant change must have been the arrival of the telephone. Curiously it is mentioned only once in Volume 5 (1845–1914) of the Black Books. It appears that in 1886 the Metropolitan Fire Brigade recommended that for the protection of the Great Hall and Library 'telephone communication ... be at once established [with] our Fire Engine Station in Theobald's Road'. Certainly by 1961 most chambers, and probably most members, were on the phone, though I do recollect that the clerk of a leading silk was reputed always to apologize to any solicitor asking to talk to his principal by replying, 'I am very sorry, Sir, Sir Andrew does not come to the telephone.'

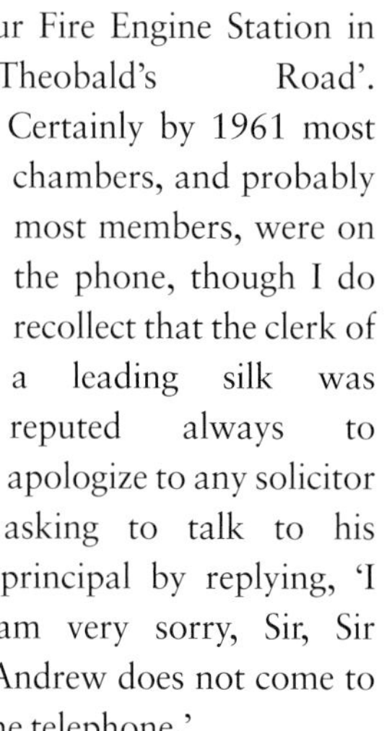

After the general, if not universal, acceptance of individual telephones by practitioners there followed the telex (mainly for communications overseas, the costs of which were frequently shared between sets), and the photocopier (initially very primitive and the paper smelly), followed rapidly by electric typewriters, fax machines, word processors, the web, e-mail, laptops, mobile phones, and electronic information. But a barrister's seemingly eternal need to browse and thus to have available law reports, textbooks and other reference material in 'hard copy' means that the need for chambers' libraries and, as the great fall back resource, the Inn's Library, is still as great as ever. Some things do not change.

Above: The Gatehouse from Chancey Lane, c1874.

Left: Lamplighters.

LEGAL FAMILIES

Martin Nourse

In their annual messages Treasurers often refer affectionately to the Lincoln's Inn family, by which they mean the bench, Bar, students and the staff. But as family connection is often influential in the choice of an Inn, the Inn is also notable for the many families who, through several generations, have contributed to its membership. It should perhaps be added that in recent times such connections have played no part in later success either within the Inn or in the profession at large.

Impracticabilities of research and space necessitate that mention be made only of families who, in the last 150 years, have given three or more successive generations to the Inn. The list may not be exhaustive. Top of it come the Clarkes, whose five generations start with Sir Edward Clarke KC (1841-1931), an outstanding common law leader of the Victorian period, who was Solicitor General from 1886 to 1892. He had two sons. His grandson was Judge Edward Clarke QC (1908-1989). His great-grandson is Peter Clarke QC, whose daughter Jessica, was called in 2006.

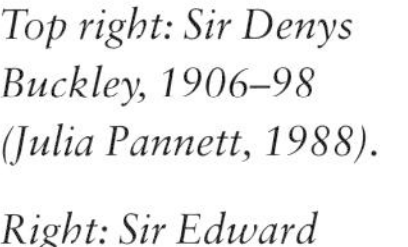

Top right: Sir Denys Buckley, 1906–98 (Julia Pannett, 1988).

Right: Sir Edward Clarke KC, 1841–1931, the first of five generations to be members of the Inn.

Next there are the Hoggs, who have produced two Lord Chancellors, father and son: Douglas, first Viscount Hailsham (1872–1950) and Quintin, Lord Hailsham of St Marylebone (1907–2001). (This feat has been equalled only by the Yorkes: Lord Hardwicke (1690–1764) and Charles Yorke (1722–1770) both Lincoln's Inn men of whom the latter survived his appointment by only three days). In the third generation are the Rt Hon Douglas Hogg QC, MP and Dame Mary Hogg, a judge of the Family Division.

When he retired from the Court of Appeal in 1915 Sir Henry Burton Buckley (1845–1935) became the first Lord Wrenbury. Two of his sons and one of his daughters were members of the Inn, the youngest son, Denys (1906–1998), himself becoming a Lord Justice. Sir Denys's daughter Jane is married to another former Lord Justice, Sir Christopher Slade. Their son, Richard, is a member of the Inn, as is Martin Buckley, a grandson of Lord Wrenbury and formerly Chief Registrar of the Companies Court.

There have been three successive generations of Parkers and four of Harmans. The first Lord Parker of Waddington (1857–1918) was a Lord of Appeal and the second (1900–1972) was Lord Chief Justice. The latter's nephew is Sir Roger Parker, a former Lord Justice. The second Harman, Sir Charles (1894-1970), son of a bencher, was a Lord Justice and the third, Sir Jeremiah, a judge of the Chancery Division. His daughter, Sarah is in practice at the Chancery Bar.

Other families with three successive generations are the Cassels, of whom the present representative is Sir Timothy Cassel QC; the Cohens, of whom the first, Lionel (1888-1973), was a Lord of Appeal: and the Lightmans, of whom the second, Sir Gavin, is a judge of the Chancery Division.

Some Lincoln's Inn families have themselves been interrelated. In an article of April 1928 announcing the retirement of my grandfather (Lord Justice Sargant), his replacement by Mr Justice (Frank) Russell and the replacement of the latter by FH Maugham KC (afterwards Lord Chancellor), the *Daily Mail* was able to point out that Mrs Maugham was a daughter of the late Lord Justice Romer and a sister of Mr Justice Romer, who himself married a sister-in-law of Lord Justice Russell.

The Maughams are now represented by the Lord Chancellor's grandson, His Honour Frederick

Above: 24 Old Buildings 1883 (Waldo Sargeant). John Cudworth Whitebrook lived and practised here for over fifty years.

A Child in Old Square

I was born in Lincoln's Inn in 1920. My father, John Cudworth Whitebrook, practised there and my parents lived in what was then 24 Old Square, now 24 Old Buildings. The turret room was my bedroom. It had eight walls and gas lamps as there was no electricity. We occupied the top floor; lower down Captain Stott, an equerry to George V, had a very elegant suite, including a ballroom and a large drawing room. Growing up in the Inn was paradise. The fruit man, who used to have a stand by the entrance, always gave me an apple when I got back from school. I had to pick my key up from the Porter's Lodge as it was too large to carry about. I did my homework in the gardens and went to sleep nightly with the 9 pm toll bell. At school everyone thought my father was a publican as I lived at Lincoln's Inn.

Apparently Cromwell's secretary, John Thurloe, used to live in our rooms. There was a ghost who made strange creaks in the building and we found hiding places where papers might once have been secreted behind the panelling. Mr Morley, who was in charge of maintenance, found human bones in the attic above our kitchen. It was thought they belonged to someone holed in at the time of the plague. Mr Morley refused to go up again and it took a bomb several years later to decide their fate.

My father had to move out after the bomb but returned to No. 24 when it had been repaired, continuing to live and practise there until his death, aged 87,in 1960.

Theresa Gibbs (née Whitebrook)

Above: A garden party for the America Bar Association 1924.

Above right: East side of New Square looking north c1922.

Marr-Johnson. The Russells and the Romers each enjoy the remarkable distinction of having produced three successive generations of appellate judges. The first Lord Russell of Killowen (1832-1900) was Lord Chief Justice, and the second and third (1867-1946 and 1908-1986 respectively) were Lords of Appeal. Sir Nicholas Bratza, a grandson of the second Lord Russell, is a judge of the European Court of Human Rights. Sir Robert Romer (1840-1918) was a Lord Justice of Appeal, his son Mark (1866-1944) was a Lord of Appeal and the latter's son Charles (1897-1969) was also a Lord Justice. His son is Ian Romer, who practised at the Chancery Bar.

It is likely that several overseas families have given, or will have before long, three successive generations to the Inn. Research is difficult because the Inn's database only starts in 1993 and so the Inn is dependent on memory and members keeping in touch for earlier details. However, the Amin family of Kenya are well on the way to three generations with Shaikh Amin, who was called by the Inn in 1952, appointed to the High Court of Kenya in 1985 and whose children Farah (called 1991) Omar (also called 1991) and Salah-El-din (called 1993) are all practising at the Bar; Farah in London, Omar and Salah-El-din in Kenya.

A 1950s PUPILLAGE

Peter Graham

My first encounter with Lincoln's Inn was in the spring of 1958. Although called to Gray's Inn, a fascination with real property law drew me to pupillage in 3 New Square. My pupil-master, Walter Wigglesworth, was one of the six counsel who made up the chambers on the first floor.

Badge porters, so named as they wore silver badges engraved with the Inn's arms to distinguish them as permanent members of staff, were traditionally responsible for keeping order. J.H. Buckthorpe, the last of them, retired in 1935.

As was the custom, the fee (paid by, not to, the pupil) was a hundred guineas. The whole atmosphere was old fashioned even by the standards of the 1950s. I was the only pupil and the pupil room was in the basement. I do not recall any natural light: illumination was provided by a single bulb in the centre of the room over the desk. Our clerk was president of the Barristers' Clerks Association. He was always every bit as formally dressed as the rest of the chambers. He lived in Woking – as I did; he travelled first class – I did not. During term-time, the dress code was strict: black short jacket and waistcoat, striped trousers and a 'silver' tie. Outside term-time, a business or, on Fridays, a country suit was called for. Of course no one ever told the pupil about this change and I duly turned up on the day after the end of my first term still wearing formal dress. Our clerk soon put me right – though I was not sent home to change.

My pupillage coincided with many acquisitions by the City of London for what became the Barbican development. There were some wonderful old titles to sort out, including, for example, a foreclosed long lease from around 200 years ago. We were also involved in the conveyancing that gave rise to the John Lewis site in Oxford Street and the Knightsbridge Green development. There were wills, some of which I was allowed to do 'almost by myself'. I most enjoyed the work on landed settlements, though it meant I had to acquire, on the run, a working knowledge of estate duty. The clients would complain about their high rates of tax: I would wish I was in a bracket that paid half that rate. Typically the conferences consisted of the instructing solicitor relaxing quietly in a chair in the corner – the accountant whom he had brought along would spar knowledgeably with Mr Wigglesworth. We hardly ever went into court – though it could not have been nearer. Very occasionally, however, we would be galvanized into action when it became necessary to rush across the road to get some heiress made a ward of court: I got to know the names of at least a couple of the rakes who sought to take these girls out of the country. The task done, we returned to our conveyancing books.

At the time I was commuting at weekends to Cambridge to take supervisions in pre-1925 real property. So the ultimate delight was working in chambers on a resettlement of land in the Republic of Ireland. The law there was still the 'English' pre-1925 law and we actually had to draft a disentailing deed. I took a copy of this to show those being supervised – perhaps pretending that it

was still part of the every day life of chambers. I doubt that any of them ever saw such a document again.

From the very beginning it had been made clear to me that I would not be able to take a seat in chambers and, towards the end of my pupillage, I was interviewed by the set 'downstairs', that is, on the ground floor of 3 New Square. But, passing the notice board in the Inn on my way to lunch one day, I saw an advertisement for a vacancy in the Office of the Parliamentary Counsel. And so began a career which was to give me a very different life, which I have much enjoyed. But, for many years, I used to wonder what life would have been like had I stayed in 3 New Square – one floor or the other. That was the most important reason why I subsequently applied to, and was fortunate to be accepted as an *ad eundem* member of, Lincoln's Inn.

REMEMBERING THE 1960s

Cenydd Howells

I was admitted to the Inn as a student in 1960 in the middle of my university career. In 1963, I enrolled in the graduates' course for the Bar finals run by the Council of Legal Education, then ensconced in the basement of 7

Stone Buildings. There we had excellent tuition from bright young practitioners such as Robert Walker, Gordon Slynn, and Peter Millett (all later law lords) and William Goodhart, now a peer. In June 1964 I was called to the Bar in Lincoln's Inn by the Treasurer, Lord Denning, already a judicial legend. An introduction quickly led to a six-month pupillage. No formal applications to chambers' pupillage committees and rules for selection in those days!

Once launched, work was thin. I regarded myself lucky to get one case a month at first and occupied the rest of my time in chambers editing part of a legal periodical, indexing legal books, and also preparing tutorials and lectures, which I delivered at various educational institutions in the evenings and at weekends. In time I became involved in variation of trusts and administration actions. The great bulk of work in chambers and, indeed, at the Chancery Bar, was squarely based on land law in all its aspects: trusts and estates and capital taxation (ie estate duty and the new capital gains tax). To draft a lease of a large city property was fairly common, as was the drafting of conveyances, settlements and wills. What now seems an oddity was the occasional wardship case, then dealt with in the Chancery Division, which introduced an element of variety and spice.

All fees were calculated in guineas. County Court work was not very common, but there was some. I recall one greyhound stadium company which was such a stickler for principle that it frequently sued dog owners for kennel fees of as little as £5, in respect of which I received a brief fee of 'three and two' (guineas).

Although the Second World War had ended 20 years before, memory of it remained. My head of chambers, Alfred Baden Fuller, had served in the Air Ministry, his very aged father (called in the 1890s) holding the fort until after the war. One senior member had been evacuated from Dunkirk and another had used his boat in this evacuation. Our clerk had served in Europe in the army. In one incident his life had been saved by his best friend, another clerk in the Inn. One very clear memory from the 1960s is of the sound of medals clanging as the new silks bowed to the judges on the first day of term after Easter. A substantial number of senior practitioners had distinguished war records.

Chambers were much smaller then than now. I do not recall any chambers of as few as two or three members, but sets of eight or nine were the average. Notably, there were few women practising at the Chancery Bar. We have in our present chambers today as many women tenants as there were in the whole of Lincoln's Inn for most of the 1960s.

Monday mornings were when judges dealt with 'chambers matters', that is, appeals from masters or matters referred by masters to them. On Wednesdays, one judge presided over the Companies Court, hearing petitions for winding up and other matters. On Tuesdays and Fridays, motions were heard, usually by other judges. On appointment, judges were assigned to one of two groups – A or B. *The White Book* contained strict tables of succession. Every writ and originating summons would on issue be allocated to one group or the other strictly alternately. Stories circulated that some solicitors in the 1950s frequently issued two writs or originating summons in the same case in order to avoid certain judges.

Long gone is the confinement of chambers matters to Monday and motions to particular days, as is the division into groups of judges. The flood of variations of trusts has almost ceased and estate duty has long been replaced. Virtually gone, but not quite, are the will construction cases. I have not heard of any administration action for a long time. Commercial contracts and injunctions (now called 'freezing orders') are much commoner.

So practice proceeds and changes.

POTPOURRI

Edna Chayen

Only in the mind's eye
Not in the place
Can you take from the peg
A student's gown,
Smile at the notice
Of 'spurs and sword
To be left outside'
And enter the hall

Vast but comfortable,
Softened by panelled wood
Overseen by portraits
Rich, gilt-framed,
Scarlet-robed judges.
Polished beams,
The tables
Stretch to infinity;
The benchers' dais.
Companionable,
Messes of four
From all the world,
Dine together

Call Day,
Waiting,
Name called,
Step forward,
Shake hands,
Bow.
Now a barrister,
Qualified to stand in court.
A pupil,
To be dropped in the deep end
And swim or .....

Dining in hall,
In your own gown,
With friends
In your messes of four.
Guest nights,
Grand nights and
Grandest of all,
Princess Margaret in gleaming pink,
Our new royal bencher,
How the champagne flowed.

Lunching in hall,
Year after year,
Same table,
Same faces,
Good fellowship,
Accustomed places.
Weddings in the old hall,
Weddings in the new.
Garden parties on the lawn,
Concerts in the hall.
The book-lined library;
Haven of peace.
Omniscient librarian,
Annotated volumes,
Where the clock could spin
From nine to three
In the search for a precedent.

All fragrant memories
Of the mind.

In the Library – waiting for call.

HRH The Princess Margaret, Countess of Snowdon

by Bryan Organ (b. 1935)

The portrait was commissioned by the Inn to celebrate the Princess's fortieth birthday in 1970. In 1997 I had the good fortune to discuss the painting with her. As well as having been our Royal Bencher since 1956, Princess Margaret had also been the Colonel in Chief of the regiment in which I served and which, coincidentally, had commissioned a more conventional portrait about the same time.

The Princess herself chose the artist. Bryan Organ had already made his name among a new generation of painters, his portrait of Mary Quant the previous year very much capturing the spirit of the era. In 2006 Bryan Organ told me that some at the Inn had not been happy with the choice of artist. Certainly when the painting was first put on display at the National Portrait Gallery before coming to the Inn it caused a sensation, with press coverage across the world.

On first looking at the picture the observer is struck by the depth of the background and its almost surreal imagery. In the Princess's words, the artist captured the clarity of her public life and the unseen and less public trials and tribulations of her private life. In conversation, Bryan Organ would not be drawn on how painter and sitter interacted – an artist's equivalent of legal privilege – but a successful portrait cannot be achieved without rapport. The painting is also notable for its use of devices: the outline of her bencher's gown, the line representative of the Bar and her position slightly above it, and the so-called prison bars, which the Princess certainly thought could represent the linen-fold panelling in the Old Hall, her favourite place to dine in all of London, she said. She ended her conversation with me by saying that the Organ portrait was one of many painted of her, but the only one which truly captured her spirit and her way of life.

David Hills

The Short Adjournment

by Norman Hepple RA (1908–90)

This work celebrates a remarkable event. In 1957 the Lord Chief Justice of England and Wales, the Master of the Rolls, and five out of the eight Lords Justices of Appeal then in office were all members of Lincoln's Inn. Seated from left to right are Sir Edward Holroyd Pearce, Sir Charles Romer, Lord Evershed (Master of the Rolls), Sir David Jenkins, Lord Parker of Waddington (Lord Chief Justice), Sir Tom Denning, and Sir Benjamin Ormerod. Lord Denning, as he became, is placed near the door to represent his imminent appointment to the House of Lords.

The artist has not simply produced excellent portraits of the seven Lords Justices, he has also tried to capture the atmosphere in the Benchers' Drawing Room immediately after lunch, an important time when decisions are often made. In the background can be seen three portraits later stolen from the Inn. Two of these came to light in Bermondsey Market and a lengthy saga ensued, complicated by the law of market overt.

A painting like this is unlikely to be repeated. The Court of Appeal has now grown to thirty-seven members, excluding Heads of Divisions, and it would need to have about twenty-three members of the Inn to achieve the same percentage as in this picture. The first woman member of the Court of Appeal was appointed thirty years later in 1988. Two out of three of the Lady Justices in the summer of 2006 are members of Lincoln's Inn, so a painting of the Inn's members of the Court of Appeal today would include both sexes.

Mary Arden

The World Wars

ANGELA HOLDSWORTH

The way the Inn reacted and adapted during the two world wars is striking more for its differences than similarities. In 1914 little was done to prepare for the major upheavals which lay ahead. The Inn optimistically subscribed to the popular view that the war would be over by Christmas. There was perfunctory agreement that there should be no entertainment on the next Grand Night and that a contribution of £1,000 be made to the War Relief Fund. When the government first appealed for economies, the Inn's response was merely to instruct the Kitchen Committee to arrange that dinner at the Bench Table should be simpler and that all members of the Inn should give notice of intention to dine. The Consolidated Regulations were altered to dispense with keeping terms for those on active service and to allow displaced Belgian judges and advocates to use the facilities of the Inn. Otherwise life went on and, it was assumed, would continue to go on, as normal.

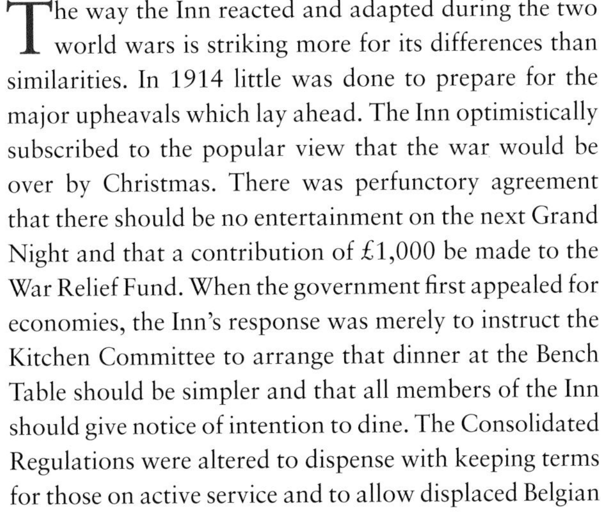

By 1915 it was clear this was not to be. The war was far from over and was cutting dramatically into the number of students and young barristers – those sitting their final exam were well under half the pre-war figures. In November 1916 only thirty-eight students were keeping terms. and it was decided to allow students to be called to the Bar on joining or leaving the armed services even if they had not taken their final exams.

As increasing numbers of barristers responded to the call to arms some chambers were forced to close. In the summer of 1916 over a fifth of the Inn's sets were empty. So, as a replacement source of rent, builders and carpenters began adapting some second and third floor sets in Stone Buildings and Old Square into residential flats.

On 13 October 1915 the Inn was hit during a Zeppelin raid. Sir Arthur Underhill, a bencher, recalls the day in his memoirs, *Change and Decay* (1938). His parlour maid told him at breakfast that she had heard from the milkman that Lincoln's Inn had been entirely destroyed. Sceptical of the reliability of such a newsgathering process, Sir Arthur went off to investigate. He found all the buildings still standing, though many windows in New Square had lost their glass and the roof of No. 8 had been blown off. An old gentleman occupying a flat on the top floor of No. 7 had been found by the fire brigade still in bed. When they expressed surprise at finding him there, he replied that he considered it the safest place, 'as the odds were strongly against another bomb being dropped in the same spot'.

Above: Sir Arthur Underhill, who witnessed the Zeppelin raid in December 1917, made a sketch of the benchers (including himself – A.U.) sheltering in the wine cellar.

The worst damage was the shattering of all the windows in the Chapel, including the priceless original Van Linge glass. Fortunately, Sir Arthur noted, enough fragments survived to reconstruct six of them, using a painting of the windows as a guide – the glass that had survived the Puritans in the seventeenth century survived the Germans too. Benchers suggested that the depression caused by the bomb should be preserved and encircled by a railing to provide an enduring record. This somewhat inconvenient idea was never adopted, but the spot is marked by a steel stud in the road on the north-west corner of the Chapel and with a plaque on the outside Chapel wall opposite it.

The only other hit suffered by the Inn was on 18 December 1917. This time Sir Arthur was on the spot. In the middle of a Council meeting the Steward rushed in warning of an expected raid. All the assembled benchers were ushered to the wine cellar. 'The scene was a curious one. Lord Muir Mackenzie sitting at a small table ladened with oysters which were being sent in opened from the kitchen, while Lord Muir Mackenzie himself acted as butler and filled our glasses with champagne.' After a while, finding the cellar too cold, Sir Arthur went up to the Drawing Room and was there when the bomb went off, rocking the Hall. The bomb, which fell outside the drill hall in Stone Buildings, was felt by everyone in the Great Hall but not by those sheltering in the basement in Old Square. Fortunately no one was injured but many windows and exterior stonework and pipes were badly damaged.

Cost-cutting and thrift were now taken far more seriously and a special Economy Committee was set up which recommended further ways of saving. It pointed out it was wasteful to have separate joints just so that one could be carved at each table. In future all meat would be sliced ahead in the kitchen. However, this meant there would no longer be broken meat left over to feed the staff. Instead, it was suggested, they could be given less expensive joints from a different butcher ('not having an address in or about Piccadilly') charging more moderate prices. It was not only staff who made sacrifices. Benchers approved the sale of fifty dozen 1904 Veuve Cliquot and

H.H. Asquith former Prime Minister and Treasurer of the Inn (on the left) unveiling the War Memorial 1921.

thirty dozen Pommery 1906, for which they were confident they would get a good price.

At the outbreak of the war the Inns of Court Officer Training Corps (later known as the Inns of Court Regiment), based at 10 Stone Buildings, was a small territorial unit recruiting from barristers and Bar students, and other public school men. It was rapidly transformed into a major recruiting centre for anyone of 'officer material'. At its peak 1,200 candidates a day were being interviewed and it had to expand into Nos 2, 4 and 7 Stone Buildings and 12 Old Square. Training was moved out to a camp in Berkhamsted, but during the first months of the war, and again briefly in 1915 when a measles epidemic closed the camp, the gardens of the Inn became drilling grounds. Predictably, the lawns were ruined.

By the end of the war 1,438 barristers had enlisted in the services, of whom 190 were killed. Sixty-eight members of Lincoln's Inn died, their lives remembered by the War Memorial to the west of the Chapel, and the Roll of Honour, still displayed outside the Library. There is also an inscribed silver rose bowl, 'to commemorate the Barristers who dined at this Table and gave their lives in the War'. In 1924 the bowl was placed on the Bar Table at dinner with the two places on either side laid but left unoccupied. Originally this was quite near the junior end, representing an absent 'mess' of those killed. It went up from time to time in recognition of the increasing seniority those commemorated would have achieved had they survived.

The Memorial Mess rose bowl.

A ROLL OF THE MEMBERS
BOTH BARRISTERS AND STUDENTS
OF THE HONOURABLE SOCIETY
OF LINCOLN'S INN
WHO SERVED IN THE NAVAL
MILITARY OR AIR FORCES
IN THE WAR
1914–1919

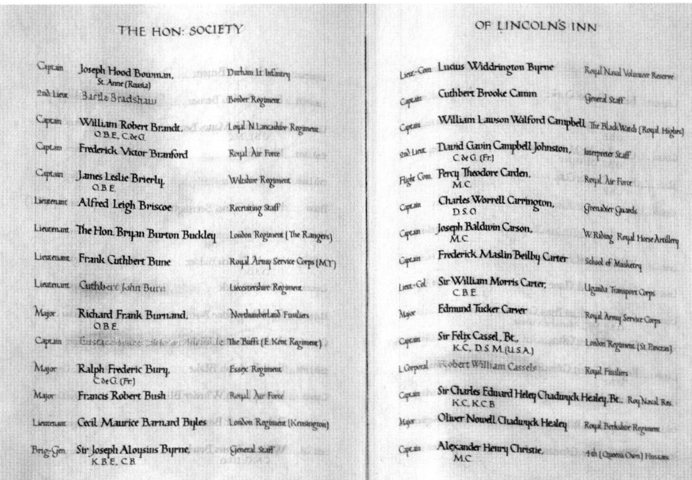
THE HON: SOCIETY

Captain	Joseph Hood Bowman, St. Anne (Russia)	Durham Lt. Infantry
2nd Lieut.	Bartle Bradshaw	Border Regiment
Captain	William Robert Brandt, O.B.E., C.de G.	Loyal N. Lancashire Regiment
Captain	Frederick Victor Branford	Royal Air Force
Captain	James Leslie Brierly, O.B.E.	Wiltshire Regiment
Lieutenant	Alfred Leigh Briscoe	Recruiting Staff
Lieutenant	The Hon. Bryan Burton Buckley	London Regiment (The Rangers)
Lieutenant	Frank Cuthbert Bune	Royal Army Service Corps (M.T.)
Lieutenant	Cuthbert John Burn	Leicestershire Regiment
Major	Richard Frank Burnand, O.B.E.	Northumberland Fusiliers
Captain	[illegible]	The Buffs (E. Kent Regiment)
Major	Ralph Frederic Bury, C. de G. (Fr.)	Essex Regiment
Major	Francis Robert Bush	Royal Air Force
Lieutenant	Cecil Maurice Barnard Byles	London Regiment (Kensington)
Brig.-Gen.	Sir Joseph Aloysius Byrne, K.B.E., C.B.	General Staff

OF LINCOLN'S INN

Lieut.-Com.	Lucius Widdrington Byrne	Royal Naval Volunteer Reserve
Captain	Cuthbert Brooke Camm	General Staff
Captain	William Lawson Walford Campbell	The Black Watch (Royal Highrs.)
2nd Lieut.	David Gavin Campbell Johnston, C. de G. (Fr.)	Interpreter Staff
Flight Com.	Percy Theodore Carden, M.C.	Royal Air Force
Captain	Charles Worrell Carrington, D.S.O.	Grenadier Guards
Captain	Joseph Baldwin Carson, M.C.	W. Riding Royal Horse Artillery
Captain	Frederick Maslin Beilby Carter	School of Musketry
Lieut.-Col.	Sir William Morris Carter, C.B.E.	Uganda Transport Corps
Major	Edmund Tucker Carver	Royal Army Service Corps
Captain	Sir Felix Cassel, Bt., K.C., D.S.M. (U.S.A.)	London Regiment (St. Pancras)
L. Corporal	Robert William Cassels	Royal Fusiliers
Captain	Sir Charles Edward Heley Chadwyck Healey, Bt., K.C., K.C.B.	Roy. Naval Res.
Major	Oliver Nowell Chadwyck Healey	Royal Berkshire Regiment
Captain	Alexander Henry Christie, M.C.	4th (Queen's Own) Hussars

The Roll of Honour, a work by the calligrapher Graily Hewitt (called 1889), displayed outside the Library.

In contrast to 1914, the start of the Second World War found the Inn ready for action. For several weeks during the summer of 1939, before war was declared, the Inn was busy mobilizing. Valuable pictures and silver were put in the strong room or wine cellar, scaffolding was erected to remove the east Chapel window, trenches were dug in the North Garden, fire-fighting equipment and large amounts of blankets, lint, bandages, and iodine were ordered. Fresh water was placed in shelters each day, volunteers from the Inn filled sandbags, and the gardener was instructed not to order any more plants or bulbs.

During the first year of the war, despite having no air raids on London, preparations sensibly went on. Dinners were discontinued, staff sent for fire-fighting training, a first aid post set up and various economies made. Meanwhile, chambers emptied and numbers of students keeping terms dwindled. As in 1914 regulations were relaxed.

German air raids on London began in September 1940. Over the next four years the Inn was hit twenty-six times by bombs, fire, or explosives. On 10 October 1940 a bomb crashed through 9 Stone Buildings, exploding as it hit the basement, gutting the bottom three floors. Sefton Delmer, a journalist and broadcaster, lived on the top floor and was giving a dinner party at the time. 'It had been a cheerful evening', he recounts in his autobiography, *Black Boomerang*, 'and none of us had thought of descending to the air-raid shelter, not even when we could hear the bombers overhead. The bombs had fallen all around in previous raids without hitting us ... We were sublimely confident that the bombs would continue to fall around but miss us and our flat.' He was entertaining that evening, among others, the daughter of the Belgian Prime Minister, Prince Bernhard of the Netherlands, and Ian Fleming, then Personal Assistant to the Director of Naval Intelligence. Delmer was busy persuading Prince Bernhard to stay and have one last drink when, 'what seemed an end-of-the-world explosion sent us all sprawling. The building heaved as in an earthquake. The lights were gone. Smoke and brick dust covered everyone and everything.' The bomb left a large hole where the staircase had been. The party continued by torchlight as if nothing had happened until an Inn official who was the ARP warden demanded they come down. The next day Sefton Delmer was approached by two CID officers. Apparently there had been an informer – his guests had been speaking foreign languages and signalling to the

War damage to 9 Stone Buildings. As the bomb struck, the journalist Sefton Delmer was holding a dinner party on the top floor.

On duty 1940.

raiders with electric torches! Would he please give them an account of what happened and a list of his guests. 'Snob that I am,' says Delmer, 'I did so with relish.'

Stone Buildings were unlucky. Delmer's experience was one of several direct hits. Two buildings had to be entirely demolished, as did 11 New Square. Old Buildings, the Old Gateway, Old Hall, and the Chapel were all damaged but reparable. Fortunately, some of the Chapel's best stained glass had been removed. But all the glass windows in the Great Hall and Library were destroyed in 1940. They were replaced 'in the cheapest way', perhaps just as well as they were blown out again in 1944. Shortly after the Blitz began the Inn's paintings were removed to the country house of a bencher, for supposed safety. Two years later they were inspected and it was discovered that damp and mildew had reduced them to a deplorable condition – a further six months of such humidity would have destroyed them all. But there was a positive outcome as they were successfully restored, some to a far higher standard than their pre-war state.

The war was particularly tough on the staff. Those not called up had to shoulder additional duties as well as the burden of air raid precautions. Norman Marriott, the Under Treasurer, in his reports to benchers, frequently praised the staff for their bravery and hard work, singling out, for instance, the courage of Chief Porter Hearn, who climbed on to the roof of the Great Hall where an incendiary bomb had fallen and, 'picked up the bomb with his naked hands and threw it on to the terrace'. Fortunately he was not injured. Marriott looked after his fire fighters well. Minutes of a Council Meeting in 1941 show the Under Treasurer having taken from the wine cellar for his own use six dozen bottles of sherry, five dozen bottles of whisky, and eighteen bottles of gin. Anxious this should not be open to misinterpretation by

Squatters in the Undercroft.

posterity, Marriott amplified the entry in the original Black Book. In the margin he has written, 'It should be noted that these wines and spirits were used almost entirely for the benefit of the fire fighters and those tenants who took refuge in the basement of the Hall during the bombing of London at a time of great stress.'

Basements were used as temporary shelters by people working or passing near the Inn when air raid warnings sounded. But there were some more permanent occupants. Three elderly sisters migrated from Battersea, after their house was bombed, and turned the Chapel Undercroft into their new home. They spread an old carpet on the stone floor, slept on barristers' benches and made cups of tea in the porter's lodge. The milkman left milk each day by the sandbags at the entrance. It seems there was no objection from the Inn – presumably the spirit of wartime cooperation prevailed.

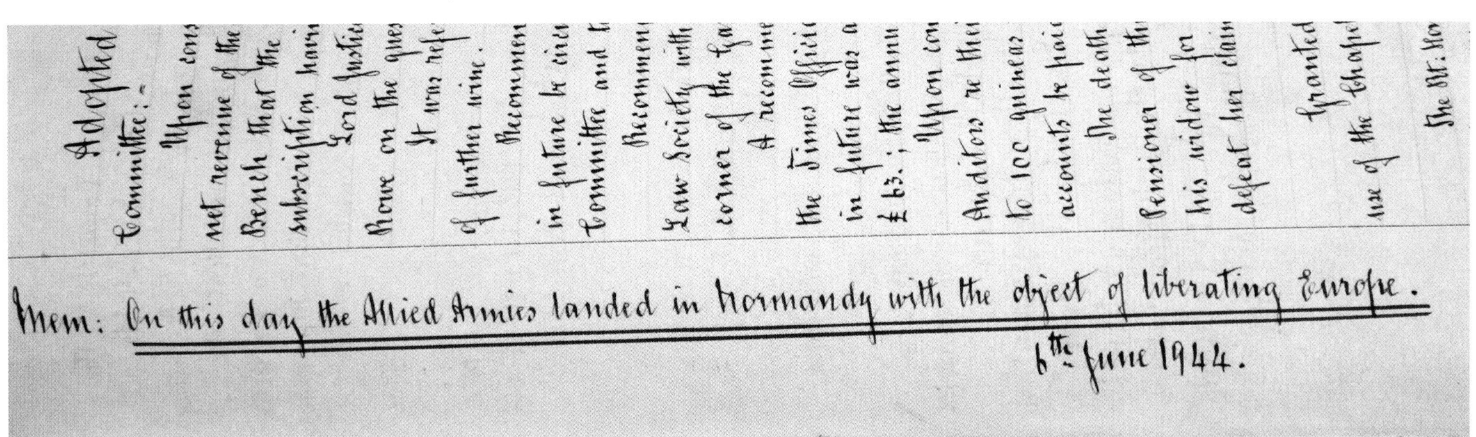

Mem: On this day the Allied Armies landed in Normandy with the object of liberating Europe.
6th June 1944.

While Council considers a report from the Finance Committee (Black Book 46).

Rededication of the War Memorial in 1950.

In this war, no troops trained on the lawns. The Inns of Court Regiment was reshaped as an armoured car regiment in 1940 and moved out of London, and the Drill Hall was taken over by the Home Guard. Their presence proved useful in 1940, when heavy-handed demolition work being carried out by London County Council in Chancery Lane was destabilizing Stone Buildings and Old Square. When the Council did not respond to the Under Treasurer's requests to stop blasting, the Home Guard was ordered out. 'Major Rose paraded his men with truncheons and this brought matters to a head ... as Mr Scott undertook not to explode any more of the Chancery Lane Front.'

During the course of the war, twenty-nine members of the Inn lost their lives on active service. Their names were added to the War Memorial. At the unveiling in 1950 an embarrassing blunder was discovered. The minutes of a Council Meeting shortly afterwards merely allude to a necessary 'addition to the War Memorial'. What is not stated is that a name had been omitted, that of the Duke of Kent, our royal bencher, killed on active service in an air crash in 1942.

The effects of the war continued long after it ended. The social programme did not get back to normal for some years as rationing restricted food, and financial resources were stretched by depleted income and the restoration programme. The last of the war damage to be repaired was the replacement of the stained glass in the Great Hall and Library in 1951.

A Wartime Memory

I went up to London daily by train to Liverpool Street. There was often no public transport from the terminus and I used to jog in about twenty minutes to Lincoln's Inn (where I then worked at a solicitors' firm in New Square), passing on the way scenes of destruction from the night before, such as the huge gas main flaring in front of the ruined Guildhall. Lincoln's Inn survived with comparatively little major damage but the other Inns suffered greatly, losing chapels and halls. I saw the pillars of the Temple Church lying in a semi-circle as they had fallen, and had great difficulty in locating the ruins of some chambers with which we had been doing business.

After the major Blitz of 1940–41, fire-watching was started for Lincoln's Inn, and those of us who volunteered would spend one night a week in teams of three. Mine was quartered in the basement of Trower Still, next door to No.6. We were equipped with gumboots and stirrup-pumps and slept, if no alarm was on, fully dressed on mattresses on the floor. There was a rule that no female fire-watcher should be on duty when someone failed to arrive, as she would then be alone with one man. Incendiary bombs, if spotted immediately, could be easily extinguished with a stirrup-pump. I was never on duty when any bombs fell and what frightened us more was to be caught asleep by the head warden, Ronald Roxburgh, later a High Court judge, who was extremely fierce. We went to work the next morning as usual. I used to get a really good breakfast at the Charing Cross Hotel and have my shoes polished by one in the row of shoe-blacks outside. I can remember now the soreness of one's toes after a night in gum-boots, and it is a reminder of how trimly people dressed in London during the war. If you saw anyone really dishevelled you assumed he had been bombed the night before, but now you see quite a lot of people looking like that, and shoe-blacks are rare indeed.

As the war went on, more and more staff were called up and it was increasingly difficult to replace them. Someone reckoned that at one time we were down to fifteen 'not counting partners and charladies'. We recruited an elderly typist with a very grand manner. One day I put my head into the typists' room to say I would want to dictate some letters after lunch. She was alone, and replied, 'You may dictate, Miss Lawrence, but not to me. I never take dictation from women.' Throughout all this time, the difficulties of transport, rationing and shortages grew ever greater and the war news was mostly very bad, although one was really too busy to worry much about it. Fortunately our coal ration was not reduced. We still had roaring fires, the only form of heating, in our rooms, though there might be snow on the inside sills of windows which had been broken so often they were glazed with a synthetic material with large gaps.

Apart from bombs, London was very safe during the war as criminals had either been called up or were pursuing black market businesses, far more lucrative than street crime. There was very little traffic and no danger until the Americans arrived and drove lorries on the wrong side of the road. There was also 24-hour supervision by police and air-raid wardens, and many premises were open all night. One Sunday night I woke with a bang, remembering that last thing on the previous Friday, instructions for drafting a will had been put on my desk. It had to be signed at 11 am on the Monday by an officer going on active service to an unspecified destination. It was 4 am and I bicycled through almost empty streets to New Square. I got into the office, open all night for fire-watching, drafted the will, and got it out to the Law Stationer for fair-copying first thing in the morning. It was on the partner's desk for execution at 11 am. I am sure the outer office never gave me away.

Lesley Lewis (née Lawrence)

Great Figures

Lord Denning (Edward Irvine Halliday 1974).

LORD DENNING 1899–1999

Through this book there have been short appreciations of the work of great men who have been members of the Inn, chosen to cover the full chronological span of our history. For the twentieth century the choice of Lord Denning is obvious. His name is known to every student of the common law, and he had a profile as a judge which few if any of his predecessors in this Inn can have matched. He died after a long and active life only a few years ago, and many of his close friends and colleagues are still active in the law and the Inn. It is much too early to attempt a full assessment of his work and its value in the development of the law. What is clear is that he evoked love and loyalty from people of widely different backgrounds, as the reminiscences below confirm.

Working with Lord Denning

In the library of the late Lord Denning's house in Whitchurch there sits a framed citation presented to him when he attended the annual meeting of the State Bar of California. It sets out the words of Francis Bacon which Lord Denning so frequently quoted: '… hold every man a debtor to his profession; from which as men of course do seek to receive countenance and profit, so ought they of duty to endeavor themselves, by way of amends, to be a help and ornament thereunto' – and it was simply inscribed, '… he rekindled our deep pride and gratitude as inheritors of the precious rights of Englishmen.'

Could it possibly be that Lord Denning was a debtor to the profession he loved and to which he gave so much? For many years I had the honour, as his clerk, of observing his attitudes, his industry, his methods, his discipline, his commitment and (though some may disagree) his humility. I stand four square with most of the accolades heaped upon him over many diverse attributes.

He held high judicial office for thirty-eight years, twenty of them as Master of the Rolls. He sat as an arbitrator both before and after his retirement. He chaired governmental committees. He was appointed to the prestigious Order of Merit, a personal honour accorded by Her Majesty the Queen. He wrote seven books between 1976 and 1986. The comparatively few judgments which were not delivered *ex tempore* he wrote by hand, always outside court hours, at weekends, or in his room after court. I have many of his originals to this day, most of them indicative of his thoroughness with their insertions, alterations and grammatical refinements. His sentences were famously short, and verbs were not always regarded as essential.

Despite a wide variety of commitments, he still found much time for law students, with whom he had great empathy and rapport. After just a few minutes with him, students would feel relaxed and left happy, enchanted and enriched. He visited his nonagenarian ex-housekeeper in her old people's home when he was an octogenarian himself. He attended the annual cricket match between Lincoln's Inn and Whitchurch. As president of both he was never on the losing side.

He was indefatigable, giving speeches, delivering lectures, writing articles. He seldom missed taking Holy Communion at 8 am on Sundays. Only on the rarest of occasions would Lord Denning rise from court early and even then would make up any time lost either by sitting earlier or later, or both, the next day. Daily at 9.30 he would tip onto his desk an apparently incomprehensible and dishevelled pile of papers, the contents of the briefcase that he had taken home the previous evening. He then gleefully dealt with as much of it as possible in the hour prior to going enthusiastically into court promptly at 10.30. This pre-court frantic hour had always to include hearing my rundown of the work for the day of the other four Courts of Appeal, reciting what they were doing, with what cases, on what subject matter, and for what estimated length of hearing. They were all 'his' cases in 'his' Court of Appeal (of which he was the President) and he therefore wanted to know everything that was going on in it.

Lord Denning sometimes told me, 'I shall pop into Lincoln's Inn Library on the way home. They've got *Hansard* there.' But he was roundly rebuked in the House of Lords for his referral to *Hansard* in one or two judgments, '*Hansard* not being suitable or permissible for recital in our courts'. Years later it was acknowledged that reference to debates and Parliamentary material which preceded Bills becoming Laws of the Land could be helpful. It is true that the motto *fiat justitia, ruat coelum* ('let justice be done though the heavens fall') was often interpreted as 'let justice be done even if the House of Lords disagrees'.

So, a debtor to his profession? He was called by Lincoln's Inn in 1923 and his work for the Inn included membership of committees for many years, serving as a bencher from 1944 and as Treasurer of the Inn in 1964. His work rate was staggering, prolific. Yet through it all he kept a polite serenity in all he did. I never saw a temper lost, never heard a harsh word uttered; no reprimand delivered; he never drank alcohol and never smoked; courtesy, with a very human touch, oozed throughout the period in which I was privileged to clerk the Master of the Rolls who set much new law in stone, if not entirely in the statutes. And for seventeen years after his retirement, he threw himself into multifarious activities, from advising laymen who could not afford to litigate, to making sterling speeches in debates in the House of Lords. He lived for 100 years and six weeks. I was 'with' him for nearly a quarter of that time as I continued to work with him after his retirement, and he made me one of his two executors. Few would disagree, to conclude with Bacon, that Lord Denning made much amends of any debt to his profession by help and ornament thereunto.

Peter Post

A Special Letter

When I was 17 and at boarding school in Cumberland, I received a letter from my mother, who was at the time a widow in her early forties. You will need no reminding that in those days there was no e-mail, no mobile phones, and for a schoolgirl no access to a telephone. My mother wrote:

Lord Denning with his wife and his stepdaughter, Hazel Fox.

October 11th 1942, Tuesday
My darling Hazel,
This is rather a special letter with some special news, so take a large breath and be ready for a shock You will have gathered from my last letter that my friendship with Mr Justice Denning was maturing rather rapidly, well the long and the short of it is that he wants us to get married and help each other make a home for you all ...His full name is the Hon Sir Alfred Thompson Denning (The Hon because he is a Judge, the Sir a knighthood). It sounds very grand but he is so simple with it all that it doesn't seem to matter, in fact we are quite in love.

The letter continues:

I call him Tom, his name with his family; he is 1 year older than me, tall, and I fear bald perhaps from wearing a wig so much! He has very bright keen brown eyes and a mind as quick as mercury (why he should choose me with my bad memory etc I can't think) but we have lots in common.

The very next day I received a second letter:

My darling Hazel,
This is just to let you know that after all we find it best to announce our news this Saturday. The reason is that we have met several friends etc travelling to town together and there will only be gossip if we don't come out in the open. This is undesirable as Tom is judging divorce cases from today.

My mother and Tom Denning were married two months later, living up to his family motto 'Denning for speed'. Thereafter Tom had a profound effect both on me, on my private life, and on my career as a lawyer.

Hazel Fox

The Future

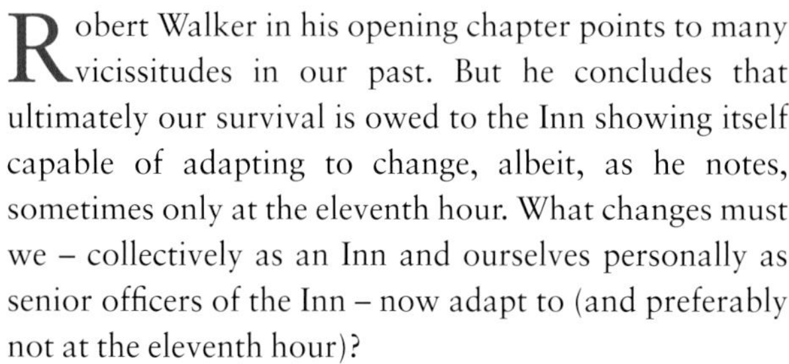

ROY AMLOT *Treasurer 2007*
and ELIZABETH APPLEBY *Master of the Library and of the Walks 2007*

Robert Walker in his opening chapter points to many vicissitudes in our past. But he concludes that ultimately our survival is owed to the Inn showing itself capable of adapting to change, albeit, as he notes, sometimes only at the eleventh hour. What changes must we – collectively as an Inn and ourselves personally as senior officers of the Inn – now adapt to (and preferably not at the eleventh hour)?

One is sheer increase in numbers. We have by far the largest intake of any of the Inns: 724 commenced the Bar Vocational Course in September 2006. Proposals on deferral of call and revalidation of the delivery of training for the Bar Vocational Course are other areas which will have a deep impact on students and how the Inn supports them. As will be seen from an earlier chapter, the Inn values enormously its overseas connections, and is anxious that they are not disrupted by changes in the pattern of legal education for the Bar. It is heartening that thriving alumni associations have been established in Malaysia and Hong Kong, and that plans are well advanced for establishing such associations in Ghana, the Caribbean, Singapore, and the Indian subcontinent.

The restructuring of the governance of the profession under the Legal Services Board (to be established under the Legal Services Bill) will also bring change to the way the Inn conducts its business. The strengthening of the provision of education both to students and pupils, and continuing professional development for barristers, to some extent already underway, will be a particular focus of our strategy. A strategy for change also necessitates a realistic approach to prioritizing our substantial, but far from limitless, funds. One priority is scholarships – only by attracting the brightest and the best, regardless of background, can a strong and dedicated membership be maintained. Another is ensuring the durability of the estate, not just as an exercise in heritage preservation, but also as a matter of sound economics – after all, the rent is what pays for most of the facilities we enjoy.

Of the preceding chapters, all we hope enjoyable and varied, one that naturally struck a personal chord with one of us was that on women. The battle for the admission of women is now thankfully long over, but it still gives pause for thought that a change instituted over eighty years is only about to come to a conclusion in one respect. It will indeed be a rather special honour when, as we hope will be the case in 2008, we have the first woman, as an ordinary bencher, to be Treasurer. It is also particularly pleasing that our fellow bencher, Janet Smith, has been appointed the first woman President of the Council of the Inns of Court.

Six hundred years are gone. Whether or not we have six hundred years to go, it is our belief that the Inn will continue to offer, as Sir Robert Megarry described, 'all that is needed for practice at the Bar … chambers to live and work in, a hall to eat and drink in, a chapel or church to pray in, and a library to consult books in', as it has done over the preceding centuries, for a very long time indeed.

List of Subscribers

Lionel Abel-Smith
Hester R. Nicola Adams
Palwasha Khan Afridi
Mr Zubair Ahmad
Anees Ahmed
Sabrina Ifthikar Ahmed
Saima Ahmed
Christie Ahweyevu
David Ainger
Neil M. Aitken LLB, Barrister at Law
Remi Aiyela
Timothy J. Akeroyd Esq
Jonathan Akrush
Zainab Alamgir
Charles Aldous QC
Vaji Aleemi
His Honour Judge Ian Alexander QC
Barrister Ishtiyaq Ali and Barrister Waqas Rashid
Brian Alland
Sebastian Allen
Peter Allsop CBE
Muhammad Abdullah Almamun
David Altaras
Danish Ameen
Mahmudul Hoque Amin
Roy Amlot QC
Tim Amos
Kathleen B. Anderson
Peter Andrews QC
Prince Lawrence Olatide Anifalaje
Thaddeus Marc Antoine Esq
Dr Samuel Appiah-Anane
Mr and Mrs P.B. Appleby
Rosemary Argente
Kwabena Asare
Dr Jur. Regina Asariotis LLM
John M. Ashley
Julie Anne Ashley
Ravi Girdharilal Aswani
Ryan Bradley Atkinson
Ruth Atkinson-Lyon
Satvir Kaur Aujla
Miangul Hassan Aurangzab
Rachel Jane Avery
Abid Azeem
Abdul Ghani Aziz and Sarah Aziz
Wan Azlian
James Badenoch QC
Nawabzada Waseem Khan Badozai
William J. Baillieu
Mary Susan Bain
Professor Sir John Baker QC
Nicholas Bridgman Baker
His Honour P.V. Baker QC
Siti Loreley (Laura) Bakri
Anne Louise Balestrino
Hairat A. Balogun (née Alatishe)
R.G. Bamford
Keith Barber
Francis Barlow
Lynne Barnett
Prashanta B. Barua
Eric I. Baskind
Desire Ignace Basset SC and Jean-Gael Alexandre Basset
Dr S. Bassett
Graham Battersby
Mark Baxter
Martin D.E. Bayntun
Professor Hugh Beale
His Honour Judge Peter Beaumont QC
David Beckenham
Alexis Beckford
Eve Bedell
Miss Alaha Begum
Stephen H. Bellamy QC
Mrs Frances Bellis
The Revd Paul J. Benfield
Graham Bentley
Philip Bentley QC
M.J.E. Berry
Nicholas Berry Esq
Ismail Bin Ibrahim
Miss Meral Birinci
Miss Diane Zamina Bisbrown-Lee
Christine Bispham LLB
Sir William Blackburne
His Honour A.J. Blackett-Ord
Leslie William Blake
John C. Blakeley
Psa Blincow
James M. Bonnett
Chia Boon Teck
Fiona Louise Bowden

Miss Joanna Louise Bowling
Ian D. Boyes
Alan Boyle QC
Mrs Irène Bradburn
Reginald H. Braddon
Dr M.A. Branthwaite
G.R. Bretten QC
His Honour Judge A.N.J. Briggs
James Brightwell
John Brisby Esq QC
A.L.C. Broadberry
His Honour Judge Brodrick
John Brookes
Graham S. Brown
Miss Ceri Bryant
Nicholas Bryars
Martin Christopher Burton Buckley
Richard A. Buckley
J.M. Burbidge
Roy Anthony Burgess
Philip Burke
Professor E.H. Burn
Linda Ann Burns
Paul Andrew Burns
Martin Burr
Frances Burton
Natalie Grace Campbell
Howard B. Caney
Ian Caplin
Jamie Carr
Captain Malcolm Carver
Peter Castle
Gordon B. Catford
Georgina Chambers
Vivian Chapman
Sir William Charles
Edna Chayen (née Greenburgh)
N.P. Cheah
Julia Cheetham
Chen Tsui Hua, Lesley
Alvin Cheng Sun Cheok
Ho Wai Cheong
Kwai Cheong Chen
Chen Cheong Heng
Nicholas Cherryman
P.K. Chew
Keith Chin Hsiun
Owen H.S. Chio
Mr Chul Choi
Chan Chee Choong
Ronald D. Christie
Theodora A. Christou
Christopher Chuah Chee Kian
Christopher John Clark
Aisling Clarke
Ian Clarke
Peter William Clarke QC
Simon Clarke
Dan Cocker
Oswaldo Coelho
Jonathan Cohen QC
The Honour L.H.L. Cohen OBE
Dr William Coker
Richard Coleman
Ian R. Coles
His Honour Judge Andrew Collender QC
Liam Needham Collens
Stephen J. Collier
His Honour Judge Simon Colart
The Honour Mr Justice Cooke
Judge John D. Cooke
His Honour Roger Cooke
Mark Graeme Cooper
His Honour Anura Cooray
Dr Justin Corfield
Michael Corkery QC
David Cotterell
A.J.P. Cousins
Edward Cousins
T. Gordon Coutts QC
Kenneth Craig
Jock Craven
His Honour Peter Crawford QC
Jonathan Crow
Terence Cullen
Emily Culverhouse
Joseph Curl
Mohammad Nabeel Khan Dahir
J.C.P. Davies
Julie Davies
Sir Mervyn Davies MC TD
Janet Davis
Malcom Davis-White QC
Mr Giovanni P. D'Avola
Miss Laura Dawes
Ian Grant Dawson Esq
Douglas Day QC
Francis Hilary D'Cruz
M.P. Debono
Nicholas Dee
Richard Deery
Leon Fernando Del Canto
Raul Antonio DeMenezes
Miss Suzan Demirates
His Honour Neil Denison QC
Dr John Dennis
Mrs E. Denza
James Parkyns Derriman
Anne Derwin
Ben-Jacob Diewitz
Lady Dillon
H.J. Dingwall
Alastair G. Dobbie
Louise A. Doble
Mr A.N. Dobson
Suzanne Dobson FRSA, ACIM
Nicholas Doherty
Miss Nancy Dooher
Andrew Dowden

James Drake
Rebecca Drake
Maurice J.D. Drummond
Garry Dunlop
His Honour Hubert Dunn QC
Philip Dykes SC
Nicholas Easterman
Richard Eaton
Jeremy Eccles
Sir Alfred O. Eghobamien San
Baroness Elles
Miss Eleni Ellina
Barry C. Ellis
Andrew Emery
Adam Nicholas Emilianou
Seah Suat Eng
Miss A.M. England
Johanne Enright
Eddy H.B.-Enyinnaya Oyouwa-Oko Jaja
Kow Abaka Essuman Esq
Sir Terence Etherton
Rt Hon Sir Edward Eveleigh
Mr Solomon Jonathan Ezekiel
Miss H.C. Farley
How Su Fen
Tamsin V. Ferri
Sir Francis Ferris
Anthony W. Finch
Roy Dunsmore Fitzsimmons
Vernon Flynn
Robert Fookes
John Wilson Forman
Timothy Paul Brian Found
Hazel Fox QC
Judith Fox
Lynn Fox
Nicholas Fox
Angela Fozzard
Andrew Francis
Anthony Fraser
Miss Fiona Elizabeth Frazer
Jonathan Gabriel French
Mr Michael A. Fuller
Eugene Fung
Lim Wai Henry Fung
S. Wendy Gallagher
Adrien Galy
Yvonne Gan Ai Wah
Mrs Joan Gandolfi
Mr David C. Gardner, LLB (hons) Barrister
Jennifer Garn
Julia M. Garratt
June Gascoine
His Honour Judge George
William George
Emily Aphrodite Georgiades
Michael P. Gerard
Syed Hur Riahi Gardezi
A. Gersch
Seth Benjamin Gibbard
James Gibbons
Julia Elizabeth Gibbons
Sir Peter Gibson
His Honour Judge Francis Gilbert QC
R.G. Gilbert
Matthew C. Gilks Esq
Rt Hon Lord Gill
Amritpal A.K. Gill
The Rt Hon Justice Pajan Singh Gill
Aurelie-Anne Gilly
Gerald Godfrey CBE QC
David J. Goldberg
Joseph Goldsmith
Miss Marion Goldstraw
G.S. Goodchild
Julian Leigh Alexander Goode
Mr Nigel Gore BA Hons LLM
Anna Gotts
Lord Grabiner QC
Sir Peter Graham KCB QC
Charles Gray
Colin Green
David Cameron Green
Peter Griffiths
John A.R. Grove
Mweemba Benedict Haamadibula
Erlend Haaskjold SC
Adrian Hamilton QC
Eben Hamilton QC
Jemma Elizabeth Hamlin
Derrick G. Hanson
Muhammed Luthful Haque
Stephen T. Hardy
Adele Alexis Harris
David R. Harris
John Henry Harris
Norson B. Harris
Ralph Harris
Paul Harrison
Victoria Harrison
Louise Barbara Harvey
Lesley Jean Harwood
Tay Guan Hau
Michael P. Hayton
Madeleine Heal
David G. Heap
Michael Ambrose Heather
Mr B.S. Heil
Paul Heim
Barrister Mir Mohammed Helal Uddin
Mr Clive B.H. Heng
Mark Herbert QC
Amabel Herrera Sanz
Mr R. Hidson
G. Hill
Jason Hill
Colonel D.H. Hills MBE

Miss Margaret Rose Hilson
Mrs Nirmala Hind (née Kulasekaram)
F.P. Hinks
David Hodge QC
Paul Hoffman
Dame Mary Hogg DBE
Jack Holborn
Holly Holden
Mr R.T. Holden JP
Justice Randy J. Holland
Andrew C. Holmes
H.H.J. John Holt
Professor J.A. Hornby
Nigel A.F.J. Horner
K.E. Horrex
Philip J. Hoser
Mrs Susan R. Howdle
Mr John Howe
Cenydd I. Howells
Pamela Ann Howes
His Honour Judge Michael Hucker
C.A. and E. Hughes
Ms Julie Hughes
Stephen Hunt
David Alexander Hunter
Thomas Edward Hurst
M. Asker Husain
Amjad Hussain, Barrister at Law
Lalarukh Hussain
Dr Philip Hutcheon
Josephine Hutchings
Michael J. Huxley-Evans
Serena Chiew Hwa Lim
Sir Robin Ibbs KBE
M. Jaman Ibrahim
Danish Iftikhar
Barrister Sana Iftikhar
Mr N.D. Ing
Justice David Ipp
Miss Shabnam Ishaque
Mohammed Ishaque Khan
Keiko Iwakawa
Adrian P. Jackson
Bernadette Jackson
Mrs Sabine Jacobs
Geoffrey Jaques
A.H.R. Jahanshahi-Qajar
Adil Jamal
Stephanie A. Jarrett
John Jarvis QC
Mrs Dharamshila Jayaswal
Dr Kashi Prasad Jayaswal
Michael Jefferis
A.B. Jenkins
Tee Keng Jin
Victor Joffe QC
James K. Juggapah
Nicholas R. Johnson
Lindsay A.M. Johnston
Robert J.M. Johnstone
Clifford Jones
Darius W. Jones
Elaine Thomson Jones
Jennifer Jones
Lawrence Victor Jones
Alison M. Judd
Veena Kapila
Julie Kathuria
Atif Waheed Kaudri
Dennis Kavanagh
Mrs Jervis Kay
R. Jervis Kay QC
Kevin P. Kearns
Wong Kee Them
Brian Keegan
Benjamin Keith Kelly
Mr Yee Mei Ken
Sir Sydney Kentridge QC
Mr A. Keskisaari
James Kessler
Thomas Leopold Kew
Lee Khai
Ikhtiar Khan
Mubasher Khan, Barrister at Law
Rasab Khan Esquire
Howard King Chian Hwa
Julie Catherine King
Michael King
Sir Timothy King
Mike A. Klonaris
Judy Knight
Darren N.T. Koh
His Honour Dr Colin Kolbert
Andrew Konecki
Robert G. Kotewall
Siva S. Krishnasamy
Surendra Kumar Kapur
Dato' K Kumeraendran
Kwok Tung-Ming, Eric SC
Christian L.J. Landeg-John
Andrew R. Lane
Abigail L. Langford
Tam Latymer
Dennis Lau Yee Meng
George Laurence QC
Nicholas Lavender
Marina Lavithia
Tristan James Law Smith
Georgia Lay
The Hon Justice Le Pichon, JA
Nicholas Le Poidevin
Elaine Leadbetter MBA
Peter G.F. Leader
Peter Leaver QC
Peter Lee Kong Chung
Shin Jie Lee
Thomas Kang Bor Lee
Wei En Lee
His Honour Norman Lees

His Honour Judge Leigh QC
Kevin Leigh LLB (Hons)
Lord Lester of Herne Hill QC
Pakkia Letchumi
Mrs Lesley Lewis
Mark Lewis BA LLB Hons LLM
Sir Kim Lewison
Miss Edite Ligere
Jeremy Alexander Lightfoot
Song Sing Lik
Christopher Lim Su Heng
His Honour Judge Crawford Lindsay QC
Sir John Lindsay
Bernard Livesey QC
David Charles Lloyd
Sir Timothy Lloyd
Andrew Lloyd-Davies
Oliver R.W.W. Lodge
Ramanath Lokanath
Stephen K. Lomax
Paul Lonergan
Keith Loney
Julie-Anne Luck
His Honour David Lynch
Edward Lyons QC
Timothy Lyons
E.A. Machin QC
Judith-Anne MacKenzie
John MacLennan
His Honour Judge Bruce Macmillan
Dame Julia Macur DBE
Graham Adrian Madeley
Ann C. Mahabir
Rachel Ann Mahony
Alan Christopher Mait LLB
Andrew Y.S. Mak
Devadessen Malay
Ola P. Malik
Ben Daniel Maltz
Martin Mann QC
Mrs (Justice) Sujata Manohar (retd)
His Honour F.J.M. Marr-Johnson
Graham Marsh
Hedley Marten
Daniel James Martin
Thomas Martin
John Mathew QC
Jan Matthews
Professor Stephen Mayson
Catherine McArdle
Sir Richard McCombe
Hugh McKay, In Memoriam
Ducibel Jenkins McKenzie
James McKeon
Miss Tracey McLevy
Louise McQuoid
Mrs Rowena Meager
Mark Meier
B.T. Mellors Esq
Maurice Mendelson QC
Her Honour Judge Mensah
Jack Meredith
Waheed ur Rehman Mian
Michael Michell
The Rt Hon The Lord Millett
Judge Milmo
David Milne QC
Michael Milne
Dr Stephen Milner
Dennis Balfour Minns
Julianna Mitchell
Mitsue Miyajima
Andlib Mohsin
David Mohyuddin
Prof. John Warwick Montgomery, Ph.D, D.Theol., LLD
Caroline Moonan
John F. Moore
Sir Paul Morgan
Gerald Moriarty QC
His Honour Judge David Morris
The Rt Hon Sir Andrew Morritt CVO
Rupert A.C. Mosley
John Mowbray QC
Miss Alexandra Moyler
Khairuzzaman Muhammad
Morgan Ann Mulay
Mr Mustafa Mumtaz, Esq
Dr Yegappan Muthupalaniyappan
Kanakavalli Nadarajan
Mr Satish P.S. Nair
Rosemary Anne Nand LLB (Hons)
Mr S.M. Nasser
Lord Neuberger of Abbotsbury
Dr Trevessa Heidi Moesha Newton
Ng Fook Loy (Thomas)
Aminatta Lois Runeni N'gum
David Nicholls
Rebecca Nieto
Canon William Norman
The Rt Hon Sir Martin Nourse
Nzo Tarh Lucas
H.H. Judge O'Brien
Mr Anthony J. O'Carroll
Mark Ockelton
Bridget C. O'Donovan
Mr Lanre Oke
Julie Anne Okine
Miss Tessa Okposuogu
Elder S.M. Olakunri San FCIAB
Ms Michele O'Leary
Laurence Olphin
Christina Ayinke Omideyi
David Ong Mung Pang
Dr Victor Onipede
Faisal Osman
Howard Page QC
Michael Paget
Christopher Papaloizou

Sunita Sonya Parhar
Matthew Parish
Sir Andrew Park
Naz Parveen and Jefri Rahman
Alpesh B. Patel
Tan Kar Peng
Christopher Perry
His Honour Francis Petre
Miss Kim Pham
Deborah Phillips-Hallam
Anthony Pickford
David Pickup
Anthony Hart Piercy GM
Adrian Polak
Professor Jill Poole
Lorna A. Pope
Michael Douglas Pope
Miss Janette Porteous
Sir Humphrey Potts
Dr Michael J. Powers QC
Nicola Preston
Leolin Price CBE QC
Anna Luise Pryde
John Purcell
Kathryn Purkis and Sinead Agnew
MD Ruhul Quddus (Kazal)
Roland Quinault
Anthony P. Quinn FCI ARB
Victoria K. Quinn
Mrs Hafsa Rafique-Laskar
Miss T.L. Ranales-Cotos
John Randall QC
Stephen J. Randall
Sir Donald Rattee
Peter Rawson
Mohammad Ali Raza
T.M.L. Reading
Esmerelda Reasbeck
Gareth D. Reeds
Robert Reid
Simon J. Reevell
W.M. Rial
Caroline Kapur Richardson
Mr Ryan R. Richter
Miss C.A. Roberts
Gary Robinson
Allan Rogers
Hafizur Rohman
Suzanne Rose
Murray Rosen QC
Mr Simon Hadleigh Ross
John and Beryl Ross Martyn
Martin Roth
The Revd Peter and Mrs Elizabeth Rowe
Coopoosamy N. Rungasamy
Regina V. Saga
Sarah Louise Salmon
R.M.A. Sampson
Glyn Ross Samuel
His Honour John Samuels QC
Antonella and Paulo Santos
Mrs Asmin-Nighat-Sarwar-Khan
David W.J. Scorey
Gary Scrivener
Hanif Adam Secretary, Barrister at Law
Jonathan Seitler QC
Collin Lawrence Sequerah
Bryan R. Shacklady
Mohammed Shamim
Amar Saeed Sheikh
Sarah Alexandra Shellard
Jude Shepard
Mrs Louise Shooter
Elaine Siggery
Prodromos V. Sikiaridis
Donald Anton Silcock
Keng Huan Eric Sim
Matthew David James Simmonds Esq
Mrs Heidi L. Simpson
His Honour Judge P.R. Simpson
Sir Patrick Sinclair, Bt.
Balbir Singh
His Honour Mota Singh QC
Rabinder Singh QC
Shilpa Singh
Sukhwant Singh
Sir Christopher Slade
Michael Sladen
Mr Iain James Slater
George Boleyne Smedley
Dame Janet Smith
M.V. Smith
Mr Justice Peter Smith
Dr Peter M. Smith
Mr Justice T.C. Smyth
Marcus R.F. Soanes
C.J.F. Sokol QC
Efrosyni Soumelidis
David Southern
Emma Southern
Margaret M. Spencer
Peter Spooner
Gordon Stables
Simon Stanley
Alan Steinfeld QC
John A. Stenhouse
Sir Thomas Stockdale Bt
Christopher Stoner
Chris Stott
Timothy Straker QC
Katharine Anne Streatfield LLB(Cantab), LLM
Richard J.M. Stubbs
Mark Studer
Prosper Honore Sugewe
The Revd T.H.W. Swan
Colin L.K. Swee
Glinton Sweeting O'Brien

Colin Sydenham
Mohammed Hussain Syed
Syed Zulfqar Ali
Richard Sykes QC
Darren J. Sylvester
Eunice Sze Yin Tan
Jun Ling Tan
Rock Tansey QC
Miss Leanne Targett-Parker
Daniel and Emma Tate
Geoffrey Tattersall QC
David C. Taylor, Esq
Miss Eve Rebecca Taylor
William Taylor QC
Athena R.Taylor-Carrol de Mueller
Teh Eik Chween
Lay Teik Soon Vincent
Balaskanda Thamotharam
Thevarani Pushparasah
Tony Thorndike
Daren Timson-Hunt
Anthony Tolan
John Tomaschek
Anthony Towner
Stephanie Tozer
Peter Trevett QC
William Trower QC
Mr B.M.P. Tuck
Sir Richard Tucker
Sir Haydn Tudor-Evans
Mr James Tunley
Linda Angela Turnbull
Rowena M. Turner
Uduak Ukpeh Esq
Miss Ofonimeh Nseobong Umoh
Ian S. Unsworth
Mrs M. Van Der Beugel-Krutswyk
John Venmore
Mary Vitoria QC
Wan Mohd Firdaus Wan Mohd Fuaad
David Wagstaff, Esq
Ling Tien Wah
H.H. Judge Stephen Waine
Geoffrey P. Wakem
Mohammad Waliuddin Tanvir
Lord Walker of Gestingthorpe
Andrew P.D. Walker
Nicolas and Naomi Walker
Patrick Walker
Paul Mackenzie Walker
John N. Wall
Richard Wallington
Alderman Simon Walsh
Carolyn M. Walton
Stephen Walton
Shan Warnock-Smith QC
Rodney B. Wasserson
Malcolm Waters QC
Mr P.W. Watkins
His Honour Brian Watling QC
Anthony Watson
Atif Latif Wattoo
Andrew Waugh QC
Lord Weatherill
Edward Brett Welch
Commander Anthony R. Wells RN
Mark West
Clara Nieves Westbrook
Julie Anne Whitby
Andrew White QC
Nicholas Whitsun-Jones
Mark Whittaker
Peter Whitworth
Simon Wickens Esq
Wildy and Sons Ltd
David A.R. Williams QC
Michael 'Tiger' Williams
Stanley Williams
Brett Williamson
Chief Master Jonathan Winegarten
Paul Winter
Oliver Wise
Paul Woffenden
Miss Gen Q. Wong
Wong, Yat Ming Michael
James Maitland Wood
Sir John Wood
Sir Michael Wright
Robert Wright QC
Malik Muhammad Yaqub
Mr Umar Yasin, Esq
Katrina M. Yates
Yeap Chin Pho
Yee Shin Ching
Willie Yeo S.K.
Mun Yi Lee
Winnie Yii Graham
(aka Winnie Lay Hong Yii)
Michael Yin, Esq
Lim Ying Hui
Junichiro Yoshinaga
Conrad Young
Qamar Zaman, Esq
Mohammad M. Zuberi
Saleem Zulfiqar Kahn

Index of Names

T
W D
1697
T
W D
1697
T
N. G. C.
1818.
WILDY & SONS
Established 1850

Picture credits

Unless an acknowledgement appears below, the illustrations in this volume have been provided by Lincoln's Inn. Every effort has been made to contact the copyright holders of all works reproduced in this book. However, if acknowledgements have been omitted, the publishers ask those concerned to contact Third Millennium Publishing.

Julian Andrews: 11, 58, 84, 91 (all), 94, 99, 117 (right), 130, 131, 147, 151, 152, 153, 164, 166, 167, 177; **Dame Mary Arden:** 152 (top left); **Professor Sir John Baker:** 18; **British Cartoon Archive:** 149 (bottom left); **British Museum:** 53, 106; **Chancery Bar Association:** 26 (bottom right); **Denning Archives at Whitchurch:** 174; **Nick Easterman:** 21 (bottom), 24, 27, 35 (all), 113 (top); **Hazel Fox:** 175; **Getty Images:** 65 (bottom right), 149 (top right), 173; **Guildhall Library:** 10; **Danish Iftikhar:** 142; **Sir John Soane's Museum:** 32 (top and centre); **Ian Jones:** front cover, title verso, 25, 30, 31, 37 (all), 42, 44, 45, 61, 132, 160 (bottom left); **Judicial Communications Office:** 152 (top right); **The Secretary of the Institute:** 54; **Mary Evans Picture Library:** 63 (bottom right), 69, 76, 77 (bottom left), 78, 79, 80 (bottom right), 81, 117 (left), 146; **Museum of London:** 56 (left); **Mark Ockelton:** 135 (top right); **Peter Spooner:** 35; **Supreme Court of New South Wales:** 136; **Matthew Wilson:** title page, 21, 29 (bottom), 35 (bottom), 38–9, 45 (top right), 71, 108, 114 (top), 123, 124 (all), 154, 163.

Hogarth's *Second Stage of Cruelty* p57 reproduced by courtesy of the **University Librarian and Director, John Rylands Library, University of Manchester,** image file courtesy of the **British Cartoon Archive.** The Inigo Jones design p126 (bottom left) **Devonshire Collection, Chatsworth,** reproduced by courtesy of the **Chatsworth Settlement Trustees.** The Supreme Court of Madras p135 reproduced by courtesy of **Rajan Jaykar,** advocate and solicitor, Mumbai, India. The Court House Singapore p138 reproduced from *The Malaysian Judiciary* by James Foong courtesy of **LexisNexis Malaysia.**

Other acknowledgements
Remembering the 1970s by Cenydd Howells is based on an article previously published in *Trusts and Estates Law Journal* (Legalease Publishing), 2003, no.50.